ISBN 978-1-330-89221-3
PIBN 10117899

For support please visit www.forgottenbooks.com

1 MONTH OF
FREE
READING

at

www.ForgottenBooks.com

By purchasing this book you are eligible for one month membership to ForgottenBooks.com, giving you unlimited access to our entire collection of over 700,000 titles via our web site and mobile apps.

To claim your free month visit:

www.forgottenbooks.com/free117899

English
Français
Deutsche
Italiano
Español
Português

www.forgottenbooks.com

Mythology Photography **Fiction**
Fishing Christianity **Art** Cooking
Essays Buddhism Freemasonry
Medicine **Biology** Music **Ancient
Egypt** Evolution Carpentry Physics
Dance Geology **Mathematics** Fitness
Shakespeare **Folklore** Yoga Marketing
Confidence Immortality Biographies
Poetry **Psychology** Witchcraft
Electronics Chemistry History **Law**
Accounting **Philosophy** Anthropology
Alchemy Drama Quantum Mechanics
Atheism Sexual Health **Ancient History**
Entrepreneurship Languages Sport
Paleontology Needlework Islam
Metaphysics Investment Archaeology
Parenting Statistics Criminology
Motivational

Vanishing Roads

And Other Essays

By

Richard Le Gallienne

G. P. Putnam's Sons

New York   London

The Knickerbocker Press

BY

RICHARD LE GALLIENNE

———

Third Impression

The Knickerbocker Press, New York

ROBERT HOBART DAVIS

DEAR BOB: It is quite a long time now since you and I first caught sight of each other and became fellow wayfarers on this Vanishing Road of the world. O quite a lot of years now, Bob! Yet I control my tendency to shiver at their number from the fact that we have travelled them, always within hailing distance of each other, I with the comfortable knowledge that near by I had so good a comrade, so true a friend.

For this once, by your leave, we won't "can" the sentiment,—to use an idiom in which you are the master-artist on this continent,— but I, at least, will luxuriate in retrospect, as I write your name by way of dedication to this volume of essays, for some of which your quick-firing mind is somewhat more than editorially responsible. You were one of the first to make me welcome to a country of which, even as a boy, I used prophetically to dream as my "promised land," little knowing that it was indeed to be my home, the home of my spirit, as well as the final resting-place of my household gods; and, having you so early for my friend, is it to be wondered at if I soon came to regard the American humourist as the noblest work of God?

There is yet, I trust, much left of the Vanishing Road for us to travel together; and I hope that, when the time comes for us both to vanish over the horizon line, we may exit still within hail of each other,—so that we may have a reasonable chance of hitting the trail together on the next route, whatever it is going to be.

Always yours,
RICHARD LE GALLIENNE.

Rowayton, December 25, 1914.

iii

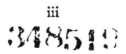

For their discernment in giving the following essays their first opportunity with the reader the writer desires to thank the editors of *The North American Review, Harper's Magazine, The Century, The Smart Set, Munsey's, The Out-Door World,* and *The Forum.*

CONTENTS

Contents

Vanishing Roads

Vanishing Roads

VANISHING ROADS

THOUGH actually the work of man's hands— or, more properly speaking, the work of his travelling feet,—roads have long since come to seem so much a part of Nature that we have grown to think of them as a feature of the landscape no less natural than rocks and trees. Nature has adopted them among her own works, and the road that mounts the hill to meet the sky-line, or winds away into mystery through the woodland, seems to be veritably her own highway leading us to the stars, luring us to her secret places. And just as her rocks and trees, we know not how or why, have come to have for us a strange spiritual suggestiveness, so the vanishing road has gained a meaning for us beyond its use as the avenue of mortal wayfaring, the link of communication between village and village and city and city; and some roads indeed seem so lonely, and so beautiful in their loneliness, that one feels they were meant to be travelled only by the soul. All roads indeed lead to Rome, but theirs also is a more mystical destination, some bourne of which no traveller knows the name, some city, they all seem to hint, even more eternal.

Never more than when we tread some far-spreading solitude and mark the road stretching on and on into infinite space, or the eye loses it in some wistful curve behind the fateful foliage of lofty storm-stirred trees, or as it merely loiters in sunny indolence through leafy copses and ferny hollows, whatever its mood or its whim, by moonlight or at morning; never more than thus, eagerly afoot or idly contemplative, are we impressed by that something that Nature seems to have to tell us, that something of solemn, lovely import behind her visible face. If we could follow that vanishing road to its far mysterious end! Should we find that meaning there? Should we know why it stops at no mere market-town, nor comes to an end at any seaport? Should we come at last to the radiant door, and know at last the purpose of all our travel? Meanwhile the road beckons us on and on, and we walk we know not why or whither.

Vanishing roads do actually stir such thoughts, not merely by way of similitude, but just in the same way that everything in Nature similarly stirs thoughts beyond the reaches of our souls; as moonlit waters stir them, or the rising of the sun. As I have said, they have come to seem a part of natural phenomena, and, as such, may prove as suggestive a starting-point as any other for those speculations which Nature is all the time provoking in us as to why she affects us thus and thus. These mighty hills of multitudinous rock, piled confusedly against the sky—so much granite and iron and copper and crystal, says one. But to the soul, strangely something besides, so much more. These rolling shapes of cloud, so fantastically massed and moulded, moving in rhythmic change like painted music in the heaven, radiant with ineffable glories or monstrous with inconceivable doom. This sea of silver, "hushed and halcyon," or this sea of wrath and ravin, wild as Judgment Day. So much vapour and sunshine and wind and water, says one.

Yet to the soul how much more!

And why? Answer me that if you can. There, truly, we set our feet on the vanishing road.

Whatever reality, much or little, the personifications of Greek Nature-worship had for the ancient world, there is no doubt that for a certain modern temperament, more frequently met with every day, those personifications are becoming increasingly significant, and one might almost say veritably alive. Forgotten poets may, in the first instance, have been responsible for the particular forms they took, their names and stories, yet even so they but clothed with legend presences of wood and water, of earth and sea and sky, which man dimly felt to have a real existence; and these presences, forgotten or banished for a while in prosaic periods, or under Puritanic repression, are once more being felt as spiritual realities by a world coming more and more to evoke its divinities by individual meditation on, and responsiveness to, the mysterious so-called natural influences by which it feels itself surrounded. Thus the first religion of the world seems likely to be its last. In other words, the modern tendency, with spiritually sensitive folk, is for us to go direct to the fountain-head of all theologies, Nature herself, and, prostrating ourselves before her mystery, strive to interpret it according to our individual "intimations," listening, attent, for ourselves to her oracles, and making, to use the phrase of one of the profoundest of modern Nature-seers, our own "reading of earth." Such was Wordsworth's initiative, and, as some one has said, "we are all Wordsworthians today." That pagan creed, in which Wordsworth passionately wished himself suckled, is not "outworn." He himself, in his own austere way, has, more than any one man, verified it for us, so that indeed we do once more nowadays

> Have sight of Proteus rising from the sea;
> Or hear old Triton blow his wreathèd horn.

Nor have the dryads and the fauns been frighted away for good. All over the world they are trooping back to the woods, and whoso has eyes may catch sight, any summer day, of "the breast of the nymph in the brake." Imagery, of course; but imagery that is coming to have a profounder meaning, and a still greater expressive value, than it ever had for Greece and Rome. All myths that are something more than fancies gain rather than lose in value with time, by reason of the accretions of human experience. The mysteries of Eleusis would mean more for a modern man than for an ancient Greek, and in our modern groves of Dodona the voice of the god has meanings for us stranger than ever reached his ears. Maybe the meanings have a purport less definite, but they have at least the suggestiveness of a nobler mystery. But surely the Greeks were right, and we do but follow them as we listen to the murmur of the wind in the lofty oaks, convinced as they of the near presence of the divine.

> The word by seers or sibyls told
> In groves of oak or fanes of gold,
> Still floats upon the morning wind,
> Still whispers to the willing mind.

Nor was it a vain thing to watch the flight of birds across the sky, and augur this or that of their strange ways. We too still watch them in a like mood, and, though we do not interpret them with a like exactitude, we are very sure that they mean something important to our souls, as they speed along their vanishing roads.

This modern feeling of ours is quite different from the outworn "pathetic fallacy," which was a purely sentimental attitude. We have, of course, long since ceased to think of Nature as the sympathetic mirror of our moods, or to imagine that she has any concern with the temporal affairs of man. We no longer seek to appease her in her terrible moods with prayer and sacrifice. We know that she is not thinking of us, but we do know that for all her moods there is in us an answering thrill of correspondence, which is not merely fanciful or imaginative, but of the very essence of our beings. It is not that we are reading our thoughts into her. Rather we feel that we are receiving her thoughts into ourselves, and that, in certain receptive hours, we are, by some avenue simpler and profounder than reason, made aware of certitudes we cannot formulate, but which nevertheless siderealize into a faith beyond the reach of common doubt—a faith, indeed, unelaborate, a faith, one might say, of one tenet: belief in the spiritual sublimity of all Nature, and, therefore, of our own being as a part thereof.

In such hours we feel too, with a singular lucidity of conviction, that those forces which thus give us that mystical assurance are all the time moulding us accordingly as we give up ourselves to their influence, and that we are literally and not fancifully what winds and waters make us; that the poetry, for instance, of Wordsworth was literally first somewhere in the universe, and thence transmitted to him by processes no less natural than those which produced his bodily frame, gave him form and feature, and coloured his eyes and hair.

It is not man that has "poetized" the world, it is the world that has made a poet out of man, by infinite processes of evolution, precisely in the same way that it has shaped a rose and filled it with perfume, or shaped a nightingale and filled it with song. One has often heard it said that man has endowed Nature with his own feelings, that the pathos or grandeur of the evening sky, for instance, are the illusions of his humanizing fancy, and have no real existence. The exact contrary is probably the truth—that man has no feelings of his own that were not Nature's first, and that all that stirs in him at such spectacles is but a translation into his own being of cosmic emotions which he shares in varying degrees with all created things. Into man's strange heart Nature has distilled her essences, as elsewhere she has distilled them in colour and perfume. He is, so to say, one of the nerve-centres of cosmic experience. In the process of the suns he has become a veritable microcosm of the universe. It was not man that placed that tenderness in the evening sky. It has been the evening skies of millions of years that have at length placed tenderness in the heart of man. It has passed into him as that "beauty born of murmuring sound" passed into the face of Wordsworth's maiden.

Perhaps we too seldom reflect how much the

life of Nature is one with the life of man, how un-important, or indeed merely seeming, the difference between them. Who can set a seed in the ground, and watch it put up a green shoot, and blossom and fructify and wither and pass, without reflecting, not as imagery but as fact, that he has come into existence, run his course, and is going out of exist-ence again, by precisely the same process? With so serious a correspondence between their vital experience, the fact of one being a tree and the other a man seems of comparatively small import-ance. The life process has but used different material for its expression. And as man and Nature are so like in such primal conditions, is it not to be supposed that they are alike too in other and subtler ways, and that, at all events, as it thus clearly appears that man is as much a natural growth as an apple-tree, alike dependent on sun and rain, may not, or rather must not, the thoughts that come to him strangely out of earth and sky, the sap-like stirrings of his spirit, the sudden inner music that streams through him before the beauty of the world, be no less authentically the working of Nature within him than his more obvi-ously physical processes, and, say, a belief in God be as inevitable a blossom of the human tree as apple-blossom of the apple?

If this oracular office of Nature be indeed a truth, our contemplation of her beauty and marvel is seen to be a method of illumination, and her varied spectacle actually a sacred book in picture-writing, a revelation through the eye to the soul of the stupendous purport of the universe. The sun and the moon are the torches by which we study its splendid pages, turning diurnally for our perusal, and in star and flower alike dwells the lore which we cannot formulate into thought, but can only come indescribably to know by loving the pictures. "The meaning of all things that are" is there, if we can only find it. It flames in the sunset, or flits by us in the twilight moth, thunders or moans or whispers in the sea, unveils its bosom in the moonrise, affirms itself in mountain-range and rooted oak, sings to itself in solitary places, dreams in still waters, nods and beckons amid sunny foliage, and laughs its great green laugh in the wide sincerity of the grass.

As the pictures in this strange and lovely book are infinite, so endlessly varied are the ways in which they impress us. In our highest moments they seem to be definitely, almost consciously, sacerdotal, as though the symbolic acts of a solemn cosmic ritual, in which the universe is revealed visibly at worship. Were man to make a praetice of rising at dawn and contemplating in silence and alone the rising of the sun, he would need no other religion. The rest of the day would be hallowed for him by that morning memory and his actions would partake of the largeness and chastity of that lustral hour. Moonlight, again, seems to be the very holiness of Nature, welling out ecstatically from fountains of ineffable purity and blessedness. Of some moonlight nights we feel that if we did what our spirits prompt us, we should pass them on our knees, as in some chapel of the Grail. To attempt to realize in thought the rapture and purification of such a vigil is to wonder that we so seldom pay heed to such inner promptings. So much we lose of the best kind of joy by spiritual inertia, or plain physical sloth; and some day it will be too late to get up and see the sunrise, or to follow the white feet of the moon as she treads her vanishing road of silver across the sea. This involuntary conscience that reproaches us with such laxity in our Nature-worship witnesses how instintive that worship is, and how much we unconsciously depend on Nature for our impulses and our moods.

Another definitely religious operation of Nature within us is expressed in that immense gratitude which throws open the gates of the spirit as we contemplate some example of her loveliness or grandeur. Who that has stood by some still lake and watched a stretch of water-lilies opening in the dawn but has sent out somewhere into space a profound thankfulness to "whatever gods there be" that he has been allowed to gaze on so fair a sight. Whatever the struggle or sorrow of our lives, we feel in such moments our great good fortune at having been born into a world that contains such marvels. It is sufficient success in life, whatever our minor failures, to have beheld such beauty; and mankind at large witnesses to this feeling by the value it everywhere attaches to scenes in Nature exceptionally noble or exquisite. Though the American traveller does not so express it, his sentiment toward such natural spectacles as the Grand Cañon or Niagara Falls is that of an intense reverence. Such places are veritable holy places, and man's heart instinctively acknowledges them as sacred. His repugnance to any violation of them by materialistic interests is precisely the same feeling as the horror with which Christendom regarded the Turkish violation of the Holy Sepulchre. And this feeling will increase rather than decrease in proportion as religion is recognized as having its shrines and oracles not only in Jerusalem, or in St. Peter's, but wherever Nature has erected her altars on the hills or wafted her incense through the woodlands.

After all, are not all religions but the theological symbolization of natural phenomena; and the sacraments, the festivals, and fasts of all the churches have their counterparts in the mysterious processes and manifestations of Nature? and is the contemplation of the resurrection of Adonis or Thammuz more edifying to the soul than to meditate the strange return of the spring which their legends but ecclesiastically celebrate? He who has watched and waited at the white grave of winter, and hears at last the first faint singing among the boughs, or the first strange "peeping" of frogs in the marshes; or watches the ghost-like return of insects, stealing, still half asleep, from one knows not where—the first butterfly suddenly fluttering helplessly on the window-pane, or the first mud-wasp crawling out into the sun in a dazed, bewildered way; or comes upon the violet in the woods, shining at the door of its wintry sepulchre: he who meditates these marvels, and all the magic processional of the months, as they march with pomp and pathos along their vanishing roads, will come to the end of the year with a lofty, illuminated sense of having assisted at a solemn religious service, and a realization that, in no mere fancy of the poets, but in very deed, "day unto day uttereth speech and night unto night sheweth knowledge."

Apart from this generally religious influence of Nature, she seems at times in certain of her aspects and moods specifically to illustrate or externalize states of the human soul. Sometimes in still, moonlit nights, standing, as it were, on the brink of the universe, we seem to be like one standing on the edge of a pool, who, gazing in, sees his own soul gazing back at him. Tiny creatures though we be, the whole solemn and majestic spectacle seems to be an extension of our own reverie, and we to enfold it all in some strange way within our own infinitesimal consciousness. So a self-conscious dewdrop might feel that it enfolded the morning sky, and such probably is the meaning of the Buddhist seer when he declares that "the universe grows I."

Such are some of the more august impressions

made upon us by the pictures in the cosmic picture-book; but there are also times and places when Nature seems to wear a look less mystic than dramatic in its suggestiveness, as though she were a stage-setting for some portentous human happening past or to come—the fall of kings or the tragic clash of empires. As Whitman says, "Here a great personal deed has room." Some landscapes seem to prophesy, some to commemorate. In some places not marked by monuments, or otherwise definitely connected with history, we have a curious haunted sense of prodigious far-off events once enacted in this quiet grassy solitude—prehistoric battles or terrible sacrifices. About others hangs a fateful atmosphere of impending disaster, as though weighted with a gathering doom. Sometimes we seem conscious of sinister presences, as though veritably in the abode of evil spirits. The place seems somehow not quite friendly to humanity, not quite good to linger in, lest its genius should cast its perilous shadow over the heart. On the other hand, some places breathe an ineffable sense of blessedness, of unearthly promise. We feel as though some hushed and happy secret were about to be whispered to us out of the air, some wonderful piece of good fortune on the edge of happening. Some hand seems to beckon us, some voice to call, to mysterious paradises of inconceivable green freshness and supernaturally beautiful flowers, fairy fastnesses of fragrance and hidden castles of the dew. In such hours the Well at the World's End seems no mere poet's dream. It awaits us yonder in the forest glade, amid the brooding solitudes of silent fern, and the gate of the Earthly Paradise is surely there in yonder vale hidden among the violet hills.

Various as are these impressions, it is strange and worth thinking on that the dominant suggestion of Nature through all her changes, whether her mood be stormy or sunny, melancholy or jubilant, is one of presage and promise. She seems to be ever holding out to us an immortal invitation to follow and endure, to endure and to enjoy. She seems to say that what she brings us is but an earnest of what she holds for us out there along the vanishing road. There is nothing, indeed, she will not promise us, and no promise, we feel, she cannot keep. Even in her tragic and bodeful seasons, in her elegiac autumns and stern winters, there is an energy of sorrow and sacrifice that elevates and inspires, and in the darkest hours hints at immortal mornings. She may terrify, but she never deadens, the soul. In earthquake and eclipse she seems to be less busy with destruction than with renewed creation. She is but wrecking the old, that

> . . . there shall be
> Beautiful things made new, for the surprise
> Of the sky-children.

As I have thus mused along with the reader, a reader I hope not too imaginary, the manner in which the phrase with which I began has recurred to my pen has been no mere accident, nor yet has it been a mere literary device. It seemed to wait for one at every turn of one's theme, inevitably presenting itself. For wherever in Nature we set our foot, she seems to be endlessly the centre of vanishing roads, radiating in every direction into space and time. Nature is forever arriving and forever departing, forever approaching, forever vanishing; but in her vanishings there seems to be ever the waving of a hand, in all her partings a promise of meetings farther along the road. She would seem to say not so much *Ave atque vale*, as *Vale atque ave*. In all this rhythmic drift of things, this perpetual flux of atoms flowing on and on into Infinity, we feel less the sense of loss than of a musical progression of which we too are notes.

We are all treading the vanishing road of a song in the air, the vanishing road of the spring flowers and the winter snows, the vanishing roads of the winds and the streams, the vanishing road of beloved faces. But in this great company of vanishing things there is a reassuring comradeship. We feel that we are units in a vast ever-moving army, the vanguard of which is in Eternity. The road still stretches ahead of us. For a little while yet we shall experience all the zest and bustle of marching feet. The swift-running seasons, like couriers bound for the front, shall still find us on the road, and shower on us in passing their blossoms and their snows.   For a while the murmur of the running stream of Time shall be our fellow-wayfarer—till, at last, up there against the sky-line, we too turn and wave our hands, and know for ourselves where the road wends as it goes to meet the stars.   And others will stand as we to-day and watch us reach the top of the ridge and disappear, and wonder how it seemed to us to turn that radiant corner and vanish with the rest along the vanishing road.

WOMAN AS A SUPERNATURAL BEING

THE boy's first hushed enchantment, blent with a sort of religious awe, as in his earliest love affair he awakens to the delicious mystery we call woman, a being half fairy and half flower, made out of moonlight and water lilies, of elfin music and thrilling fragrance, of divine whiteness and softness and rustle as of dewy rose gardens, a being of unearthly. eyes and terribly sweet marvel of hair; such, too, through life, and through the ages, however confused or overlaid by use and wont, is man's perpetual attitude of astonishment before the apparition woman.

Though she may work at his side, the comrade of his sublunary occupations, he never, deep down, thinks of her as quite real. Though his wife, she remains an apparition, a being of another element, an Undine. She is never quite credible, never quite loses that first nimbus of the supernatural.

This is true not merely for poets; it is true for all men, though, of course, all men may not be conscious of its truth, or realize the truth in just this way. Poets, being endowed with exceptional sensitiveness of feeling and expression, say the wonderful thing in the wonderful way, bring to it words more nearly adequate than others can bring; but it is an error to suppose that any beauty of expression can exaggerate, can indeed more than suggest, the beauty of its truth. Woman is all that poets have said of her, and all that poets can never say:

> Always incredible hath seemed the rose,
> And inconceivable the nightingale—

and the poet's adoration of her is but the articulate voice of man's love since the beginning, a love which is as mysterious as she herself is a mystery.

However some may try to analyse man's love for woman, to explain it, or explain it away, belittle it, nay, even resent and befoul it, it remains an unaccountable phenomenon, a "mystery we make darker with a name." Biology, cynically pointing at certain of its processes, makes the miracle rather more miraculous than otherwise. Musical instruments are no explanation of music. "Is it not strange that sheep's guts should hale souls out of men's bodies?" says Benedick, in *Much Ado About Nothing*, commenting on Balthazar's music. But they do, for all that, though no one considers sheep's gut the explanation. To cry "sex" and to talk of nature's mad preoccupation with the species throws no light on the matter, and robs it of no whit of its magic. The rainbow remains a rainbow, for all the sciences. And woman, with or without the suffrage, stenographer or princess, is of the rainbow. She is beauty made flesh and dwelling amongst us, and whatever the meaning and message of beauty may be, such is the meaning of woman on the earth—her meaning, at all events, for men. That is, she is the embodiment, more than any other creature, of that divine something, whatever it may be, behind matter, that spiritual element out of which all proceeds, and which mysteriously gives its solemn, lovely and tragic significance to our mortal day.

If you tell some women this of themselves, they will smile at you. Men are such children. They are so simple. Dear innocents, how easily they are fooled! A little make-up, a touch of rouge, a dash of henna—and you are an angel. Some women seem really to think this; for, naturally, they know nothing of their own mystery, and imagine that it resides in a few feminine tricks, the superficial cleverness with which some of them know how to make the most of the strange something about them which they understand even less than men understand it.

Other women indeed resent man's religious attitude toward them as sentimental, old-fashioned. They prefer to be regarded merely as fellow-men. To show consciousness of their sex is to risk offence, and to busy one's eyes with their magnificent hair, instead of the magnificent brains beneath it, is to insult them. Yet when, in that old court of law, Phryne bared her bosom as her complete case for the defence, she proved herself a greater lawyer than will ever be made by law examinations and bachelor's degrees; and even when women become judges of the Supreme Court, a development easily within sight, they will still retain the greater importance of being merely women. Yes, and one can easily imagine some future woman President of the United States, for all the acknowledged brilliancy of her administration, being esteemed even more for her superb figure.

It is no use. Woman, if she would, "cannot shake off the god." She must make up her mind, whatever other distinctions she may achieve, to her inalienable distinction of being woman; nothing she can do will change man's eternal attitude toward her, as a being made to be worshipped and to be loved, a being of beauty and mystery, as strange and as lovely as the moon, the goddess and the mother of lunatics. What a wonderful destiny is hers! In addition to being the first of human beings, all that a man can be, to be so much else as well; to be, so to say, the president of a railroad and yet a priestess of nature's mysteries; a stenographer at so many dollars a week and yet a nymph of the forest pools—woman, "and yet a spirit still." Not without meaning has myth endowed woman with the power of metamorphosis, to change at will like the maidens in the legend into wild white swans, or like Syrinx, fleeing from the too ardent pursuit of Pan, into a flowering reed, or like Lamia, into a jewelled serpent——

Eyed like a peacock, and all crimson barr'd;
And full of silver moons.

Modern conditions are still more favourable
than antique story for the exhibition of this
protean quality of woman, providing her with
opportunities of still more startling contrasts of
transformation. Will it not be a wonderful sight
in that near future to watch that woman judge of
the Supreme Court, in the midst of some learned
tangle of inter-state argument, turn aside for a
moment, in response to a plaintive cry, and, un-
fastening her bodice, give the little clamourer
the silver solace it demands! What a hush will
fall upon the assembled court! To think of such
a genius for jurisprudence, such a legal brain,
working in harmony—with such a bosom! So
august a pillar of the law, yet so divine a mother.

As it is, how piquant the contrast between
woman inside and outside her office hours! As
you take her out to dinner, and watch her there
seated before you, a perfumed radiance, a dewy
dazzling vision, an evening star swathed in gauzy
convolutions of silk and lace—can it be the same
creature who an hour or two ago sat primly with
notebook and pencil at your desk side, and took
down your specification for fireproofing that new
steel-constructed building on Broadway? You,
except for your evening clothes, are not changed;
but she—well, your clients couldn't possibly
recognize her. As with Browning's lover, you

are on the other side of the moon, "side unseen" of office boy or of subway throng; you are in the presence of those "silent silver lights and darks undreamed of" by the gross members of your board of directors. By day—but ah! at evening under the electric lights, to the delicate strains of the palm-shaded orchestra! Man is incapable of these exquisite transformations. By day a gruff and hurried machine—at evening, at best, a rapt and laconic poker player. A change with no suggestion of the miraculous.

Do not let us for a moment imagine that because man is ceasing to remove his hat at her entrance into crowded elevators, or because he hustles her or allows her to hang by the straps in crowded cars, that he is tending to forget this supernaturalism of woman. Such change in his manners merely means his respect for her disguise, her disguise as a business woman. By day she desires to be regarded as just that, and she resents as untimely the recognition of her sex, her mystery, and her marvel during business hours. Man's apparent impoliteness, therefore, is actually a delicate modern form of chivalry. But of course his real feelings are only respectfully masked, and, let her be in any danger or real discomfort, or let any language be uttered unseemly for her ears, and we know what promptly happens. Barring such accidents, man tacitly understands that her incognito is to be respected—till the charming moment comes when she chooses to put it aside and take at his hands her immemorial tribute.

So, you see, she is able to go about the rough ways, taking part even in the rough work of the world, literally bearing what the fairy tales call a charmed life. And this, of course, gives her no small advantage in the human conflict. So protected, she is enabled, when need arises, to take the offensive, with a minimum of danger. Consider her recent campaign for suffrage, for example. Does any one suppose that, had she been anything but woman, a sacrosanct being, immune from clubs and bullets, that she would have been allowed to carry matters with such high victorious hand as in England—and more power to her!—she has of late been doing. Let men attempt such tactics, and their shrift is uncomplimentarily short. It may be said that woman enjoys this immunity with children and curates, but, even so, it may be held that these latter participate in a less degree in that divine nature with which woman is so completely armoured.

> How with this rage shall beauty hold a plea,
> Whose action is no stronger than a flower?

exclaims Shakespeare.

But there is indeed the mystery, for, though its "action is no stronger than a flower," the power wielded by beauty in this world, and therefore by woman as its most dynamic embodiment, is as undeniable as it is irresistible. "Terrible as an army with banners" was no mere figure of love-sick speech. It is as plain a truth as the properties of radium, and belongs to the same order of marvel. Such scientific discoveries are particularly welcome as demonstrating the power of the finer, as contrasted with the more brutally obvious, manifestations of force; for they thus illustrate the probable nature of those spiritual forces whose operations we can plainly see, without being able to account for them. A foolish phrase has it that "a woman's strength is in her helplessness." "Helplessness" is a curious term to use for a mysteriously concentrated or super-refined form of strength. "Whose action is no stronger than a flower." But is the action of a flower any less strong because it is not the action of a fist? As a motive force a flower may be, and indeed has time and again been, stronger than a thousand fists. And what then shall we say of the action of that flower of flowers that is woman—that flower that not only once or twice in history has

> . . . launched a thousand ships
> And burned the topless towers of Ilium.

Woman's helplessness, forsooth! On the contrary, woman is the best equipped fighting machine that ever went to battle. And she is this, not from any sufferance on the part of man, not from any consideration on his part toward her "weakness," but merely because he cannot help himself, because nature has so made her.

No simple reasoning will account for her influence over man. It is not an influence he allows. It is an influence he cannot resist, and it is an influence which he cannot explain, though he may make believe to do so. That "protection," for example, which he extends to her from the common physical perils with which he is more muscularly constituted to cope—why is it extended? Merely out of pity to a weaker being than himself? Does other weakness always command his pity? We know that it does not. No, this "protection" is but a part of an instinctive reverence, for which he can give no reason, the same kind of reverence which he has always given to divine beings, to any manifestation or vessel of the mysteriously sacred something in human life. He respects and protects woman from the same instinct which makes him shrink from profaning an altar or robbing a church, or sends him on his knees before any apparition supposedly divine. Priests and women are often classed together, but not because the priests are regarded as effeminately "helpless"; rather because both are recognized as ministers of sacred mysteries, both belong to the spiritual sphere, and have commerce with the occult holiness of things. Also be it remarked that this "protection" is chiefly needed against the brutality and bestiality of man's own heart, which woman and religion alike rather hold in subjection by their mysterious influence than have to thank for any favours of self-control. Man "protects" woman because he first worships her, because, if she has for him not always the beauty of holiness, she at least always suggests the holiness of beauty.

Now when has man ever suggested holiness to the most adoring woman? I do not refer to the professional holiness of saints and ecclesiastics, but to that sense of hallowed strangeness, of mystic purity, of spiritual exquisiteness, which breathes from a beautiful woman and makes the touch of her hand a religious ecstasy, and her very garments a thrilling mystery. How impossible it is to imagine a woman writing the *Vita Nuova*, or a girl feeling toward a boy such feelings of awe and worship as set the boy Dante a-tremble at his first sight of the girl Beatrice.

At that moment [he writes], I say most truly that the spirit of life, which hath its dwelling in the secretest chamber of the heart, began to tremble so violently that the least pulse of my body shook therewith; and in trembling it said these words: "*Ecce deus fortior me, qui veniens dominabitur mihi.* (Here is a deity stronger than I, who, coming, shall rule over me.)"

And, loverlike, he records of "this youngest of the angels" that "her dress on that day was of a most noble colour, a subdued and goodly crimson, girdled and adorned in such sort as best suited with her very tender age." Ah! that "little frock," that sacred little frock we first saw her in! Don't we all know it? And the little handkerchief, scented like the breath of heaven, we begged as a sacred relic!   And——

> Long after you are dead
> I will kiss the shoes of your feet. . . .

Yes! anything she has worn or touched; for, as a modern writer has said:

Everything a woman wears or touches immediately incarnates something of herself. A handkerchief, a glove, a flower—with a breath she endows them with immortal souls.

Waller with his girdle, Donne with "that subtle wreath of hair about his arm," the mediæval knight riding at tourney with his lady's sleeve at his helm, and all relic-worshipping lovers through the ages bear witness to that divine supernaturalism of woman. To touch the hem of that little frock, to kiss the mere imprint of those little feet, is to be purified and exalted. But when did man affect woman in that way? I am tolerably well read in the poetry of woman's emotions, but I recall no parallel expressions of feeling. No passionate apostrophes of his golf stockings come to my mind, nor wistful recollections of the trousers he wore on that never-to-be-forgotten afternoon. The immaculate collar that spanned his muscular throat finds no Waller to sing it:

> A narrow compass—and yet there
> Dwelt all that's good, and all that's fair,

and probably the smartest negligée shirt that ever
sported with the summer winds on a clothes-line
has never caused the smallest flutter in feminine
bosoms. The very suggestion is, of course, absurd
—whereas with women, in very deed, it is as with
the temple in Keats's lines:

> . . . even as the trees
> That whisper round a temple become soon
> Dear as the temple's self.

Properly understood, therefore, the cult of the
skirt-dancer has a religious significance, and man's
preoccupation with petticoats is but the popular
recognition of the divinity of woman. All that
she is and does and wears has a ritualistic character, and she herself commands our reverence
because we feel her to be the vessel of sacred
mysteries, the earthly representative of unearthly
powers, with which she enjoys an intimacy of
communication denied to man. It is not a reasonable feeling, or one to be reasoned about; and that
is why we very properly exempt woman from the
necessity of being reasonable. She is not, we say,
a reasonable being, and in so saying we pay her a
profound compliment. For she transcends reason,
and on that very account is mysteriously wise, the
wisest of created things—mother-wise. When we
say "mother-wit," we mean something deeper than
we realize—for what in the universe is wiser than
a mother, fed as she is through the strange channels
of her being with that lore of the infinite which

seems to enter her body by means of organs subtler than the brain?

A certain famous novelist meant well when recently he celebrated woman as "the mother of the male," but such celebration, while ludicrously masculine in its egotistic limitation, would have fallen short even if he had stopped to mention that she was the mother of the female, too; for not merely in the fact that she is the mother of the race resides the essential mystery of her motherhood. We do not value woman merely, if one may be permitted the expression, as a brood mare, an economic factor controlling the census returns. Her gift of motherhood is stranger than that, and includes spiritual affinities and significances not entirely represented by visible babes. Her motherhood is mysterious because it seems to be one with the universal motherhood of nature, one with the motherhood that guards and warms to life the eggs in the nest and the seeds in the hollows of the hills, the motherhood of the whole strange vital process, wherever and howsoever it moves and dreams and breaks into song and flower. And, as nature is something more than a mother, so is woman. She is a vision, an outward and visible sign of an inward and spiritual grace and goodness at the heart of life; and her beauty is the sacred seal which the gods have set upon her in token of her supernatural meaning and mission; for all beauty is the message of the immortal to mortality. Always when man has been in doubt concerning his gods, or in despair amid the darkness of his destiny, his heart has been revived by some beatific vision;

> Some shape of beauty moves away the pall
> From our dark spirits.

Woman is our permanent **Beatific Vision** in the darkness of the world.

III

THE LACK OF IMAGINATION AMONG MILLIONAIRES

CONSIDERING the truly magical power of money, it must often have struck the meditative mind—particularly that class of meditative mind whose wealth consists chiefly in meditation—to what thoroughly commonplace uses the modern millionaire applies the power that is his: in brief, with what little originality, with what a pitiful lack of imagination, he spends his money. One seldom hears of his doing a novel or striking thing with it.

On the contrary, he buys precisely the same things as his fellow-millionaires, the same stereotyped possessions—houses in Fifth Avenue and Newport, racehorses, automobiles, boxes at the opera, diamonds and dancing girls; and whether, as the phrase is, he makes good use of his wealth, or squanders it on his pleasures, the so-called good or bad uses are alike drearily devoid of individuality. Philanthropist or profligate, the modern millionaire is one and the same in his lack of initiative. Saint or sinner, he is one or the other in the same tame imitative way.

The rich men of the past, the splendid spend-
thrifts of antiquity, seem usually to have combined
a gift of fancy with their wealth, often even something like poetry; and their extravagances, however extreme, had usually a saving grace of personal
whim to recommend them to lovers of the picturesque. Sardanapalus and Heliogabalus may have
been whatever else you please, but they were
assuredly not commonplace; and the mere mention of their names vibrates with mankind's
perennial gratitude for splendour and colossal
display, however perverse, and even absurd. The
princes of the Italian Renaissance were, of course,
notable examples of the rich man as fantast,
probably because they had the good sense to seek
the skilled advice of poets and painters as to how
best to make an artistic display of their possessions.
Alas, no millionaire today asks a poet's or painter's
assistance in spending his money; yet, were the
modern millionaire to do so, the world might once
more be delighted with such spectacles as Leonardo
devised for the entertainments at the Villa Medici
—those fanciful banquets, where, instead of a
mere vulgar display of Medici money—"a hundred
dollars a plate," so to say—whimsical wit and
beauty entered into the creation of the very dishes.
Leicester's famous welcoming of Elizabeth to
Kenilworth was perhaps the last spectacular
"revel" of its kind to strike the imagination;
though we must not fail to remember with gratitude the magnificent Beckford, with his glorious

"rich man's folly" of Fonthill Abbey, a lordly pleasure house which naturally sprang from the same Aladdin-like fancy which produced "Vathek."

I but mention one or two such typical examples at random to illustrate the difference between past and present. At present the rich man's paucity of originality is so painful that we even welcome a certain millionaire's *penchant* for collecting fleas— he, it is rumoured, having paid as much as a thousand dollars for specimens of a particularly rare species. It is a passion perhaps hard to understand, but, at least, as we say, it is "different." Mr. Carnegie's more comprehensible hobby for building libraries shows also no little originality in a man of a class which is not as a rule devoted to literature. Another millionaire I recently read of, who refused to pay the smallest account till it had run for five years, and would then gladly pay it, with compound interest at five per cent., has something refreshing about him; while still another rich eccentric, who has lived on his yacht anchored near the English coast for some fifteen years or so in order to avoid payment of his American taxes, and who occasionally amuses himself by having gold pieces heated white hot and thrown into the sea for diving boys to pick them up, shows a quaint ingenuity which deserves our gratitude. Another modern example of how to spend, or waste, one's money picturesquely was provided by the late Marquis of Anglesey, a young lord generally regarded as crazy by an ungrateful

England.   Perhaps it was a little crazy in him to spend so much money in the comparatively commonplace adventure of taking an amateur dramatic company through the English provinces, he himself, I believe, playing but minor rôles; but lovers of Gautier's *Le Capitaine Fracasse* will see in that but a charmingly boyish desire to translate a beloved dream into a reality—though his creditors probably did not take that view.   Neither, one can surmise, did those gentlemen sufficiently appreciate his passion for amassing amazing waistcoats, of which some seven hundred were found in his wardrobe at his lamented death; or strange and beautiful walking sticks, a like prodigious collection of which were among the fantastic assets which represented his originally large personal fortune on the winding up of his earthly affairs.   Among these unimaginative creditors were, doubtless, many jewellers who found it hard to sympathize with his lordship's genial after-dinner habit, particularly when in the society of fair women, of plunging his hand into his trousers pocket and bringing it forth again brimming over with uncut precious stones of many colours, at the same time begging his companion to take her choice of the moonlit rainbowed things.   The Marquis of Anglesey died at the early age of twenty-nine, much lamented, as I have hinted— by his creditors, but no less sincerely lamented, too, by those for whom his flamboyant personality and bizarre whims added to that gaiety of nations sadly in need today of such figures. A friend of mine owns two of the wonderful waistcoats. Sometimes he wears one as we lunch together, and on such occasions we always drink in silence to the memory of his fantastic lordship.

These examples of rich men of our own time who have known how to spend their money with whim and fancy and flourish are but exceptions to my argument, lights shining, so to say, in a great darkness. As a general rule, it is the poor or comparatively poor man, the man lacking the very necessary material of the art, who is an artist of this kind. It is the man with but little money who more often provides examples of the delightful way of spending it. I trust that Mr. Richard Harding Davis will not resent my recalling a charming feat of his in this connection. Of course Mr. Davis is by no means a poor man, as all we who admire his writings are glad to know. Still, successful writer as he is, he is not yet, I presume, on a Carnegie or Rockefeller rating; and, at the time which I am about to recall, while already famous and comparatively prosperous, he had not attained that security of position which is happily his today. Well, I suppose it was some twelve or fifteen years ago—and of course I am only recalling a story well known to all the world— that, chancing to be in London, and wishing to send a surprise message to a lady in Chicago who afterward became his wife, he conceived the idea of sending it by messenger boy from Charing

Cross to Michigan Avenue; and so the little lad, in the well-known uniform of hurry, sped across the sea, as casually as though he were on an errand from Charing Cross to Chancery Lane, raced across nearly half the continent, as casually as though he were on an errand from Wall Street to Park Row, and finding the proper number in Michigan Avenue, placed the far travelled letter in the lady's hand, no doubt casually asking for a receipt.   This I consider one of the most romantic compliments ever paid by a lover to his lady. What millionaire ever had a fancy like that?

Or what millionaire ever had a fancy like this? There was living in New York some ten years ago a charming actor, not unknown to the public and much loved by his friends for, among his other qualities, his quaint whims. Good actor as he was, like many other good actors he was usually out of an engagement, and he was invariably poor. It was always his poorest moment that he would choose for the indulgence of an odd, and surely kindly, eccentricity. He would half starve himself, go without drinks, forswear tobacco, deny himself car fares, till at last he had saved up five dollars. This by no means easy feat accomplished, he would have his five-dollar bill changed into five hundred pennies, filling his pockets with which, he would sally forth from his lodging, and, seeking neighbourhoods in which children most abound, he would scatter his arduously accumulated largess among the scrambling boys and girls, literally happy as a king to watch the glee on the young faces at the miraculous windfall. We often wondered that he was not arrested for creating a riot in the public streets, a disturber of the public traffic. Had some millionaire passed by on one of those ecstatic occasions, there is no question but that he would have been promptly removed to Bellevue as a dangerous lunatic.

. Or what millionaire ever had a fancy like this? Passing along Forty-second Street one afternoon, I came upon a little crowd, and joining it I found that it was grouped in amused curiosity, and with a certain kindness, round an old hatless Irishman, who was leaning against a shop front, weeping bitterly, and, of course, grotesquely. The old man was very evidently drunk, but there was something in his weeping deeply pitiful for all that. He was drunk, for certain; but no less certainly he was very unhappy—unhappy over some mysterious something that one or two kindly questioners tried in vain to discover. As we all stood helplessly looking on and wondering, a tall, brisk young man, of the lean, rapid, few-worded American type, pushed in among us, took a swift look at the old man, thrust a dollar bill into his hand, said "Forget it"—no more—and was gone like a flash on his way. The old man fumbled the note in a daze, but what chiefly interested me was the amazed look on the faces of the little crowd. It was almost as if something supernatural had happened. All eyes turned quickly to catch sight of that strange young man; but he was already far off striding swiftly up the street. I have often regretted that I checked my impulse to catch up with him—for it seemed to me, too, that I had never seen a stranger thing. Pity or whim or whatever it was, did ever a millionaire do the like with a dollar, create such a sensation or have so much fun with so small a sum? No; millionaires never have fancies like that.

Another poor man's fancy is that of a friend of mine, a very poor young lawyer, whose custom it is to walk uptown from his office at evening, studying the faces of the passers-by. He is too poor to afford dollar bills. He must work his miracles with twenty-five-cent pieces, or even smaller coins; but it is with this art of spending money as with any other art: the greatness of the artist is shown by his command over an economy of material; and the amount of human happiness to be evoked by the dispensation of a quarter into the carefully selected hand, at the artistically chosen moment, almost passes belief. Suppose, for example, you were a sandwich man on a bleak winter day, an old weary man, with hope so long since faded out of your heart that you would hardly know what the word meant if you chanced to read it in print. Thought, too, is dead within you, and feeling even so numbed that you hardly suffer any more. Practically you are a man who ought to be in your coffin—at peace in Potter's field—who, by the mere mechanic habit of existence, mournfully parades the public streets, holding up a banner with some strange device, the scoff of the pitiless wayfarer—as like as not supporting against an empty stomach the savoury advertisement of some newly opened restaurant. Suppose you were that man, and suddenly through the thick hopelessness, muffling you around as with a spiritual deafness, there should penetrate a kind voice saying: "Try and keep up your heart, friend; there are better days ahead"; and with the voice a hand slipping into yours a coin, and with both a kind smile, a cheery "Good-bye," and a tall, broad-shouldered figure, striding with long, so to say, kindly legs up the street—gone almost before you knew he was there. I think it would hardly matter to you whether the coin were a quarter or a dime; but what would matter would be your amazement that there still was any kindness left on the earth; and perhaps you might almost be tempted to believe in God again. And then—well, what would it matter to any one what you did with your miraculous coin? This is my friend's favourite way of spending his money. To the extent of his poor means he has constituted himself the Haroun Al Raschid of the sandwich men.

After all, I suppose that most of us, if put into the possession of great wealth, would find our greatest satisfaction in the spending of it much after the fashion of my poor lawyer friend—that is, in the artistic distribution of human happiness.

I do not, of course, for a moment include in that phrase those soulless systems of philanthropy by which a solid block of money on the one side is applied to the relief of a solid block of human misery on the other, useful and much to be appreciated as such mechanical charity of course is.   It is not, indeed, the pious use of money that is my theme, but rather how to get the most fun, the most personal and original fun, out of it.

The mention of the great caliph suggests a rôle which is open to any rich man to play, the rôle of the Haroun Al Raschid of New York. What a wonderful part to play! Instead of loitering away one's evenings at the club, to doff one's magnificence and lose oneself in the great nightly multitude of the great city, wandering hither and thither, watching and listening, and, with one's cheque-book for a wand, play the magician of human destinies—bringing unhoped-for justice to the oppressed, succour as out of heaven to the outcast, and swift retribution, as of sudden lightning, to the oppressor. To play Providence in some tragic crisis of human lives; at the moment when all seemed lost to step out of the darkness and set all right with a touch of that magic wand. To walk by the side of lost and lonely men, an unexpected friend; to scribble a word on a card and say, "Present this tomorrow morning at such a number Broadway and see what will happen," and then to disappear once again into the darkness. To talk with sad, wandering girls, and arrange that wonderful new hats and other forms of feminine hope shall fall out of the sky into their lonely rooms on the morrow. To be the friend of weary workmen and all that toil by night while the world is asleep in soft beds. To come upon the hobo as he lies asleep on the park bench and slip a purse into his tattered coat, and perhaps be somewhere by to see him wake up in the dawn, and watch the strange antics of his joy—all unsuspected as its cause. To go up to the poor push-cart man, as he is being hurried from street corner to street corner by the police, and say: "Would you like to go back to Italy? Here is a steamer ticket. A boat sails for Genoa tomorrow. And here is a thousand dollars. It will buy you a vineyard in Sicily. Go home and bid the signora get ready." And then to disappear once more, like Harlequin, to flash your wand in some other corner of the human multitude. Oh, there would be fun for one's money, something worth while having money for!

I offer this suggestion to any rich man who may care to take it up, free of charge. It is a fascinating opportunity, and its rewards would be incalculable. At the end of the year how wise one would be in the human story—how filled to overflowing his heart with the thought of the joy he would thus have brought to so many lives—all, too, in pure fun, himself having had such a good time all the while!

IV

THE PASSING OF MRS. GRUNDY

"DEATH of Mrs. Grundy!" Imagine opening one's newspaper some morning and finding in sensational headlines that welcome news. One recalls the beautiful old legend of the death of Pan, and how—false report though it happily was—there once ran echoing through the world a long heartbroken sigh, and a mysterious voice was heard wailing three times from land to land, "Great Pan is dead!" Similarly, on that happy morning I have imagined, one can imagine, too, another sigh passing from land to land, the sigh of a vast relief, of a great thankfulness for the lifting of an ineffable burden, as though the earth stretched its limbs and drew great draughts of a new freedom. How wildly the birds would sing that morning! And I believe that even the church bells would ring of themselves!

Such definite news is not mine to proclaim, but if it cannot be announced with certitude that Mrs. Grundy is no more, it may, at all events, be affirmed without hesitation that she is on her deathbed, and that surely, if slowly, she is breath-

ing her last.   Yes, that poisonous breath, which
has so long pervaded like numbing miasma the
free air of the world, will soon be out of her foolish, hypocritical old body; and though it may still
linger on here and there in provincial backwoods
and suburban fastnesses, from the great air centres
of civilization it will have passed away forever.

The origin of Mrs. Grundy is shrouded in
mystery.   In fact, though one thus speaks of her
as so potent a personification, she has of course
never had any real existence.   For that very
reason she has been so hard to kill.   Nothing is so
long-lived as a chimera, nothing so difficult to
lay as a ghost.   From her first appearance, or
rather mention, in literature, Mrs. Grundy has
been a mere hearsay, a bugaboo being invented to
frighten society, as "black men" and other
goblins have been wickedly invented by nurses
to frighten children.   In the old play itself where
we first find her mentioned by name, she herself
never comes on the stage.   She is only referred to
in frightened whispers.   *"What will Mrs. Grundy
say?"* is the nervous catchword of one of the
characters, much in the same way as Mrs. Gamp
was wont to defer to the censorious standards of
her invisible friend "Mrs. Harris."   In the case of
the last named chimera, it will be recalled that the
awful moment came when Mrs. Gamp's boon
companion, Batsey Prig, was sacrilegious enough
to declare her belief that no such person as "Mrs.
Harris" was, or ever had been, in existence.   So the

awful atheistic moment has come for Mrs. Grundy, too, and an oppressed world at last takes courage to say that no such being as Mrs. Grundy has ever really existed, or that, even if she has, she shall exist no more. *What will Mrs. Grundy say?* Who cares nowadays—and so long as nobody cares, the good lady is as dead as need be.

Mrs. Grundy, of course, is man's embodied fear of his neighbour, the creation of timid souls who are afraid of being themselves, and who, instead of living their lives after their own fashion and desires, choose to live them in hypocritical discomfort according to the standards of others, standards which in their turn may be held insincerely enough from fear of someone else, and so on without end—a vicious circle of insincere living being thus created, in which no man is or does anything real, or as he himself would naturally prefer to be and to do. It is evident that such a state of mutual intimidation can exist only in small communities, economically interdependent, and among people with narrow boundaries and no horizons. If you live in a village, for example, and are dependent on the good opinion of your neighbours for your means of existence, your morals and your religious belief must be those of the village, or you are liable to starve. It is only the rich man in a village who can do as he pleases. The only thing for the dependent individualist in a village to do is to go somewhere else, to some place where a man may at the same time hold his job and his own opinions, a place too big to keep track of its units, too busy to ask irrelevant questions, and so diverse in its constituents as to have generated tolerance and free operation for all.

Now, in spite of its bigness, the world was till quite recently little more than a village, curiously held in subjection by village superstitions and village ethics, narrow conceptions of life and conduct; but the last twenty years have seen a remarkable enlargement of the human spirit, a reassertion of the natural rights of man as against the figments of prurient and emasculate conventions, to which there is no parallel since the Renaissance. Voices have been heard and truths told, and multitudes have listened gladly that aforetime must take shelter either in overawed silence or in utterance so private that they exerted no influence; and the literature of the day alone, literature of wide and greedy acceptance, is sufficient warrant for the obituary announcement which, if not yet, as I said, officially made, is already writing in the hearts, and even in the actions, of society. The popularity of such writers as Meredith and Hardy, Ibsen and Nietzsche, Maeterlinck and Walt Whitman, constitutes a writing on the wall the significance of which cannot be gainsaid. The vogue alone of Mr. Bernard Shaw, apostle to the Philistines, is a portent sufficiently conclusive. To regard Mr. Shaw either as a great dramatist or an original philosopher is, of course,

absurd. He, of all men, must surely be the last
to imagine such a vain thing about himself; but
even should he be so self-deluded, his immense
coarse usefulness to his day and generation remains, and the value of it can hardly be over-
estimated. What others have said for years as in
a glass darkly, with noble seriousness of utterance,
he proclaims again through his brazen megaphone,
with all the imperturbable *aplomb* of an impudent
showman, having as little self-respect as he has
respect for his public; and, as a consequence, that
vast herd of middle-class minds to whom finer
spirits appeal in vain hear for the first time truths
as old as philosophy, and answer to them with as-
senting instincts as old as humanity. Truth, like
many another excellent commodity, needs a vulgar
advertisement, if it is to become operative in the
masses. Mr. Shaw is truth's vulgar advertisement.
He is a brilliant, carrying noise on behalf of freedom
of thought; and his special equipment for his peculiar revivalist mission comes of his gift for revealing
to the common mind not merely the untruth of
hypocrisy, but the laughableness of hypocrisy, first
of all. He takes some popular convention, that of
medicine or marriage or what you will, and shows
you not merely how false it is but how ludicrously
false. He purges the soul, not with the terror
and pity of tragedy, but with the irresistible
laughter of rough-and-tumble farce. To think
wrongly is, first of all, so absurd. He proves it
by putting wrong thinking on the stage, where

you see it for yourself in action, and laugh immoderately. Perhaps you had never thought how droll wrong thinking or no thinking was before; and while you laugh with Shaw at your side-splitting discovery, the serious message glides in unostentatiously—wrong thinking is not merely laughable; it is also dangerous, and very uncomfortable. And so the showman has done his work, the advertiser has sold his goods, and there is so much more truth in circulation in unfamiliar areas of society.

That word "society" naturally claims some attention at the hands of one who would speak of Mrs. Grundy, particularly as she has owed her long existence to a general misconception as to what constitutes "society," and to a superstitious terror as to its powers over the individual. Society —using the word in its broad sense—has heretofore been regarded as a vague tremendous entity imposing a uniformity of opinion and action on the individual, under penalty of a like vague tremendous disapproval for insubordination. Independent minds, however, have from time to time, and in ever increasing numbers, ventured to do their own will and pleasure in disregard of this vague tremendous disapproval, and have, strange to say, found no sign of the terrible consequences threatened them, with the result that they, and the onlookers, have come to the conclusion that this fear of society is just one more bugaboo of timorous minds, with no power over the courageous spirit. From a multitude of such observations men and women have come more and more to draw the conclusion that the solidarity of society is nothing but a myth, and that so-called society is merely a loosely connected series of independent societies, formed by natural selection among their members, each with its own codes and satisfactions; and that a man not welcome in one society may readily find a home for himself in another, or indeed, if necessary, and if he be strong enough, rest content with his own society of one.

There was a time when a doubt as to the credibility of the book of Genesis or a belief in the book of Darwin made the heretic a lonely man, but nowadays he is hardly likely to go without friends. Besides, men and women of strong personal character are not usually indiscriminately gregarious. On the contrary, they are apt to welcome any disparity between them and their neighbours which tends to safeguard their leisure and protect them against the social inroads of irrelevant persons. I recall the case of a famous novelist, who, himself jealous of his own proper seclusion, permitted the amenities of his neighbours to pleasure his wife who was more sociably inclined, and smilingly allowed himself to be sacrificed once a week on the altar of a domestic "at home" day. It was amusing to see him in his drawing-room on Fridays, surrounded by every possible form of human irrelevancy—men and women well enough in their way, of course, but absolutely unrelated, if

not antipathetic to him and all he stood for—
heroically doing his best to seem really "at home."
But there came a time when he published a book
of decidedly "dangerous" tendencies, if not worse,
and then it was a delight to see how those various
nobodies fled his contact as they would the plague.
His drawing-room suddenly became a desert, and
when you dropped in on Fridays you found there—
only the people he wanted. "Is not this," he
would laughingly say, "a triumph of natural
selection? See how simply, by one honest action,
I have cut off the bores!"

To cut off the bores! Yes, that is the desperate
attempt that any man or woman who would live
their own lives rather than the lives of others is
constantly engaged in making; and more and more
all men and women are realizing that there is only
one society that really counts, the society of people
we want, rather than the people who want us or
don't want us or whom we don't want. And nowadays the man or woman must be uncomfortable
or undesirable, indeed, who cannot find all the
society he or she can profitably or conveniently
handle, be their opinions and actions never so
anti-Grundy. Thus the one great fear that more
than any other has kept Mrs. Grundy alive, the
fear of being alone in the world, cut off from such
intercourse with our fellows as most of us feel the
need of at times, has been put an end to by the
ever increasing subdivision of "society" into
friendly seclusions and self-dependent communi-

ties of men and women with like ways and points of view, however disapproved in alien circles. What "shocks" one circle will seem perfectly natural in another; and one great truth should always be held firmly in mind—that the approval of one's neighbours has never yet paid a man's bills. So long as he can go on paying those, and retain the regard of the only society he values— that of himself and a few friends—he can tell Mrs. Grundy to go—where she belongs. And this happily is—almost—as true nowadays for woman as for man; which is the main consideration, for, it need hardly be said, that it has been on her own sex that the tyranny of Mrs. Grundy has weighed peculiarly hard.

Had that tyranny been based on a genuine moral ideal, one would have some respect for it, but, as the world has always known, it has been nothing of the sort. On the contrary, it has all along been an organized hypocrisy which condoned all it professed to censure on condition that it was done in unhealthy secrecy, behind the closed doors of a lying "respectability." All manner of unclean-ness had been sanctioned so long as it wore a mask of "propriety," whereas essentially clean and wholesome expressions of human nature, undis-guised manifestations of the joy and romance of life, have been suppressed and confounded with their base counterfeits merely because they have sought the sunlight of sincerity rather than the shade where evil does well to hide. Man's proper delight in the senses, the natural joy of men and women in each other, the love of beauty, naked and unashamed, the romantic emotions, and all that passionate vitality that dreams and builds and glorifies the human story: all this, forsooth, it has been deemed wrong even to speak of, save in colourless euphemisms, and their various drama has had to be carried on by evasion and subterfuge pitiably silly indeed in this robustly procreative world. Silly, but how preposterous, too, and no longer to be endured.

It was a gain indeed to drag these vital human interests into the arena of undaunted discussion, but things are clearly seen to have already passed beyond that stage. Discussion has already set free in the world braver and truer ideals, ideals no longer afraid of life, but, in the courage of their joyousness, feasibly close to all its breathing facts. Men and women refuse any longer to allow their most vital instincts to be branded with obloquy, and the fulness of their lives to be thwarted at the bidding of an impure and irrational fiction of propriety. On every hand we find the right to happiness asserted in deeds as well as words. The essential purity of actions and relations to which a merely technical or superstitious irregularity attaches is being more and more acknowledged, and the fanciful barriers to human happiness are everywhere giving way before the daylight of common sense. Love and youth and pleasure are asserting their sacred natural rights, rights as elemental as those forces of the universe by which the stars are preserved from wrong, and the merely legal and ecclesiastical fictions which have so long overawed them are fleeing like phantoms at cockcrow.   It is no longer sinful to be happy— even in one's own way; and the extravagances of passion, the ebullitions of youth, and the vagaries of pleasure are no longer frowned down by a sour-visaged public opinion, but encouraged, or, if necessary, condoned, as the dramatic play of natural forces, and as welcome additions to the gaiety of nations.   The true sins against humanity are, on the other hand, being exposed and pil-loried with a scientific eye for their essential qualities.

> . . . . The cold heart, and the murderous tongue,
> The wintry soul that hates to hear a song,
> The close-shut fist, the mean and measuring eye,
> And all the little poisoned ways of wrong.

Man's virtues and vices are being subjected to a re-classification, in the course of which they are entertainingly seen, in no few instances, to be changing places.   The standards of punishment applied by Dante to his inferno of lost souls is being, every year, more closely approximated; warm-blooded sins of instinct and impulse, as having usually some "relish of salvation" in them, are being judged lightly, when they are accounted sins at all, and the cold-hearted sins of essential selfishness, the sins of cruelty and calculation and cowardice, are being nailed up as the real crimes against God and man. The individual is being allowed more and more to be the judge of his own actions, and all actions are being estimated more in regard to their special relation and environment, as the relativity of right and wrong, that most just of modern conceptions, is becoming understood. The hidden sins of the pious and respectable are coming disastrously into the light, and it no longer avails for a man to be a pillar of orthodoxy on Sundays if he be a pillar of oppression all the rest of the week; while the negative virtues of abstinence from the common human pleasures go for less than nothing in a world that no longer regards the theatre, the race course, and the card table, or even a beautiful woman, as under the especial wrath of God. No, the Grundy "virtues" are fast disappearing, and piano legs are once more being worn in their natural nudity. The general trend is unmistakable and irresistible, and such apparent contradictions of it as occasionally get into the newspapers are of no general significance; as when, for example, some exquisitely refined Irish police officer suppresses a play of genius, or blushingly covers up the nakedness of a beautiful statue, or comes out strong on the question of woman's bathing dress when some sensible girl has the courage to go into the water with somewhat less than her entire walking costume; or, again, when some crank invokes the blue laws against

Sunday golf or tennis; or some spinster association puts itself on record against woman's smoking: all these are merely provincial or parochial exceptions to the onward movement of morals and manners, mere spasmodic twitchings, so to say, of the poor old lady on her deathbed. We know well enough that she who would so sternly set her face against the feminine cigarette would have no objection to one of her votaries carrying on an affair with another woman's husband—not the least in the world, so long as she was careful to keep it out of the courts. And such is a sample of her morality in all her dealings. Humanity will lose no real sanctity or safeguard by her demise; only false shame and false morality will go—but true modesty, "the modesty of nature," true propriety, true religion—and incidentally true love and true marriage—will all be immeasurably the gainers by the death of this hypocritical, nasty-minded old lady.

V

MODERN AIDS TO ROMANCE

THERE have, of course, in all ages been those
who made a business of running down the
times in which they lived—tiresome people for
whom everything had gone to the dogs—or was
rapidly going—uncomfortable critics who could
never make themselves at home in their own
century, and whose weary shibboleth was that of
some legendary perfect past.

In Rome this particular kind of bore went by the
name of *laudator temporis acti;* and, if we have
no such concise Anglo-Saxon phrase for the type,
we still have the type no less ubiquitously with
us. The bugbear of such is "modern science,"
or "modern thought," a monster which, we are
frequently assured, is fast devouring all the
beautiful and good in human life, a Moloch fed on
the dreams and ideals and noble faiths of man.
Modernity! For such "modernity" has taken
the place of "Anti-Christ." These sad, nervous
people have no eye for the beautiful patterns and
fantasies of change, none of that faith which
rejoices to watch "the roaring loom of time"

weaving ever new garments for the unchanging eternal gods. In new temples, strangely enough, they see only atheism, instead of the vitality of spiritual evolution; in new affirmations they scent only dangerous denials. With the more grave misgivings of these folk of little faith this is not the place to deal, though actually, if there were any ground for belief in a modern decay of religion, we might seriously begin to believe in the alleged decay of romance.

Yes, romance, we not infrequently hear, is dead. Modern science has killed it. It is essentially a "thing of the past"—an affair presumably of stage-coaches, powdered wigs, and lace ruffles. It cannot breathe in what is spoken of as "this materialistic age."

The dullards who repeat these platitudes of the muddle-headed multitude are surely the only people for whom they are true. It is they alone who are the materialists, confusing as they do the spirit of romance with its worn-out garments of bygone fashions. Such people are so clearly out of court as not to be worth controverting, except for the opportunity they give one of confidently making the joyous affirmation that, far from romance being dead in our day, there never was a more romantic age than ours, and that never since the world began has it offered so many opportunities, so many facilities for romance as at the present time.

In fact, a very little thinking will show that of

all those benefited by "the blessings of modern science," it is the lovers of the community who as a body have most to be thankful for. Indeed, so true is this that it might almost seem as though the modern laboratory has been run primarily from romantic motives, to the end that the old reproach should be removed and the course of true love run magically smooth. Valuable as the telephone may be in business affairs, it is simply invaluable in the affairs of love; and mechanicians the world over are absorbed in the problem of aerial flight, whether they know it or not, chiefly to provide Love with wings as swift as his desire.

Distance may lend enchantment to those whom we prefer to appreciate from afar, but nearness is the real enchantment to your true lover, and distance is his natural enemy. Distance and the slow-footedness of Time are his immemorial evils. Both of these modern science has all but annihilated. Consider for a moment the conditions under which love was carried on in those old days which some people find so romantic. Think what a comparatively short distance meant then, with snail-paced precarious mails, and the only means of communication horses by land, and sailing ships by sea. How men and women had the courage to go on long journeys at all away from each other in those days is hard to realize, knowing what an impenetrable curtain of silence and mystery immediately fell between them with the winding of the coach horn, or the last wave of the plumed hat as it disappeared behind the last turning of the road —leaving those at home with nothing for company but the yearning horizon and the aching, uncommunicative hours. Days, weeks, months, even years, must go by in waiting for a word—and when at last it came, brought on lumbering wheels or at best by some courier on his steaming mud-splashed mount, precious as it was, it was already grown old and cold and perhaps long since untrue.

Imagine perhaps being dependent for one's heart news on some chance soldier limping back from the wars, or some pilgrim from the Holy Land with scallop shell and staff!

Distance was indeed a form of death under such conditions—no wonder men made their wills as they set out on a journey—and when actual physical death did not intervene, how much of that slow death-in-life, that fading of the memory and that numbing of the affections which absence too often brings, was even still more to be feared. The loved face might indeed return, looking much the same as when it went away, but what of the heart that went a-journeying, too? What even of the hearts that remained at home?

The chances of death and disaster not even modern science can forestall, though even these it has considerably lessened; but that other death of the heart, which comes of the slow starvation of silence and absence, it may be held to have all but vanquished. Thanks to its weird magicians, you may be seas or continents away from her whom your soul loveth, yet "at her window bid good-morrow" as punctually as if you lived next door; or serenade her by electricity—at all hours of the night. If you sigh in New York, she can hear you and sigh back in San Francisco; and soon her very face will be carried to you at any moment of the day along the magic wires. Nor will you need to wait for the postman, but be able to read her flowerlike words as they write themselves out on the luminous slate before you, at the very moment as she leans her fragrant bosom upon her electric desk three thousand miles away. If this isn't romantic, one may well ask what is!

To take the telephone alone, surely the romance of Pyramus and Thisbe, with their primitive hole in the wall, was a tame affair compared with the possibilities of this magic toy, by means of which you can talk with your love not merely through a wall but through the Rocky Mountains. You can whisper sweet nothings to her across the sounding sea, and bid her "sleep well" over leagues of primeval forest, and through the stoniest-hearted city her soft voice will find its way. Even in mid-ocean the "wireless" will bring you news of her *mal-de-mer*. And more than that; should you wish to carry her voice with you from place to place, science is once more at your service with another magic toy—the phonograph—by which indeed she can still go on speaking to you, if you have the courage to listen, from beyond the grave.

The telegraph, the telephone, the "wireless," the phonograph, the electric letter writer—such are the modern "conveniences" of romance; and, should an elopement be on foot, what are the fastest post-chaise or the fleetest horses compared with a high-powered automobile?   And when the airship really comes, what romance that has ever been will compare for excitement with an elopement through the sky?

Apart from the practical conveniences of these various new devices, there is a poetic quality about the mere devices themselves which is full of fascination and charm.   Whether we call up our sweetheart or our stockbroker, what a thing of enchantment the telephone is merely in itself! Such devices turn the veriest prose of life into poetry; and, indeed, the more prosaic the uses to which we put them, the more marvellous by contrast their marvel seems.   Even our businesses are carried on by agencies more mysterious and truly magical than anything in the *Arabian Nights*, and all day long we are playing with mysterious natural laws and exquisite natural forces as, in a small way, when boys we used to delight in our experiments with oxygen and hydrogen and Leyden jars.   Science has thus brought an element of romantic "fun," so to speak, even into our stores and our counting-houses.   I wonder if "Central" realizes what a truly romantic employment is hers?

But, pressed into the high service of love, one sees at once what a poetic fitness there is in their employ, and how our much-abused modern science has found at last for that fastidious god an appropriately dignified and beautiful ministrant. Coarse and vulgar indeed seem the ancient servitors and the uncouth machinery by which the divine business of the god was carried on of old. Today, through the skill of science, the august lightning has become his messenger, and the hidden gnomes of air and sea hasten to do his bidding.

Modern science, then, so far from being an enemy of romance, is seen on every hand to be its sympathetic and resourceful friend, its swift and irresistible helper in its serious need, and an indulgent minister to its lighter fancies. Be it whim or emergency, the modern laboratory is equally at the service of romance, equally ready to gratify mankind with a torpedo or a toy.

Not only, however, has modern science thus put itself at the service of romance, by supplying it with its various magic machinery of communication, but modern thought—that much maligned bugbear of timorous minds—has generated an atmosphere increasingly favourable to and sympathetic with the romantic expression of human nature in all its forms.

The world has unmistakably grown younger again during the last twenty years, as though—which, indeed, is the fact—it had thrown off an accumulation of mopishness, shaken itself free from imaginary middle-aged restrictions and preoccupations. All over the world there is a wind

of youth blowing such as has not freshened the
air of time since the days of Elizabeth. Once
more the spring of a new Renaissance of Human
Nature is upon us.   It is the fashion to be young,
and the age of romance both for men and women
has been indefinitely extended.   No one gives up
the game, or is expected to, till he is genuinely
tired of playing it.   Mopish conventions are less
and less allowed to restrict that free and joyous
play of vitality dear to the modern heart, which is
the essence of all romance.   More and more the
world is growing to love a lover, and one has only
to read the newspapers to see how sympathetic
are the times to any generous and adventurous
display of the passions.

This more humane temper is the result of many
causes.   The disintegration of religious superstition, and the substitution in its stead of spiritual
ideals closer to the facts of life, is one of these.
All that was good in Puritanism has been retained
by the modern spirit, while its narrowing and
numbing features, its anti-human, self-mortifying,
provincial side have passed or are passing in the
regenerating sunlight of what one might call a
spiritual paganism, which conceives of natural
forces and natural laws as inherently pure and
mysteriously sacred.   Thus the way of a man
with a maid is no longer a shamefaced affair, but
it is more and more realized that in its romance and its multifarious refinements of development are the "law and the prophets," the

"eternal meanings" of natural religion and social spirituality.

Then, too, the spread of democracy, resulting in the breaking down of caste barriers, is all to the good of romance. Swiftly and surely Guelph and Ghibelline and break-neck orchard walls are passing away. If Romeo and Juliet make a tragedy of it nowadays, they have only to blame their own mismanagement, for the world is with them as it has never been before, and all sensible fathers and mothers know it.

Again, the freer intercourse between the sexes tends incalculably to smooth that course of true love once so proverbially rough, but now indeed in danger of being made too unexcitingly smooth. Yet if, as a result, certain old combinations of romance are becoming obsolete, new ones, no less picturesque, and even more vital in their drama, are being evolved every day by the new conditions. Those very inroads being so rapidly and successfully made by woman into the immemorial business of man, which are superficially regarded by some as dangerous to the tenderer sentiments between men and women, are, on the contrary, merely widening the area of romance, and will eventually develop, as they can be seen already developing, a new chivalry and a new poetry of the sexes no less deep and far more many-sided than the old. The robuster comradeship between the two already resulting from the more active sharing of common interests cannot but tend to a deeper and more exhilarating union of man and woman, a completer, intenser marriage literally of true minds as well as bodies than was possible in the old régime, when the masculine and feminine "spheres" were kept so jealously distinct and only allowed to touch at the elementary points of relationship. There has always been a thrill of adventure when either has been admitted a little farther into the other's world than was customary. How thrilling, therefore, will it be when men and women entirely share in each other's lives, without fictitious reserves and mysteries, and face the whole adventure of life squarely and completely together, all the more husband and wife for being comrades as well—as many men and women of the new era are already joyously doing.

And, merely on the surface, what a new romantic element woman has introduced into the daily drudgery of men's lives by her mere presence in their offices! She cannot always be beautiful, poor dear, and she is not invariably gracious, it is true; yet, on the whole, how much the atmosphere of office life has gained in amenity by the coming of the stenographer, the typewriter, and the telephone girl, not to speak of her frequent decorative value in a world that has hitherto been uncompromisingly harsh and unadorned! Men may affect to ignore this, and cannot afford indeed to be too sensitive to these flowery presences that have so considerably supplanted those misbegotten young miscreants known as office-boys, a vanishing race of human terror; yet there she is, all the same, in spite of her businesslike airs and her prosaic tasks, silently diffusing about her that eternal mystery which she can never lose, be her occupations never so masculine.

There she is with her subtly wreathed hair and her absurd little lace handkerchiefs and her furtive powder puff and her bits of immemorial ornaments and the soft sound of her skirts and all the rest of it. Never mind how grimly and even brusquely you may be dictating to her specifications for steel rails or the like, little wafts of perfume cannot help floating across to your rolltop desk, and you are a man and she is a woman, for all that; and, instead of having her with you at fag ends of your days, you have her with you all day long now— and your sisters and your sweethearts are so much the nearer to you all day for her presence, and, whether you know it or not, you are so much the less a brute because she is there.

Where the loss to romance comes in in these admirable new arrangements of modern commerce it is hard to see. Of course a new element of danger is thus introduced into the routine of our daily lives, but when was danger an enemy to romance? The "bright face" of this particular "danger" who would be without? The beloved essayist from whom that last phrase is, of course, adapted, declared, as we all know, that to marry is "to domesticate the recording angel." One might say that the modern business man has officialized the ministering angel—perhaps some other forms of angel as well.

In their work, then, as in their play, men and women are more and more coming to share with each other as comrades, and really the fun of life seems in no wise diminished as a consequence. Rather the contrary, it would seem, if one is to judge from the "Decameron" of the newspapers. Yet it is not very long ago that man looked askance at woman's wistful plea to take part even in his play. He had the old boyish fear that she would spoil the game. However, it didn't take him long to find out his mistake and to know woman for the true "sport" that she can be. And in that discovery it was another invention of that wicked modern science that was the chief, if humble seeming, factor, no less than that eclipsed but inexpressibly useful instrument (of flirtation) in the hands of a kind providence, the bicycle.

The service of the bicycle to the "emancipation of woman" movements has perhaps never been acknowledged by the philosopher; but a little thought will make evident how far-reaching that service has been. When that near day arrives on which woman shall call herself absolutely "free," should she feel inclined to celebrate her freedom by some monument of her gratitude, let the monument be neither to man nor woman, however valiant in the fight, but simply let it take the form of an enthroned and laurelled bicycle—for the moment woman mounted that apparently innocent machine, it carried her on the high-road to freedom. On that she could go not only where she pleased, but—what is even more to the point—with whom she pleased. The free companionship of man and woman had begun. Then and forever ended the old system of courtship, which seems so laughable and even incredible today. One was no longer expected to pay court to one's beloved, sitting stiffly on straight-backed chairs in a chill drawing-room in the non-conducting, or non-conducive, presence of still chillier maiden aunts. The doom of the *duenna* was sounded; the chill drawing-room was exchanged for "the open road" and the whispering woodland; and soon it is to come about that a man shall propose to his wife high up in the blue heavens, in an airship softly swaying at anchor in the wake of the evening star.

VI

THE LAST CALL

I DON'T know whether or not the cry "Last call for the dining-car" affects others as it affects me, but for me it always has a stern, fateful sound, suggestive of momentous opportunity fast slipping away, opportunity that can never come again; and, on the occasions when I have disregarded it, I have been haunted with a sense of the neglected "might-have-been."

Not, indeed, that the formless regret has been connected with any illusions as to the mysterious quality of the dinner that I have thus foregone. I have been well enough aware that the only actual opportunity thus evaded has been most probably that of an unusually bad dinner, exorbitantly paid for. The dinner itself has had nothing to do with my feeling, which, indeed, has come of a suggestiveness in the cry beyond the occasion, a sense conveyed by the words, in combination with the swift speeding along of the train, of the inexorable swift passage and gliding away of all things. Ah! so soon it will be the last call—for so many pleas-

ant things—that we would fain arrest and enjoy
a little longer in a world that with tragic velocity
is flowing away from us, each moment, "like the
waters of the torrent." O yes, all too soon it
will be the "last call" in dead earnest—the last
call for the joy of life and the glory of the
world. The grass is already withering, the
flower already fading; and that bird of time, with
so short a way to flutter, is relentlessly on the
wing.

Now some natures hear this call from the beginning of their lives. Even their opulent spendthrift
youth is "made the more mindful that the sweet
days die," by every strain of music, by every
gathered flower. All their joy is haunted, like
the poetry of William Morris, with the wistful
burden of mortality. Even the summer woodlands,
with all their pomp and riot of exuberant green
and gold, are anything but safe from this low
sweet singing, and in the white arms of beauty,
pressed desperately close as if to imprison the
divine fugitive moment, the song seems to come
nearest. Who has not held some loved face in
his hands, and gazed into it with an almost agon-
izing effort to realize its reality, to make eternally sure of it, somehow to wrest possession of it
and the transfiguring moment for ever, all the
time pierced with the melancholy knowledge
that tomorrow all will be as if this had never
been, and life once more its dull disenchanted
self?

Too soon shall morning take the stars away,
  And all the world be up and open-eyed,
This magic night be turned to common day—
  Under the willows on the riverside.

Youth, however, can afford to enjoy even its melancholy; for the ultimate fact of which that melancholy is a prophecy is a long way off. If one enchanted moment runs to an end, it may be reasonably sure for a long time yet of many more enchanted moments to come. It has as yet only taken a bite or two into the wonderful cake. And, though its poets may warn it that "youth's a stuff does not endure," it doesn't seriously believe it. Others may have come to an end of their cake, but its cake is going to last for ever. Alas, for the day when it is borne in upon us with a tragic suddenness, like a miser who awakens to find that he has been robbed of his hoard, that unaccountably the best part of the cake has been eaten, that perhaps indeed only a few desperate crumbs remain. A bleak laughter blends now with that once luxurious melancholy. There is a song at our window, terribly like the mockery of Mephistopheles. Our blood runs cold. We listen in sudden fear. It is life singing out its last call.

The time of this call, the occasion and the manner of it, mercifully vary with individuals. Some fortunate ones, indeed, never hear it till they lie on their deathbeds. Such have either been gifted with such a generous-sized cake of youth that it has lasted all their lives, or they have possessed a great art in the eating of it. Though I may add here that a cautious husbanding of your cake is no good way. That way you are liable to find it grown mouldy on your hands. No, oddly enough, it is often seen that those who all their lives have eaten their cake most eagerly have quite a little of it left at the end. There are no hard and fast rules for the eating of your cake. One can only find out by eating it; and, as I have said, it may be your luck to disprove the proverb and both eat your cake and have it.

For a dreary majority, however, the cake does come to an end, and for them henceforth, as Stevenson grimly put it, the road lies long and straight and dusty to the grave. For them that last call is apt to come usually before sunset—and the great American question arises: What are they going to do about it? That, of course, every one must decide for himself, according to his inclinations and his opportunities. But a few general considerations may be of comfort and even of greater value.

There is one thing of importance to know about this last call, that we are apt to imagine we hear it before we actually do, from a nervous sense that it is about time for it to sound. Our hair perhaps is growing grey, and our years beginning to accumulate. We hypnotize ourselves with our chronology, and say with Emerson:

It is time to grow old,
To take in sail.

Well and good, if it is and we feel like it; but
may be it isn't, and we don't. Youth is largely a
habit. So is romance. And, unless we allow
ourselves to be influenced by musty conventions
and superstitions, both habits may be prolonged
far beyond the moping limits of custom, and need
never be abandoned unless we become sincerely
and unregretfully tired of them. I can well
conceive of an old age like that of Sophocles, as
reported by Plato, who likened the fading of the
passions with the advance of age to "being set
free from service to a band of madmen."

When a man feels so, all is well and comfortable
with him. He has retired of his own free will from
the banquet of life, having had his fill, and is
content. Our image of the last call does not apply
to him, but rather to those who, with appetites
still keen, are sternly warned that for them, willy-
nilly, the banquet must soon end, and the prison
fare of prosaic middle age be henceforth their
portion. No more ortolans and transporting
vintages for them. Nothing but Scotch oatmeal
and occasional sarsaparilla to the end of the chapter. No wonder that some, hearing this dread
sentence, go half crazy in a frenzied effort to clutch
at what remains, run amok, so to say, in their
despairing determination to have, if need be, a
last "good time" and die. Their efforts are apt

to be either distasteful or pathetically comic, and the world is apt to be cynically contemptuous of the "romantic" outbursts of aging people. For myself, I always feel for them a deep and tender sympathy. I know that they have heard that last fearful call to the dining-car of life—and, poor souls, they have probably found it closed. Their mistake has been in waiting so long for the call. From various causes, they have mismanaged their lives. They have probably lived in a numbing fear of their neighbours, who have told them that it is bad manners to eat one's cake in public, and wicked to eat it in private; and any one who is fool enough to allow his neighbours to live his life for him instead of living it himself deserves what he gets, or rather doesn't get.

A wholesome oblivion of one's neighbours is the beginning of wisdom. Neighbours, at the best, are an impertinent encroachment on one's privacy, and, at the worst, an unnatural hindrance to our development. Generally speaking, it is the man or woman who has lived with least fear of his neighbours, who is least likely to hear that last call. Nothing in retrospect is so barren as a life lived in accordance with the hypocrisies of society. For those who have never lived, and are now fain to begin living when it is too late, that last call comes indeed with a ghastly irony. But for those who have fearlessly lived their lives, as they came along, with Catullus singing their *vivamus atque amemus*, and practising it, too; for those, if indeed the last call must come, they will be able to support it by the thought that, often as in the past life has called to them, it has never called to them in vain. We are apt sometimes to belittle our memories, but actually they are worth a good deal; and should the time come when we have little to look forward to, it will be no small comfort to have something to look back on. And it won't be the days when we *didn't* that we shall recall with a sense of possession, but the days and nights when we most emphatically *did*. Thank God, we did for once hold that face in our hands in the woodland! Thank God, we did get divinely drunk that wild night of nights in the city!

Wilt thou yet take all, Galilean? But these thou
    shalt not take,
The laurel, the palms and the pæan, the breast of the
    nymphs in the brake.

It is the fine excesses of life that make it worth living. The stalks of the days are endurable only because they occasionally break into flower. It is our sins of omission alone that we come in the end to regret. The temptations we resisted in our youth make themselves rods to scourge our middle age. I regret the paradoxical form these platitudes have unconsciously taken, for that they are the simplest truth any honest dying man would tell you. And that phrase recalls a beautiful poem by "E. Nesbit" which has haunted me all my life, a poem I shall beg leave to quote here, because,

though it is to be found in that poet's volume, it is
not, I believe, as well known as it deserves to be
by those who need its lesson. I quote it, too,
from memory, so I trust that the length of time I
have remembered it may be set to my credit
against any verbal mistakes I make.

"If, on some balmy summer night,
You rowed across the moon path white,
And saw the shining sea grow fair
With silver scales and golden hair,
What would you do?"

"I would be wise
And shut my ears and shut my eyes,
Lest I should leap into the tide
And clasp the seamaid as I died."

"But if you thus were strong to flee
From sweet spells woven of moon and sea,
Are you quite sure that you would reach,
Without one backward look, the beach?"

"I might look back, my dear, and then
Row straight into the snare again,
Or, if I safely got away—
Regret it to my dying day."

He who liveth his life shall live it. It is a grave
error to give ourselves grudgingly to our experi-
ences. Only in a whole-hearted surrender of
ourselves to the heaven-sent moment do we receive
back all it has to give us, and by the active recep-
tivity of our natures attract toward us other such

moments, as it were, out of the sky. An ever-ready romantic attitude toward life is the best preservative against the *ennui* of the years. Adventures, as the proverb says, are to **the adventurous**, and, as the old song goes:

> He either fears his fate too much
>   Or his deserts are small,
> That dares not put it to the touch
>   To gain or lose it all.

And the spirit of the times is happily growing more clement toward a greater fulness and variety of life. The world is growing kinder toward the fun and foolishness of existence, and the energetic pursuit of joy is no longer frowned down by anæmic and hypocritical philosophies. The old gods of energy and joy are coming to their own again, and the lives of strong men and fair women are no longer ruled over by a hierarchy of curates and maiden aunts; in fact, the maiden aunt has begun to find out her mistake, and is out for her share of the fun and the foolishness with the rest. Negative morality is fast becoming discredited, and many an old "Thou shalt not" is coming to seem as absurd as the famous Blue Laws of Connecticut. "Self-development, not self-sacrifice,"— a favourite dictum of Grant Allen's,—is growing more and more to be the formula of the modern world; and, if a certain amount of self-sacrifice is of necessity included in a healthy self-development, the proportion is being reduced to a rational limit.

One form of self-sacrifice, at all events, is no longer demanded of us—the wholesale sacrifice of our own opinions. The possibility that there may be two opinions or a dozen or a hundred on one matter, and that they may be all different, yet each one of them right in its proper application, has dawned forcibly on the world, with the conception of the relativity of experience and the modification of conditions. Nowadays we recognize that there are as many "rights" and as many "wrongs" as there are individuals; and to be happy in our own way, instead of somebody else's, is one of the first laws of nature, health, and virtue. Many an ancient restriction on personal vitality is going the way of the old sumptuary laws. We have all of us amusing memories of those severe old housekeepers who for no inclemency of the weather would allow a fire in the grate before the first of October, and who regarded a fire before that date as a positive breach of the moral law. Such old wives are a type of certain old-fashioned moralists whose icy clutch on our warm-blooded humanity we no longer suffer. Nowadays we light our fires as we have a mind to, and if we prefer to keep them going all the year round, it is no one's business but our own. Happy is the man who, when the end comes, can say with Landor:

> I warmed both hands before the fire of life;
> It sinks and I am ready to depart.

Such a one will have little need to fear that last
call of which I have been writing. In Kipling's
phrase, he has taken his fun where he found it,
and his barns are well stocked with the various
harvests of the years. Not his the wild regret for
having "safely got away." Rather he laughs to
remember how often he was taken captive by the
enchantments of the world, how whenever there
was any piece of wildness afoot he was always
found in the thick of it. When the bacchantes
were out on Mount Cithæron, and the mad *Evoe !
Evoe !* rang through the moonstruck woods, be
sure he was up and away, with ardent hands
clutched in the flying tresses. Ah! the vine leaves
and the tiger skins and the ivory bodies, the clash
of the cymbals and the dithyramb shrilling up to
the stars! "If I forget thee, O golden Aphrodite!"
He is no hypocrite, no weary "king ecclesiast,"
shaking his head over the orgies of sap and song in
which he can no longer share. He frankly acknowledges that then came in the sweet o' the
year, and he is still as young as the youngest by
virtue of having drunk deep of the only elixir, the
Dionysiac cup of life.

At the same time, while he may not ungratefully
rejoice with Sophocles at being "set free from
service to a band of madmen," that ripening of
his nature which comes most fruitfully of a generous exercise of its powers will have instinctively
taught him that secret of the transmutation of the
passions which is one of the most precious rewards

of experience. It is quite possible for a lifelong passion for fair women to become insensibly and unregretfully transmuted into a passion for first editions, and you may become quite sincerely content that a younger fellow catch the flying maiden, if only you can catch yon flitting butterfly for your collection. And, strangest of all, your grand passion for your own remarkable self may suffer a miraculous transformation into a warm appreciation for other people. It is true that you may smile a little sadly to find them even more interesting than yourself. But such passing sadness has the relish of salvation in it. Self is a weary throne, and the abdication of the ego is to be free of one of the burdens rather than the pleasures of existence.

But, to conclude, it is all too possible that you who read this may have no such assets of a wilful well spent life to draw on as he whom I have pictured. It may be that you have starved your emotions and fled your opportunities, or you may simply have had bad luck. The golden moments seldom came your way. The wilderness of life has seldom blossomed with a rose. "The breast of the nymph in the brake" and "the chimes at midnight" were not for you. And there is a menacing murmur of autumn in the air. The days are shortening, and the twilight comes early, with a chilly breath. The crickets have stopped singing, and the garden is sad with elegiac blooms. The chrysanthemum is growing on the grave of the rose. Perhaps already it is too late—too late for life and joy. You must take to first editions and entomology and other people's interests in good earnest. But no! Suddenly on the wind there comes a cry—a sound of cymbals and flutes and dancing feet. It is life's last call. You have one chance left. There is still Indian summer. It is better than nothing. Hurry and join the music, ere it be too late. For this is the last call!

When time lets slip a little perfect hour,
Take it, for it will not come again.

VII

THE PERSECUTIONS OF BEAUTY

ALL religions have periods in their history which are looked back to with retrospective fear and trembling as eras of persecution, and each religion has its own book of martyrs. The religion of beauty is no exception. Far from it. For most other religions, however they may have differed among themselves, have agreed in fearing beauty, and even in Greece there were stern sanctuaries and ascetic academes where the white bosom of Phryne would have pleaded in vain. Christianity has not been beauty's only enemy, by any means; though, when the Book of Martyrs of Beauty comes to be written, it will, doubtless, be the Christian persecutions of beauty that will bulk largest in the record—for the Beauty of Holiness and the Holiness of Beauty have been warring creeds from the beginning.

At the present moment, there is reason to fear, or to rejoice—according to one's individual leanings—that the Religion of Beauty is gaining upon its ancient rival; for perhaps never since the Renaissance has there been such a widespread impulse to assert Beauty and Joy as the ideals of human life. As evidence one has but to turn one's eyes on the youth of both sexes, as they rainbow the city thoroughfares with their laughing, heartless faces, evident children of beauty and joy, "pagan" to the core of them, however ostensibly Christian their homes and their country. In our time, at all events, Beauty has never walked the streets with so frank a radiance, so confident an air of security, and in her eyes and in her carriage, as in her subtly shaped and subtly scented garments, so conspicuous a challenge to the musty, out-worn, proprieties to frown upon her all they please. From the humblest shop-girl to the greatest lady, there is apparent an intention to be beautiful, sweet maid, and let who will be hum-drum, at whatever cost, by whatever means. This, of course, at all periods, has been woman's chief thought, but till recently, in our times, she has more or less affected a certain secrecy in her intention. She has hinted rather than fully expressed it, as though fearing a certain flagrancy in too public an exhibi-tion of her enchantments. It has hardly seemed proper to her heretofore to be as beautiful in the public gaze as in the sanctuary of her boudoir. But now, bless you, she has no such misgivings, and the flower-like effect upon the city streets is as dazzling as if, some fine morning in Constanti-nople, all the ladies of the various harems should suddenly appear abroad without their yashmaks, setting fire to the hearts and turning the heads of the unaccustomed male.   Or, to make comparison nearer home, it is almost as startling as if the ladies of the various musical comedies in town should suddenly be let loose upon our senses in broad daylight, in all the adorable sorceries of "make-up" and diaphanous draperies.   I swear that it can be no more thrilling to penetrate into that mysterious paradise "behind the scenes," than to walk up Fifth Avenue one of these summer afternoons, in the present year of grace,—humming to one's self that wistful old song, which goes something like this:

> The girls that never can be mine!
>   In every lane and street
> I hear the rustle of their gowns,
>   The whisper of their feet;
> The sweetness of their passing by,
>   Their glances strong as wine,
> Provoke the unpossessive sigh—
>   Ah! girls that never can be mine.

So audacious has Beauty become in these latter days, so proudly she walks abroad, making so superb an appeal to the desire of the eye, thighed like Artemis, and bosomed like Aphrodite, or at whiles a fairy creature of ivory and gossamer and fragrance, with a look in her eyes of secret gardens; and so much is the wide world at her feet, and one with her in the vanity of her fairness— that I sometimes fear an impending *dies iræ*, when the dormant spirit of Puritanism will reassert itself, and some stern priest thunder from the pulpit of worldly vanities and the wrath to come. Indeed, I can well imagine in the near future some modern Savonarola presiding over a new Bonfire of Vanities in Madison Square, on which, to the droning of Moody and Sankey's hymns, shall be cast all the fascinating Parisian creations, the puffs and rats, the powder and the rouge, the darling stockings, and all such concomitant be-witcheries that today make Manhattan a veri-table Isle of Circe, all to go up in savage sectarian flame, before the eyes of melancholy young men, and filling all the city with the perfume of beauty's holocaust. At street corners too will stand great books in which weeping maidens will sign their names, swearing before high heaven, to wear nothing but gingham and bed-ticking for the dreary remainder of their lives. Such a day may well come, as it has often come before, and certainly will, if women persist in being so deliberately beautiful as they are at present.

It is curious how, from time immemorial, man seems to have associated the idea of evil with beauty, shrunk from it with a sort of ghostly fear, while, at the same time drawn to it by force of its hypnotic attraction. Strangely enough, beauty has been regarded as the most dangerous enemy of the soul, and the powers of darkness that are supposed to lie in wait for that frail and fluttering psyche, so precious and apparently so perishable, are usually represented as taking shapes of beguiling loveliness—lamias, loreleis, wood nymphs, and witches with blue flowers for their eyes.   Lurking in its most innocent forms, the grim ascetic has affected to find a leaven of concupiscence, and whenever any reformation is afoot, it is always beauty that is made the first victim, whether it take the form of a statue, a stained-glass window, or a hair-ribbon.   "Homeliness is next to Godliness," though not officially stated as an article of the Christian creed, has been one of the most active of all Christian tenets.   It has always been easier far for a rich man to enter the kingdom of heaven than a gloriously beautiful woman.   Presumably such a one might be in danger of corrupting the saints, somewhat unaccustomed to such apparitions.

In this Christian fear and hatred of beauty the democratic origin of the Christian religion is suggestively illustrated, for beauty, wherever found, is always mysteriously aristocratic, and thus instinctively excites the fear and jealousy of the common people.   When, in the third century, Christian mobs set about their vandalistic work of destroying the "Pagan" temples, tearing down the beautiful calm gods and goddesses from their pedestals, and breaking their exquisite marble limbs with brutish mallets, it was not, we may be sure, of the danger to their precious souls they were thinking, but of their patrician masters who had worshipped these fair images, and paid great sums to famous sculptors for such adornment of their sanctuaries.   Perhaps it was human enough, for to those mobs beauty had long been associated with oppression.   Yet how painful to picture those golden marbles, in all their immortal fairness, confronted with the hideousness of those fanatic ill-smelling multitudes. Wonderful religionists, forsooth, that thus break with foolish hands and trample with swinish hoofs the sacred vessels of divine dreams.   Who would not

> rather be
> A Pagan suckled in a creed outworn,—
>   So might I, standing on this pleasant lea,
> Have glimpses that would make me less forlorn;
>   Have sight of Proteus rising from the sea;
> Or hear old Triton blow his wreathèd horn.

One can imagine the priest of such a violated sanctuary stealing back in the quiet moonlight, when all the mob fury had passed away, seeking amid all the wrack of fallen columns, and shattered carvings, for any poor fragments of god or goddess at whose tranquil fair-ordered altar he had ministered so long; and gathering such as he might find,—maybe a mighty hand, still the hand of a god, albeit in overthrow, or some marble curls of the sculptured ambrosial locks, or maybe the bruised breast of the goddess, white as a water-lily in the moon.   Then, seeking out some secret corner of the sacred grove, how reverently he would bury the precious fragments away from profane eyes, and go forth homeless into a mysterious changing world, from which glory and loveliness were thus surely passing away. Other priests, as we know, more fortunate than he, had forewarnings of such impending sacrilege, and were able to anticipate the mob, and bury their beautiful images in safe and secret places, there to await, after the lapse of twelve centuries, the glorious resurrection of the Renaissance. A resurrection, however, by no means free from danger, even in that resplendent dawn of intelligence; for Christianity was still the enemy of beauty, save in the Vatican, and the ignorant priest of the remote village where the spade of the peasant had revealed the sleeping marble was certain to declare the beautiful image an evil spirit, and have it broken up forthwith and ground for mortar, unless some influential scholar, or powerful lord touched with "the new learning," chanced to be on hand to save it from destruction. Yes! even at that time when beauty was being victoriously born again, the mad fear of her raged with such panic in certain minds that, when Savonarola lit his great bonfire so subtle a servant of beauty as Botticelli, fallen into a sort of religious dotage, cast his own paintings into the flames—to the lugubrious rejoicings of the sanctimonious Piagnoni — as Savonarola's followers were called; predecessors of those still gloomier zealots who, two centuries later, were to turn England into a sort of whitewashed prison, with crop-headed psalm-singing religious maniacs for gaolers. When Charles the First

> bow'd his comely head
> Down, as upon a bed,

at Whitehall, Beauty also laid her head upon the block at his side. Ugliness, parading as piety, took her place, and once more the breaking of images began, the banishment of music, the excommunication of grace, and gentle manners, and personal adornments. Gaiety became penal, and a happy heart or a beautiful smile was of the devil,—something like hanging matters—but happy hearts and beautiful smiles must have been rare things in England during the Puritan Commonwealth. Such as were left had taken refuge in France, where men might worship God and Beauty in the same church, and where it was not necessary, as at Oxford, to bury your stained-glass windows out of the reach of the mob—those

> Storied windows richly dight
> Casting a dim religious light,

which even the Puritan Milton could thus celebrate. Doubtless, that English Puritan persecution was the severest that Beauty has been called upon to endure. She still suffers from it, need one say, to this day, particularly in New England, where if the sculptured images of goddess and nymph are not exactly broken to pieces by the populace, it is from no goodwill towards them, but rather from an ingrained reverence for any form of property, even though it be nude, and where, at all events, they are under the strict surveillance of a highly proper and respectable police, those distinguished guardians of American morals.

It is worth while to try and get at the reason for this wide-spread, deep-rooted, fear of beauty: for some reason there must surely be. Such instinctive feelings, on so broad a scale, are not accidental. And so soon as one begins to analyse the attitude of religion towards beauty, the reason is not far to seek.

All religions are made up of a spiritual element and a moral element, the moral element being the temporary, practical, so to say, working side of religion, concerned with this present world, and the limitations and necessities of the various societies that compose it. The spiritual element, the really important part of religion, has no concern with Time and Space, temporary mundane laws, or conduct. It concerns itself only with the eternal properties of things. Its business is the contemplation and worship of the mystery of life, "the mystery we make darker with a name."

Now, great popular religions, designed as they are for the discipline and control of the great brute masses of humanity, are almost entirely occupied with morality, and what passes in them for spirituality is merely mythology, an element of picturesque supernaturalism calculated to enforce the morality with the multitude. Christianity is such a religion. It is mostly a matter of conduct here and now upon the earth. Its mystic side does not properly belong to it, and is foreign to, not to speak of its being practically ignored by, the average "Christian." It is a religion designed to work hand in hand with a given state of society, making for the preservation of such laws and manners and customs as are best fitted to make that society a success here and now, a worldly success in the best sense of the term. Mohammedanism is a similar religion calculated for the needs of a different society. Whatever the words or intentions of the founders of such religions, their kingdoms are essentially of this world. They are not mystic, or spiritual, or in anyway concerned with infinite and eternal things. Their business is the moral policing of humanity. Morality, as of course its name implies, is a mere matter of custom, and therefore varies with the variations of races and climates. It has nothing to do with spirituality, and, in fact, the best morals are often the least spiritual, and *vice versa*. It will be understood then that any force which is apt to disturb this moral, or more exactly speaking social, order will meet at once with the opposition of organized "religions" so called, and the more spiritual it is, the greater will be the opposition, for it will thus be the more dangerous.

Now one begins to see why Beauty is necessarily the bugbear, more or less, of all religions, or, as I prefer to regard them, "organized moralities"; for Beauty is neither moral nor immoral, being as she is a purely spiritual force, with no relations to man's little schemes of being good and making money and being knighted and so forth. For those who have eyes to see, she is the supreme spiritual vision vouchsafed to us upon the earth— and, as that, she is necessarily the supreme danger to that materialistic use and wont by which alone a materialistic society remains possible. For this reason our young men and maidens—particularly our young men—must be guarded against her, for her beauty sets us adream, prevents our doing our day's work, makes us forget the soulless occupations in which we wither away our lives. The man who loves beauty will never be mayor of his city, or even sit on the Board of Aldermen. Nor is he likely to own a railroad, or be a captain of industry. Nor will he marry, for her money, a woman he does not love. The face of beauty makes all such achievements seem small and absurd. Such so-called successes seem to him the dreariest forms of failure. In short, Beauty has made him divinely discontented with the limited human world about him, divinely incapable of taking it seriously, or heeding its standards or conditions. No wonder society should look upon Beauty as dangerous, for she is constantly upsetting its equilibrium and playing havoc with its smooth schemes and smug conventions. She outrages the "proprieties" with "the innocence of nature,"

and disintegrates "select" and "exclusive" circles
with the wand of Romance. For earthly possessions or rewards she has no heed. For her they
are meaningless things, mere idle dust and withered
leaves. Her only real estate is in the moon, and
the one article of her simple creed—"Love is
enough."

Love is enough: though the world be a-waning
And the woods have no voice but the voice of com-
    plaining,
Though the sky be too dark for dim eyes to discover
The gold-cups and daisies fair blooming thereunder,
Though the hills beheld shadows, and the sea a dark
    wonder
And this day draw a veil over all deeds passed over,
Yet their hands shall not tremble, their feet shall not
    falter;
The void shall not weary, the fear shall not alter
These lips and these eyes of the loved and the lover.

Those who have looked into her eyes see limit-
less horizons undreamed of by those who know
her not, horizons summoning the soul to radiant
adventures beyond the bounds of Space and Time.
The world is so far right in regarding beauty with
a sort of superstitious dread, as a presence almost
uncanny among our mere mortal concerns, a
dæmonic thing,—which is what the world has
meant when it has, not unnaturally, confused it
with the spirits of evil; for surely it is a supernatural stranger in our midst, a fairy element,

and, like the lorelei and the lamia, it does beckon
its votaries to enchanted realms away and afar
from "all the uses of the world." Therefore, to
them also it brings the thrill of a different and
nobler fear—the thrill of the mortal in presence
of the immortal. A strange feeling of destiny
seems to come over us as we first look into the
beautiful face we were born to love. It seems
veritably an apparition from another and lovelier
world, to which it summons us to go with it.
That is what we mean when we say that Love and
Death are one; for Death, to the thought of Love,
is but one of the gates to that other world, a gate
to which we instinctively feel Love has the key.
That surely is the meaning of the old fairy-stories
of men who have come upon the white woman in
the woodland, and followed her, never to be seen
again of their fellows, or of those who, like Hylas,
have met the water-nymph by the lilied spring,
and sunk with her down into the crystal deeps.
The strange earth on which we live is just such
a place of enchantment, neither more nor less, and
some of us have met that fair face, with a strange
suddenness of joy and fear, and followed and followed it on till it vanished beyond the limits of
the world. But our failure was that we did not
follow that last white beckoning of the hand—

And I awoke and found me here
On the cold hill's side.

VIII

AMONG the many advantages of being very young is one's absolute certainty that there is only one type of beautiful girl in the world. That type we make a religion. We are its pugnacious champions, and the idea of our falling in love with any other is too preposterous even for discussion. If our tastes happen to be for blondness, brunettes simply do not exist for us; and if we affect the slim and willowy in figure, our contempt for the plump and rounded is too sincere for expression. Usually the type we choose is one whose beauty is somewhat esoteric to other eyes. We are well aware that photographs do it no justice, and that the man in the street—who, strangely enough, we conceive as having no eye for beauty—can see nothing in it. Thank Heaven, she is not the type that any common eye can see. Heads are not turned in her wake as she passes along. Her beauty is not "obvious." On the contrary, it is of that rare and exquisite quality which only a few favoured ones can apprehend— like the beauty of a Whistler or a Corot, and we have been chosen to be its high-priest and evangelist. It is our secret, this beautiful face that we love, and we wonder how any one can be found to love the other faces. We even pity them, those rosy, rounded faces, with their bright unmysterious eyes and straight noses and dimpled chins. How fortunate for them that the secret of the beauty we love has been hidden from their lovers. Sheer Bouguereau! Neither more nor less.

In fact, the beauty we affect is aggressively spiritual, and in so far as beauty is demonstrably physical we dismiss it with disdain. Our ideal, indeed, might be said to consist in a beauty which is beautiful in spite of the body rather than by means of it; a beauty defiantly clothed, so to say, in the dowdiest of fleshly garments—radiantly independent of such carnal conditions as features or complexion. Our ideal of figure might be said to be negative rather than positive, and that "little sister" mentioned in Solomon's Song would bring us no disappointment.

We are often heard to say that beauty consists chiefly, if not entirely, in expression, that it is a transfiguration from within rather than a gracious condition of the surface, that the shape of a nose is no matter, and that a beautifully rounded chin or a fine throat has nothing to do with it—indeed, is rather in the way than otherwise. We point to the fact—which is true enough—that the most famous beauties of antiquity were plain women—

plain, that is, according to the conventional standards.

We also maintain—again with perfect truth—that mystery is more than half of beauty, the element of strangeness that stirs the senses through the imagination. These and other perfectly true truths about beauty we discover through our devotion to the one face that we love—and we should hardly have discovered them had we begun with the merely cherry-ripe. It is with faces much as it is with books. There is no way of attaining a vital catholic taste in literature so good as to begin by mastering some difficult beautiful classic, by devoting ourselves in the ardent receptive period of youth to one or two masterpieces which will serve as touchstones for us in all our subsequent reading. Some books engage all our faculties for their appreciation, and through the keen attentiveness we are compelled to give them we make personal discovery of those principles and qualities of all fine literature which otherwise we might never have apprehended, or in which, at all events, we should have been less securely grounded.

So with faces: it is through the absorbed worship, the jealous study, of one face that we best learn to see the beauty in all the other faces—though the mere thought that our apprehension of its beauty could ever lead us to so infidel a conclusion would seem heresy indeed during the period of our dedication. The subtler the type, the more caviare it is to the general, the more we learn from it. We become in a sense discoverers, original thinkers, of beauty, taking nothing on authority, but making trial and investigation always for ourselves. Such beauty brings us nearer than the more explicit types to that mysterious threshold over which beauty steps down to earth and dwells among us; that well-spring of its wonder; the point where first its shining essence pours its radiance into the earthly vessel.

The perfect physical type hides no little of its own miracle through its sheer perfection, as in the case of those masterpieces which, as we say, conceal their art. It is often through the face externally less perfect, faces, so to say, in process of becoming beautiful, that we get glimpses of the interior light in its divine operation. We seem to look into the very alembic of beauty, and see all the precious elements in the act of combination. No wonder we should deem these faces the most beautiful of all, for through them we see, not beauty made flesh, but beauty while it is still spirit. In our eager fanaticism, indeed, we cannot conceive that there can be beauty in any other types as well. Yet, because we chance to have fallen under the spell of Botticelli, shall there be no more Titian? Our taste is for a beauty of dim silver and faded stars, a wistful twilight beauty made of sorrow and dreams, a beauty always half in the shadow, a white flower in the moonlight. We cannot conceive how beauty, for others, can be a thing of the hot sun, a thing of purple and orange and the hot sun, a thing of firm outlines, superbly concrete, marmoreal, sumptuous, magnificently animal.

The beauty we love is very silent. It smiles softly to itself, but never speaks. How should we understand a beauty that is vociferously gay, a beauty of dash and dance, a beauty of swift and brilliant ways, victoriously alive?

Perhaps it were well for us that we should never understand, well for us that we should preserve our singleness of taste through life. Some contrive to do this, and never as long as they live are unfaithful to the angel-blue eyes of their boyish love. Moralists have perhaps not realized how much continence is due to a narrowness of æsthetic taste. Obviously the **man** who sees beauty only in blue eyes is securer from temptation than the man who can see beauty in brown or green eyes as well; and how perilous is his state for whom danger lurks in all beautiful eyes, irrespective of shape, size, or colour! And, alas! it is to this state of eclecticism that most of us are led step by step by the Mephistopheles of experience.

As great politicians in their maturity are usually found in the exact opposite party to that which they espoused in their youth, so men who loved blondness in boyhood are almost certain to be found at the feet of the raven-haired in their middle age, and *vice versa*. The change is but a part of that general change which overtakes us with

the years, substituting in us a catholic **apprecia-**
tion of the world as it is for idealist notions of the
world as we see it, or desire it to be. It is a part
of that gradual abdication of the ego which comes
of the slow realization that other people are quite
as interesting as ourselves—in fact, a little more
so,—and their tastes and ways of looking at
things may be worth pondering, after all. But,
O when we have arrived at this stage, what a
bewildering world of seductive new impressions
spreads for us its multitudinous snares! No
longer mere individuals, we have not merely an
individual's temptations to guard against, but
the temptations of all the world. Instead of being
able to see only that one type of beauty which
first appealed to us, our eyes have become so
instructed that we now see the beauty of all the
other types as well; and we no longer scorn as
Philistine the taste of the man in the street for
the beauty that is robustly vital and flamboyantly
contoured. Once we called it obvious. Now we
say it is "barbaric," and call attention to its
perfection of type.

The remembrance of our former injustice to it
may even awaken a certain tenderness towards it
in our hearts, and soon we find ourselves making
love to it, partly fron a vague desire to make
reparation to a slighted type, and partly from the
experimental pleasure of loving a beauty the attraction of which it was once impossible for us to
imagine. So we feel when the charm of some old

master, hitherto unsympathetic, is suddenly revealed to us. Ah! it was this they saw. How
blind they must have thought us!

Brown eyes that I love, will you forgive me that
I once looked into blue eyes as I am looking now
into yours? Hair black as Erebus, will you forgive
these hands that once loved to bathe in a brook of
rippled gold? Ah! they did not know. It was
in ignorance they sinned. They did not know.

O my beautiful cypress, stately queen of the
garden of the world, forgive me that once I gave
to the little shrub-like women the worship that is
rightly yours!

Lady, whose loveliness is like white velvet, a vineyard heavy with golden grapes, abundant as an orchard of apple blossoms, forgive that once I loved
the shadow women, the sad wreathing mists of beauty, the silvery uncorseted phantoms of womanhood.
It was in ignorance I sinned. I did not know.

Ah! That Mephistopheles of experience! How
he has led us from one fair face to another, teaching us, one by one, the beauty of all. No longer
lonely sectarians of beauty, pale prophets of one
lovely face, there is now no type whose secret is
hidden from us. The world has become a garden
of beautiful faces. The flowers are different, but
they are all beautiful. How is it possible for us,
now that we know the charm of each one, to be
indifferent to any, or to set the beauty of one above
the other? We have learned the beauty of the
orchid, but surely we have not unlearned the rose;

and would you say that orchid or rose is more beautiful than the lily? Surely not. They are differently beautiful, that is all.

Are blue eyes more beautiful than brown? I thought so once, but now I see that they are differently beautiful, that is all. Nor is gold hair more beautiful than black any more, or black than gold. They are differently beautiful, that is all. Nor is thy white skin, O Saxon lady, more beautiful than hers of tropic bronze.

Come sad, or come with laughter, beautiful faces; come like stars in dreams, or come vivid as fruit upon the bough; come softly like a timid fawn, or terrible as an army with banners; come silent, come singing . . . you are all beautiful, and none is fairer than another—only differently fair.

And yet . . . and yet . . . Experience is indeed Mephistopheles in this: We must pay him for all this wisdom. Is it the old price? Is it our souls? I wonder.

This at least is true: that, while indeed he has opened our eyes to all this beauty that was hidden to us, shown us beauty, indeed, where we could see but evil before, we miss something from our delight in these faces. We can appreciate more beauty, but do we appreciate any quite as much as in those old days when we were such passionate monotheists of the beautiful? Alas! We are priests no more,---are we even lovers? But we are wonderful connoisseurs.

It is our souls.

IX

THE SNOWS OF YESTER-YEAR

MAIS où sont les neiges d'antan? As I tran-
scribe once more that ancient sigh, perhaps
the most real sigh in all literature, it is high midsummer, and the woodland surrounding the little
cabin in which I am writing lies in a trance of
green and gold, hot and fragrant and dizzy with
the whirring of cicadæ, under the might of the
July sun. Bees buzz in and out through my door,
and sometimes a butterfly flits in, flutters a while
about my bookshelves, and presently is gone again,
in search of sweets more to his taste than those of
the muses, though Catullus is there, with

> Songs sweeter than wild honey dripping down,
> Which once in Rome to Lesbia he sang.

As I am caught by the dream-drowsy spell of the
hot murmuring afternoon, and my eyes rest on
the thick vines clustering over the rocks, and the
lush grasses and innumerable underbrush, so
spendthrift in their crowding luxuriance, I try to
imagine the ground as it was but four months ago
still in the grasp of winter, when the tiniest blade

of grass, or smallest speck of creeping green leaf, seemed like a miracle, and it was impossible to realize that under the broad snowdrifts a million seeds, like hidden treasure, were waiting to reveal their painted jewels to the April winds. Snow was plentiful then, to be had by the ton—but now, the thought suddenly strikes me, and brings home with new illuminating force Villon's old refrain, that though I sought the woodland from end to end, ransacked its most secret places, not one vestige of that snow, so lately here in such plenty, would it be possible to find. Though you were to offer me a million dollars for as much as would fill the cup of a wild rose, say even a hundred million, I should have to see all that money pass me by. I can think of hardly anything that it couldn't buy—but such a simple thing as last year's snow!

Could there be a more poignant symbol of irreclaimable vanished things than that so happily hit on by the old ballade-maker

Nay, never ask this week, fair lord,
  Where they are gone, nor yet this year,
Save with thus much for an overword—
  But where are the snows of yester-year?

Villon, as we know, has a melancholy fondness for asking these sad, hopeless questions of snow and wind. He muses not only of the drift of fair faces, but of the passing of mighty princes and all the arrogant pride and pomp of the earth—"pursuivants, trumpeters, heralds, hey!" "Ah! where is the doughty Charlemagne?" They, even as the humblest, "the wind has carried them all away." They have vanished utterly as the snow, gone—who knows where?—on the wind. "'Dead and gone'—a sorry burden of the Ballad of Life," as Thomas Lowell Beddoes has it in his *Death's Jest Book*. "Dead and gone!" as Andrew Lang re-echoes in a sweetly mournful ballade:

> Through the mad world's scene
>   We are drifting on,
> To this tune, I ween,
>   "They are dead and gone!"

"Nought so sweet as melancholy," sings an old poet, and, while the melancholy of the exercise is undouted, there is at the same time an undeniable charm attaching to those moods of imaginative retrospect in which we summon up shapes and happenings of the vanished past, a tragic charm indeed similar to that we experience in mournful music or elegiac poetry.

For, it is impossible to turn our eyes on any point of the starlit vista of human history, without being overwhelmed with a heart-breaking sense of the immense treasure of radiant human lives that has gone to its making, the innumerable dramatic careers now shrunk to a mere mention, the divinely passionate destinies, once all wild dream and dancing blood, now nought but a name huddled with a thousand such in some dusty index, seldom turned to even by the scholar, and as unknown to the world at large as the moss-grown name on some sunken headstone in a country churchyard. What an appallingly exuberant and spendthrift universe it seems, pouring out its multitudinous generations of men and women with the same wasteful hand as it has filled this woodland with millions of exquisite lives, marvellously devised, patterned with inexhaustible fancy, mysteriously furnished with subtle organs after their needs, crowned with fairy blossoms, and ripening with magic seeds,—such a vast treasure of fragrant sunlit leafage, all produced with such elaborate care, and long travail, and all so soon to vanish utterly away!

Along with this crushing sense of cosmic prodigality, and somewhat lighting up its melancholy, comes the inspiring realization of the splendid spectacle of human achievement, the bewildering array of all the glorious lives that have been lived, of all the glorious happenings, under the sun. Ah! what men this world has seen, and—what women! What divine actors have trod this old stage, and in what tremendous dramas have they taken part! And how strange it is, reading some great dramatic career, of Cæsar, say, or Luther, or Napoleon, or Byron, to realize that there was a time when they were not, then a time when they were beginning to be strange new names in men's ears, then all the romantic excitement of their developing destinies, and the thunder and lightning of the great resounding moments of their lives—moments made out of real, actual, prosaic time, just as our own moments are made, yet once so splendidly shining on the top of the world, as though to stay there forever, moments so glorious that it would seem that Time must have paused to watch and prolong them, jealous that they should ever pass and give place to lesser moments!

Think too of those other fateful moments of history, moments not confined to a few godlike individuals, but participated in by whole nations, such moments as that of the great Armada, the French Revolution, or the Declaration of American Independence. How strangely it comes upon one that these past happenings were once only just taking place, just as at the moment of my writing other things are taking place, and clocks were ticking and water flowing, just as they are doing now! How wonderful, it seems to us, to have been alive then, as we are alive now, to have shared in those vast national enthusiasms, "in those great deeds to have had some little part"; and is it not a sort of poor anti-climax for a world that has gone through such noble excitement to have sunk back to this level of every day! Alas! all those lava-like moments of human exaltation—what are they now, but, so to say, the pumice-stone of history. They have passed as the summer flowers are passing, they are gone with last year's snow.

But the last year's snow of our personal lives—what a wistful business it is, when we get thinking of that! To recall certain magic moments out of the past is to run a risk of making the happiest present seem like a desert; and for most men, I imagine, such retrospect is usually busied with some fair face, or perhaps—being men—with several fair faces, once so near and dear, and now so far. How poignantly and unprofitably real memory can make them—all but bring them back—how vividly reconstruct immortal occasions of happiness that we said could not, must not, pass away; while all the time our hearts were aching with the sure knowledge that they were even then, as we wildly clutched at them, slipping from our grasp!

That summer afternoon,—do you too still remember it, Miranda?—when, under the whispering woodland, we ate our lunch together with such prodigious appetite, and O! such happy laughter, yet never took our eyes from each other; and, when the meal was ended, how we wandered along the stream-side down the rocky glen, till we came to an enchanted pool among the boulders, all hushed with moss and ferns and overhanging boughs—do you remember what happened then, Miranda? Ah! nymphs of the forest pools, it is no use asking me to forget.

And, all the time, my heart was saying to my eyes:—"This fairy hour—so real, so magical, now —some day will be in the far past; you will sit right away on the lonely outside of it, and recall it only with the anguish of beautiful vanished things." And here I am today surely enough, years away from it, solitary on its lonely outside!

I suppose that the river, this summer day, is making the same music along its rocky bed, and the leafy boughs are rustling over that haunted pool just the same as when—but where are the laughing ripples—ah! Miranda—that broke with laughter over the divinely troubled water, and the broken reflections, as of startled water-lilies, that rocked to and fro in a panic of dazzling alabaster?

They are with last year's snow.

Meriel of the solemn eyes, with the heart and the laughter of a child, and soul like the starlit sky, where should one look for the snows of yester-year if not in your bosom, fairy girl my eyes shall never see again. Wherever you are, lost to me somewhere among the winding paths of this strange wood of the world, do you ever, as the moonlight falls over the sea, give a thought to that night when we sat together by a window overlooking the ocean, veiled in a haze of moonlit pearl, and, dimly seen near shore, a boat was floating, like some mystic barge, as we said, in our happy childishness, waiting to take us to the *Land East of the Sun and West of the Moon?* Ah! how was it we lingered and lingered till the boat was no more there, and it was too late? Perhaps it was that we seemed to be already there, as you turned and placed your hand in mine and said: "My life is in your hand." And we both believed it true. Yes! wherever we went together in those days, we were always in that enchanted land— whether we rode side by side through London streets in a hansom—"a two-wheeled heaven" we called it—(for our dream stretches as far back as that prehistoric day—How old one of us seems to be growing! You, dear face, can never grow old)—or sat and laughed at clowns in London music halls, or wandered in Surrey lanes, or gazed at each other, as if our hearts would break for joy, over the snow-white napery of some country inn, and maybe quoted Omar to each other, as we drank his red wine to the immortality of our love. Perhaps we were right, after all. Perhaps it could never die, and Time and Distance are perhaps merely illusions, and you and I have never been apart. Who knows but that you are looking over my shoulder as I write, though you seem so far away, lost in that starlit silence that you loved. Ah! Meriel, is it well with you, this summer day? A sigh seems to pass through the sunlit grasses. They are waving and whispering as I have seen them waving and whispering over graves.

Such moments as these I have recalled all men have had in their lives, moments when life seemed to have come to miraculous flower, attained that perfect fulfilment of its prom- ise which else we find only in dreams. Beyond doubt there is something in the flawless blessedness of such moments that links our mortality with super-terrestrial states of being. We do, in very deed, gaze through invisible doors into the ether of eternal existences, and, for the brief hour, live as they, drinking deep of that music of the infinite which is the divine food of the enfranchised soul. Thence comes our exaltation, and our wild longing to hold the moment for ever; for, while it is with us, we have literally escaped from the everyday earth, and have found the way into some other dimension of being, and its passing means our sad return to the prison-house of Time, the place of meetings and partings, of distance and death.

Part of the pang of recalling such moments is a remorseful sense that perhaps we might have held them fast, after all. If only we might bring them back, surely we would find some way to dwell in them for ever. They came upon us so suddenly out of heaven, like some dazzling bird, and we were so bewildered with the wonder of their coming that we stretched out our hands to seize them, only when they were already spreading their wings for flight. But O if the divine bird would but visit us again! What golden nets we would spread for him! What a golden cage of worship we would make ready! Our eyes would never leave his strange plumage, nor would we miss one note of his strange song. But alas! now that we are grown wise and watchful, that "moment eternal" comes

to us no more.   Perhaps too that sad wisdom
which has come to us with the years would least
of all avail us, should such moments by some
magic chance suddenly return.   For it is one of
the dangers of the retrospective habit that it
incapacitates us for the realization of the present
hour.   Much dwelling on last year's snow will
make us forget the summer flowers.   Dreaming
of fair faces that are gone, we will look with un-
seeing eyes into the fair faces that companion us
still.   To the Spring we say: "What of all your
blossom, and all your singing!   Autumn is already
at your heels, like a shadow; and Winter waits
for you like a marble tomb."   To the hope that
still may beckon we say: "Well, what though you
be fulfilled, you will pass, like the rest.   I shall
see you come.   We shall dwell together for a while,
and then you will go; and all will be as it was before, all as if you had never come at all."   For the
retrospective mood, of necessity, begets the anticipatory; we see everything finished before it is
begun, and welcome and valediction blend together on our lips.   "That which hath been is
now; and that which is to be hath already been."

> In every kiss sealed fast
> To feel the first kiss and forebode the last—

that is the shadow that haunts every joy, and
sicklies o'er every action of him whom life has
thus taught to look before and after.

Youth is not like that, and therein, for older eyes, lies its tragic pathos. Superficial—or, if you prefer it, more normal—observers are made happy by the spectacle of eager and confident young lives, all abloom and adream, turning towards the future with plumed impatient feet. But for some of us there is nothing quite so sad as young joy. The playing of children is perhaps the most unbearably sad thing in the world. Who can look on young lovers, without tears in their eyes? With what innocent faith they are taking in all the radiant lies of life! But perhaps a young mother with her new-born babe on her breast is the most tragical of all pictures of unsuspecting joy, for none of all the trusting sons and daughters of men is destined in the end to find herself so tragically, one might say cynically, fooled.

Cynically, I said; for indeed sometimes, as one ponders the lavish heartless use life seems to make of all its divinely precious material—were it but the flowers in one meadow, or the butterflies of a single summer day—it does seem as though a cruel cynicism inhered somewhere in the scheme of things, delighting to destroy and disillusionize, to create loveliness in order to scatter it to the winds, and inspire joy in order to mock it with desolation. Sometimes it seems as though the mysterious spirit of life was hardly worthy of the vessels it has called into being, hardly treats them fairly, uses them with an ignoble disdain. For, how generously we give ourselves up to life, how innocently we put our trust in it, do its bidding with such fine ardours, striving after beauty and goodness, fain to be heroic and clean of heart—yet "what hath man of all his labours, and of the vexation of his heart, wherein he hath laboured under the sun." Yea, dust, and fallen rose-leaves, and last year's snow.

And yet and yet, for all this drift and dishonoured decay of things, that retrospective mood of ours will sometimes take another turn, and, so rare and precious in the memory seem the treasure that it has lost, and yet in imagination still holds, that it will not resign itself to mortal thoughts of such manifest immortalities. The snows of yester-year! Who knows if, after all, they have so utterly vanished as they seem. Who can say but that there may be somewhere in the universe secret treasuries where all that has ever been precious is precious still, safely garnered and guarded for us against some wonderful moment which shall gather up for us in one transfiguring apocalypse all the wonderful moments that have but preceded us into eternity. Perhaps, as nothing is lost in the world, so-called, of matter, nothing is lost too in the world of love and dream.

O vanished loveliness of flowers and faces,
Treasure of hair, and great immortal eyes,
Are there for these no safe and secret places?
And is it true that beauty never dies?

Soldiers and saints, haughty and lovely names,
Women who set the whole wide world in flames,
Poets who sang their passion to the skies,
And lovers wild and wise:
Fought they and prayed for some poor flitting gleam
Was all they loved and worshipped but a dream?
Is Love a lie and fame indeed a breath?
And is there no sure thing in life—but death?

Ah! perhaps we shall find all such lost and lovely things when we come at length to **the Land of Last Year's Snow.**

X

THE PSYCHOLOGY OF GOSSIP

ACCORDING to the old Scandinavian fable of the cosmos, the whole world is encircled in the coils of a vast serpent. The ancient name for it was the Midgard serpent, and doubtless, for the old myth-maker, it had another significance. Today, however, the symbol may still hold good of a certain terrible and hideous reality.

Still, as of old, the world is encircled in the coils of a vast serpent; and the name of the serpent is Gossip. Wherever man is, there may you hear its sibilant whisper, and its foul spawn squirm and sting and poison in nests of hidden noisomeness, myriad as the spores of corruption in a putrefying carcass, varying in size from some hydra-headed infamy endangering whole nations and even races with its deadly breath, to the microscopic wrigglers that multiply, a million a minute, in the covered cesspools of private life.

Printed history is so infested with this vermin, in the form of secret memoirs, back-stairs diarists, and boudoir eavesdroppers, that it is almost impossible to feel sure of the actual fact of any

history whatsoever. The fame of great personages may be literally compared to the heroic
figures in the well-known group of the Laocoön,
battling in vain with the strangling coils of the
sea-serpent of Poseidon. We scarcely know what
to believe of the dead; and for the living, is it not
true, as Tennyson puts it, that "each man walks
with his head in a cloud of poisonous flies"?

What is this evil leaven that seems to have been
mixed in with man's clay at the very beginning,
making one almost ready to believe in the old
Manichean heresy of a principle of evil operating
through nature, everywhere doing battle with the
good? Even from the courts of heaven, as we
learn from the Book of Job, the gossip was not
excluded; and how eternally true to the methods
of the gossip in all ages was Satan's way of going
to work in that immortal allegory! Let us recall the familiar scene with a quoted verse or
two:

Now there was a day when the sons of God came
to present themselves before the Lord, and Satan
[otherwise, the Adversary] came also among them.

And the Lord said unto Satan, "Whence comest
thou?" Then Satan answered the Lord, and said:
"From going to and fro in the earth, and from walking
up and down in it."

And the Lord said unto Satan: "Hast thou considered my servant Job, that there is none like him
in the earth, a perfect and an upright man, one that
feareth God, and escheweth evil?"

Then Satan answered the Lord, and said, "Doth Job fear God for nought?"

Here we have in a nutshell the whole *modus operandi* of the gossip in all ages, and as he may be observed at any hour of the day or night, slimily engaged in his cowardly business. "Going to and fro in the earth, walking up and down in it," everywhere peering and listening, smiling and shrugging, here and there dropping a hint, sowing a seed, leering an innuendo; seldom saying, only implying; leaving everywhere trails of slime, yet trails too vague and broken to track him by, secure in his very cowardice.

"Doth Job fear God for nought?" He only asks, observe. Affirms nothing. Only innocently wonders. Sows a doubt, that's all—and leaves it to work.

The victim may possibly be set right in the end, as was Job; but meanwhile he has lost his flocks and his herds, his sons and his daughters, and suffered no little inconvenience from a loathsome plague of boils. Actually—life not being, like the Book of Job, an allegory—he very seldom is set right, but must bear his losses and his boils with what philosophy he can master till the end of the chapter.

The race to which Job belonged presents perhaps the most conspicuous example of a whole people burdened throughout its history with a heritage of malignant gossip. In the town of Lincoln, in England, there exists to this day, as one of its show places, the famous "Jew's House," associated with the gruesome legend of "the boy of Lincoln"—a child, it was whispered, sacrificed by the Jews at one of their pastoral feasts. Such a wild belief in child-sacrifice by the Jews was widespread in the Middle Ages, and is largely responsible, I understand, even at the present day, for the Jewish massacres in Russia.

Think of the wild liar who first put that fearful thought into the mind of Europe! Think of the holocausts of human lives, and all the attendant agony of which his diabolical invention has been the cause! What criminal in history compares in infamy with that unknown—gossip?

A similar madness of superstition, responsible for a like cruel sacrifice of innocent lives, was the terrible belief in witchcraft. Having its origin in ignorance and fear, it was chiefly the creation of hearsay carried from lip to lip, beginning with the deliberate invention of lying tongues, delighting in evil for its own sake, or taking advantage of a ready weapon to pay off scores of personal enmity. At any time to a period as near to our own day as the early eighteenth century, nothing was easier than to rid oneself of an enemy by starting a whisper going that he or she held secret commerce with evil spirits, was a reader of magical books, and could at will cast spells of disease and death upon the neighbours or their cattle.

You had but to be recluse in your habits and eccentric in your appearance, with perhaps a little more wisdom in your head and your conversation than your fellows, to be at the mercy of the first fool or knave who could gather a mob at his heels, and hale you to the nearest horse-pond. Statement and proof were one, and how ready, and indeed eager, human nature was to believe the wildest nonsense told by witless fool or unscrupulous liar, the records of such manias as the famous Salem trials appallingly evidence. Men high in the state, as well as helpless old women in their dotage, disfigured with "witch-moles" or incriminating beards on their withered faces, were equally vulnerable to this most fearful of weapons ever placed by ignorance in the hands of the malignant gossip.

In such epidemics of tragic gossip we see plainly that, whatever individuals are originally responsible, society at large is all too culpably *particeps criminis* in this phenomenon under consideration. If the prosperity of a jest be in the ears that hear it, the like is certainly true of any piece of gossip. Whoever it may be that sows the evil seed of slander, the human soil is all too evilly ready to receive it, to give it nurture, and to reproduce it in crops persistent as the wild carrot and flamboyant as the wild mustard.

There is something mean in human nature that prefers to think evil, that gives a willing ear and a ready welcome to calumny, a sort of jealousy of goodness and greatness and things of good report.

Races and nations are thus ever ready to believe

the worst of one another. In all times it has been in this field of inter-racial and international prejudice that the gossip has found the widest scope for his gleeful activity, sowing broadcast dissensions and misunderstandings which have persisted for centuries. They are the fruitful cause of wars, insuperable barriers to progress, fabulous growths which the enlightenment of the world painfully labours to weed out, but will perhaps never entirely eradicate.

Race-hatred is undoubtedly nine-tenths the heritage of ancient gossip. Think of the generations of ill-feeling that kept England and France, though divided but by a narrow strait, "natural enemies" and misunderstood monsters to each other. In a less degree, the friendship of England and America has been retarded by international gossips on both sides. And as for races and nations more widely separated by distance or customs, no lies have been bad enough for them to believe about one another.

It is only of late years that Europe has come to regard the peoples of the Orient as human beings at all. And all this misunderstanding has largely been the work of gossip acting upon ignorance.

It is easy to see how in the days of difficult communication, before nations were able to get about in really representative numbers to make mutual acquaintance, they were completely at the mercy of a few irresponsible travellers, who said or wrote what they pleased, and had no compunction about lying in the interests of entertainment. The proverbial "gaiety of nations" has always, in a great degree, consisted in each nation believing that it was superior to all others, and that the natives of other countries were invariably hopelessly dirty and immoral, to say the least. Such reports the traveller was expected to bring home with him, and such he seldom failed to bring.

Even at the present time, when intercourse is so cosmopolitan, and some approach to a sense of human brotherhood has been arrived at, the old misconceptions die hard. Nations need still to be constantly on their guard in believing all that the telegraph or the wireless is willing to tell them about other countries. Electricity, many as are its advantages for cosmopolitan *rapprochements*, is not invariably employed in the interests of truth, and newspaper correspondents, if not watched, are liable to be an even more dangerous form of international gossip than the more leisurely fabulist of ancient time.

When we come to consider the operation of gossip in the lives of individuals, the disposition of human nature to relish discrediting rumour is pitifully conspicuous. We know *Hamlet's* opinion on the matter:

Let Hercules himself do what he may,
The cat will mew, and dog will have his day.

And again:

> Be thou as chaste as ice, as pure as snow,
> Thou shalt not escape calumny.

This, it is to be feared, is merely the sad truth, for mankind, while it admires both greatness and goodness, would seem to resent the one and only half believe in the other. At all events, nothing is more to its taste than the rumour that detracts from the great or sullies the good; and so long as the rumour be entertaining, it has little concern for its truth.

Froude, in writing of Cæsar, has this to say admirably to our purpose:

In ages which we call heroic, the saint works miracles, the warrior performs exploits beyond the strength of natural man. In ages less visionary, which are given to ease and enjoyment, the tendency is to bring a great man down to the common level, and to discover or invent faults which shall show that he is or was but a little man after all. Our vanity is soothed by evidence that those who have eclipsed us in the race of life are no better than ourselves, or in some respects worse than ourselves; and if to these general impulses be added political or personal animosity, accusations of depravity are circulated as surely about such men, and are credited as readily as under other influences are the marvellous achievements of a Cid or a St. Francis.

The absurdity of a calumny may be as evident as the absurdity of a miracle; the ground for belief may

be no more than a lightness of mind, and a less par-
donable wish that it may be true.   But the idle tale
floats in society, and by and by is written down in
books and passes into the region of established
realities.

The proportion of such idle tales seriously
printed as history can never, of course, be com-
puted.   Sometimes one is tempted to think that
history is mainly "whole cloth."   Certainly the
lives of such men as Cæsar are largely made up of
what one might term illustrative fictions rather
than actual facts.   The story of Cæsar and Cleopatra is probably such an "illustrative fiction,"
representing something that might very well have
happened to Cæsar, whether it did so or not.
At all events, it does his fame no great harm, unlike another calumny, which, as it does not seem
"illustrative"—that is, not in keeping with his
general character—we are at liberty to reject.
Both alike, however, were the product of the gossip,
the embodied littleness of human nature endeavouring then, as always, to minimize and discredit
the strong man, who, whatever his actual faults,
at least strenuously shoulders for his fellows the
hard work of the world.

The great have usually been strong enough to
smile contempt on their traducers—Cæsar's answer to an infamous epigram of the poet Catullus
was to ask him to dinner—but even so, at what
extra cost, what "expense of spirit in a waste of

shame," have their achievements been bought, because of these curs that bark forever at the heels of fame!

And not always have they thus prevailed against the pack. Too often has the sorry spectacle been seen of greatness and goodness going down before the poisonous tongues and the licking jaws. Even Cæsar himself had to fall at last, his strong soul perhaps not sorry to escape through his dagger-wounds from so pitiably small a world; and the poison in the death-cup of Socrates was not so much the juice of the hemlock as the venom of the gossips of Athens.

In later times, no service to his country, no greatness of character, can save the noble Raleigh from the tongues determined to bring him to the block; and, when the haughty head of Marie Antoinette must bow at last upon the scaffold, the true guillotine was the guillotine of gossip. It was such lying tales as that of the diamond necklace that had brought her there. All Queen Elizabeth's popularity could not save her from the ribaldry of scandal, nor Shakespeare's genius protect his name from the foulest of stains.

In our own time, the mere mention of the name of Dreyfus suffices to remind us of the terrible nets woven by this dark spinner. Within the last year or two, have we not seen the loved king of a great nation driven to seek protection from the spectre of innuendo in the courts of law? But gossip laughs at such tribunals. It knows that where once it has affixed its foul stain, the mark remains forever, indelible as that imaginary stain which not all the multitudinous seas could wash from the little hand of Lady Macbeth. The more the stain is washed, the more persistently it reappears, like Rizzio's blood, as they say, in Holyrood Palace. To deny a rumour is but to spread it. An action for libel, however it may be decided, has at least the one inevitable result of perpetuating it.

Take the historical case of the Man with the Iron Mask. Out of pure deviltry, it would appear, Voltaire started the story, as mere a fiction as one of his written romances, that the mysterious prisoner was no less than a half-brother of Louis XIV; and Dumas, seeing the dramatic possibilities of the legend, picturesquely elaborates it in *Le Vicomte de Bragelonne.* Never, probably, was so impudent an invention, and surely never one so successful; for it is in vain that historians expose it over and over again. Learned editors have proved with no shadow of a doubt that the real man of the mask was an obscure Italian political adventurer; but though scholars may be convinced, the world will have nothing of your Count Matthioli, and will probably go on believing Voltaire's story to the end of time.

"At least there must have been something in it" is always the last word on such debatable matters; and the curious thing is that, whenever a doubt of the truth is expressed, it is never the victim, but always the scandal, to which the benefit of the doubt is extended.   Whatever the proven fact, the world always prefers to hold fast by the disreputable doubt.

All that is necessary is to find the dog a bad name.   The world will see that he never loses it. In this regard the oft-reiterated confidence of the dead in the justice of posterity is one of the most pathetic of illusions.   "Posterity will see me righted," cries some poor victim of human wrong, as he goes down into the darkness;   but of all appeals, the appeal to posterity is the most hopeless.

What posterity relishes is rather new scandals about its immortals than tiresome belated justifications.   It prefers its villains to grow blacker with time, and welcomes proof of fallibility and frailty in its immortal exemplars.   For rehabilitation it has neither time nor inclination, and it pursues certain luckless reputations beyond the grave with a mysterious malignity.

Such a reputation is that of Edgar Allan Poe. One would have thought that posterity would be eager to make up to his shade for the criminal animus of Rufus Griswold, his first biographer.   On the contrary, it prefers to perpetuate the lying portrait; and no consideration of the bequests of Poe's genius, or of his tragic struggles with adverse conditions, no editorial advocacy, or documentary evidence in his favour, has persuaded posterity to reverse the unduly harsh judgment of his fatuous contemporaries.

Fortunately, it all matters nothing to **Poe now.** It is only to us that it matters.

Saddening, surely, it is, to say the least, to realize that the humanity of which we are a part is tainted with so subtle a disease of lying, and so depraved an appetite for lies. Under such conditions, it is surprising that greatness and goodness are ever found willing to serve humanity at all, and that any but scoundrels can be found to dare the risks of the high places of the world. For this social disease of gossip resembles that distemper which, at the present moment, threatens the chestnut forests of America. It first attacks the noblest trees. Like it, too, it would seem to baffle all remedies, and like it, it would seem to be the work of indestructible microscopic worms.

It is this vermicular insignificance of the gossip that makes his detection so difficult, and gives him his security. A great reputation may feel itself worm-eaten, and may suddenly go down with a crash, but it will look around in vain for the social vermin that have brought about its fall. It is the cowardice of gossip that its victims have seldom an opportunity of coming face to face with their destroyers; for the gossip is as small as he is ubiquitous—

> Not half so big as a round little worm
> **Prick'd** from the lazy finger of a maid.

In all societies, there are men and women who are vaguely known as gossips; but they are seldom caught red-handed. For one thing, they do not often speak at first hand. They profess only to repeat something that they have heard—something, they are careful to add, which is probably quite untrue, and which they themselves do not believe for a moment.

Then the fact stated or hinted is probably no concern of ours. It is not for us to sift its truth, or to bring it to the attention of the individual it tarnishes. Obviously, society would become altogether impossible if each one of us were to constitute ourselves a sort of social police to arraign every accuser before the accused. We should thus, it is to be feared, only make things worse, and involuntarily play the gossip's own game. The best we can do is as far as possible to banish the tattle from our minds, and, at all events, to keep our own mouths shut.

Even so, however, some harm will have been done. We shall never be quite sure but that the rumour was true, and when we next meet the person concerned, it will probably in some degree colour our attitude toward him.

And with others, less high-minded than ourselves, the gossip will have had greater success. Not, of course, meaning any harm, they will inquire of someone else if what So-and-so hinted of So-and-so can possibly be true. And so it will go on *ad infinitum*. The formula is simple, and it is only a matter of arithmetical progression for a private lie, once started on its journey, to become a public scandal, with a reputation gone, and no one visibly responsible.

Of course, not all gossip is purposely harmful in its intention. The deliberate, creative gossip is probably rare. In fact, gossip usually represents the need of a bored world to be entertained at any price, the restless *ennui* that must be forever talking or listening to fill the vacuity of its existence, to supply its lack of really vital interests. This demand naturally creates a supply of idle talkers, whose social existence depends on their ability to provide the entertainment desired; and nothing would seem to be so well-pleasing to the idle human ear as the whisper that discredits, or the story that ridicules, the distinction it envies, and the goodness it cannot understand.

The mystery of gossip is bound up with the mysterious human need of talking. Talk we must, though we say nothing, or talk evil from sheer lack of subject-matter. When we know why man talks so much, apparently for the mere sake of talking, we shall probably be nearer to knowing why he prefers to speak and hear evil rather than good of his fellows.

Possibly the gossip would be just as ready to speak well of his victims, to circulate stories to their credit rather than the reverse, but for the melancholy fact that he would thus be left without an audience. For the world has no anxiety to hear good of its neighbour, and there is no piquancy in the disclosure of hidden virtues.

'Tis true, 'tis pity; pity 'tis, 'tis true; and the only poor consolation to be got out of it is that the victims of gossip may, if they feel so inclined, feel flattered rather than angered by its attentions; for, at all events, it argues their possession of gifts and qualities transcending the common. At least it presupposes individuality; and, all things considered, it may be held as true that those most gossiped about are usually those who can best afford to pay this tax levied by society on any form of distinction.

After all, the great and good man has his greatness and goodness to support him, though the world should unite in depreciating him. The artist has his genius, the beautiful woman has her beauty. 'Tis in ourselves that we are thus and thus; and if fame must have gossip for its seamy side, there are some satisfactions that cannot be stolen away, and some laurels that defy the worm.

XI

THE PASSING AWAY OF THE EDITOR

THE word "editor" as applied to the conductors of magazines and newspapers is rapidly becoming a mere courtesy title; for the powers and functions formerly exercised by editors, properly so called, are being more and more usurped by the capitalist proprietor. There are not a few magazines where the "editor" has hardly more say in the acceptance of a manuscript than the contributor who sends it in. Few are the editors left who uphold the magisterial dignity and awe with which the name of editor was wont to be invested. These survive owing chiefly to the prestige of long service, and even they are not always free from the encroachments of the new method. The proprietor still feels the irksome necessity of treating their editorial policies with respect, though secretly chafing for the moment when they shall give place to more manageable, modern tools.

The "new" editor, in fact, is little more than a clerk doing the bidding of his proprietor, and the proprietor's idea of editing is slavishly to truckle to the public taste—or rather to his crude conception of the public taste. The only real editors of today are the capitalist and the public. The nominal editor is merely an office-boy of larger growth, and slightly larger salary.

Innocent souls still, of course, imagine him clothed with divine powers, and letters of introduction to him are still sought after by the superstitious beginner. Alas! the chances are that the better he thinks of your MS. the less likely is it to be accepted by—the proprietor; for Mr. Snooks, the proprietor, has decided tastes of his own, and a peculiar distaste for anything remotely savouring of the "literary." His broad editorial axiom is that a popular magazine should be everything and anything but—"literature." For any signs of the literary taint he keeps open a stern and ever-watchful eye, and the "editor" or "editorial assistant"—to make a distinction without a difference—whom he should suspect of literary leanings has but a short shrift. Mr. Snooks is seldom much of a reader himself. His activities have been exclusively financial, and he has drifted into the magazine business as he might have drifted into pork or theatres—from purely financial reasons. His literary needs are bounded on the north by a detective story, and on the south by a scientific article. The old masters of literature are as much foolishness to him as the old masters of painting. In short, he is just a common, ignorant man with money invested in a magazine; and who shall blame him if he goes on the principle

that he who pays the piper calls the tune. When
he starts in he not infrequently begins by entrust-
ing his magazine to some young man with real
editorial ability and ambition to make a really
good thing. This young man gathers about him
a group of kindred spirits, and the result is that
after the publication of the second number Mr.
Snooks decides to edit the magazine himself, with
the aid of a secretary and a few typewriters. His
bright young men hadn't understood "what the
public wants" at all. They were too high-toned,
too "literary." What the public wants is short
stories and pictures of actresses; and the short
stories, like the actresses, must be no better than
they should be. Even short stories when they
are masterpieces are not "what the public wants."
So the bright young men go into outer darkness,
sadly looking for new jobs, and with its third
number *Snooks's Monthly* has fallen into line with
the indistinguishable ruck of monthly magazines,
only indeed distinguishable one from the other by
the euphonious names of their proprietors.

Now, a proprietor's right to have his property
managed according to his own ideas needs no
emphasizing. The sad thing is that such proprietors should get hold of such property. It all
comes, of course, of the modern vulgarization of
wealth. Time was when even mere wealth was
aristocratic, and its possession, more or less im-
plied in its possessors the possession, too, of refinement and culture. The rich men of the past

knew enough to encourage and support the finer arts of life, and were interested in maintaining high standards of public taste and feeling. Thus they were capable of sparing some of their wealth for investment in objects which brought them a finer kind of reward than the financial. Among other things, they understood and respected the dignity of literature, and would not have expected an editor to run a literary venture in the interests of the illiterate. The further degradation of the public taste was not then the avowed object of popular magazines. Indeed—strange as it sounds nowadays—it was rather the education than the degradation of the public taste at which the editor aimed, and in that aim he found the support of intelligent proprietors.

Today, however, all this is changed. Wealth has become democratic, and it is only here and there, in its traditional possessors, that it retains its traditional aristocracy of taste. As the commonest man can be a multi-millionaire, so the commonest man can own a magazine, and have it edited in the commonest fashion for the common good.

As a result, the editor's occupation, in the true sense, will soon be gone. There is, need one say, no lack today of men with real editorial individuality—but editorial individuality is the last thing the capitalist proprietors want. It is just that they are determined to stamp out. Therefore, your real editor must either swallow his pride and submit to ignorant dictation, or make way for the little band of automatic sorters of manuscript, which, as nine tailors make a man, nowadays constitute a sort of composite editor under the direction of the proprietor.

With the elimination of editorial individuality necessarily follows elimination of individuality in the magazine. More and more, every day, magazines are conforming to the same monotonous type; so that, except for name and cover, it is impossible to tell one magazine from another. Happily one or two—*rari nantes in gurgito vasto*—survive amid the democratic welter; and all who have at heart not only the interests of literature, but the true interests of the public taste, will pray that they will have the courage to maintain their distinction, unseduced by the moneyed voice of the mob—a distinction to which, after all, they have owed, and will continue to owe, their success. The names of these magazines will readily occur to the reader, and, as they occur, he cannot but reflect that it was just editorial individuality and a high standard of policy that made them what they are, and what, it is ardently to be hoped, they will still continue to be. Plutus and Demos are the worst possible editors for a magazine; and in the end, even, it is the best magazine that always makes the most money.

XII

THE SPIRIT OF THE OPEN

I OFTEN think, as I sit here in my green office in the woodland—too often diverted from some serious literary business with the moon or the morning stars, or a red squirrel who is the familiar spirit of my wood-pile, or having my thoughts carried out to sea by the river which runs so freshly and so truantly, with so strong a current of temptation, a hundred yards away from my window—I often think that the strong necessity that compelled me to do my work, to ply my pen and inkpot out here in the leafy, blue-eyed wilderness, instead of doing it by typewriter in some forty-two-storey building in the city, is one of those encouraging signs of the times which links one with the great brotherhood of men and women that have heard the call of the great god Pan, as he sits by the river—

> Sweet, sweet, sweet, O Pan!
> Piercing sweet by the river!
> Blinding sweet, O great god Pan!

And I go on thinking to this effect: that this impulse that has come to so many of us, and has, incidentally, wrought such a harmony in our lives, is something more than duck-shooting, trout-fishing, butterfly-collecting, or a sentimental passion for sunsets, but is indeed something not so very far removed from religion, romantic religion. At all events, it is something that makes us happy, and keeps us straight. That combination of results can only come by the satisfaction of the undeniable religious instinct in all of us: an instinct that seeks goodness, but seeks happiness too. Now, there are creeds by which you can be good without being happy; and creeds by which you can be happy without being good. But, perhaps, there is only one creed by which you can be both at once—the creed of the growing grass, and the blue sky and the running river, the creed of the dog-wood and the skunk-cabbage, the creed of the red-wing and the blue heron—the creed of the great god Pan.

Pan, being one of the oldest of the gods, might well, in an age eager for novelty, expect to be the latest fashion; but the revival of his worship is something far more than a mere vogue. It was rumoured, as, of course, we all know, early in the Christian era, that he was dead. The pilot Thomas, ran the legend, as told by Plutarch, sailing near Pascos, with a boatful of merchants, heard in the twilight a mighty voice calling from the land, bidding him proclaim to all the world that Pan was dead. "Pan is dead!"—three times ran the strange shuddering cry through the darkness, as though the very earth itself wailed the passing of the god.

But Pan, of course, could only die with the earth itself, and so long as the lichen and the moss keep quietly at their work on the grey boulder, and the lightning zigzags down through the hemlocks, and the arrowhead guards its waxen blossom in the streams; so long as the earth shakes with the thunder of hoofs, or pours out its heart in the song of the veery-thrush, or bares its bosom in the wild rose, so long will there be little chapels to Pan in the woodland—chapels on the lintels of which you shall read, as Virgil wrote: *Happy is he who knows the rural gods, Pan, and old Sylvanus, and the sister nymphs.*

It is strange to see how in every country, but more particularly in America and in England, the modern man is finding his religion as it was found by those first worshippers of the beautiful mystery of the visible universe, those who first caught glimpses of

Nymphs in the coppice, Naiads in the fountain,
Gods on the craggy height and roaring sea.

First thoughts are proverbially the best; at all events, they are the bravest. And man's first thoughts of the world and the strangely romantic life he is suddenly called up, out of nothingness, to

live, unconsulted, uninstructed, left to feel his way
in the blinding radiance up into which he has
been mysteriously thrust; those first thoughts of
his are nowadays being corroborated in every direction by the last thoughts of the latest thinker.
Mr. Jack London, one of Nature's own writers, one
of those writers too, through whom the Future
speaks, has given a name to this stirring of the
human soul—"The Call of the Wild." Following
his lead, others have written of "The Lure," of
this and that in nature, and all mean the same
thing: that the salvation of man is to be found on,
and by means of, the green earth out of which he
was born, and that, as there is no ill of his body
which may not be healed by the magic juices of
herb and flower, or the stern potency of minerals,
so there is no sickness of his soul that may not be
cured by the sound of the sea, the rustle of leaves,
or the songs of birds.

Thirty or forty years ago the soul of the world
was very sick. It had lost religion in a night
of misunderstood "materialism," so-called. But
since then that mere "matter" which seemed
to eclipse the soul has grown strangely radiant to
deep-seeing eyes, and, whereas then one had
to doubt everything, dupes of superficial disillusionment, now there is no old dream that has not
the look of coming true, no hope too wild and
strange and beautiful to be confidently entertained.
Even, if you wish to believe in fairies, science will
hardly say you nay. Those dryads and fauns,

which Keats saw "frightened away" by the prosaic times in which it was his misfortune to be alive and unrecognized, are trooping back in every American woodland, and the god whose name I have invoked has become more than ever

> the leaven
> That spreading in this dull and clodded earth
> Gives it a touch ethereal.

His worship is all the more sincere because it is not self-conscious. If you were to tell the trout-fisher, or the duck-shooter, or the camper-out, that he is a worshipper of Pan, he would look at you in a kindly bewilderment. He would seem a little anxious about you, but it would be only a verbal misunderstanding. It would not take him long to realize that you were only putting in terms of a creed the intuitive and inarticulate faith of his heart. Perhaps the most convincing sign of this new-old faith in nature is the unconsciousness of the believer. He has no idea that he is believing or having faith in anything. He is simply loving the green earth and the blue sea, and the ways of birds and fish and animals; but he is so happy in his innocent, ignorant joy that he seems almost to shine with his happiness. There is, literally, a light about him—that light which edges with brightness all sincere action. The trout, or the wild duck, or the sea bass is only an innocent excuse to be alone with the Infinite. To be alone. To be afar. Men sail precarious craft in perilous waters for no reason they could tell of. They may think that trawling, or dredging, or whaling is the explanation: the real reason is the mystery we call the Sea.

Ostensibly, of course, the angler is a man who goes out to catch fish; yet there is a great difference between an angler and a fishmonger. Though the angler catches no fish, though his creel be empty as he returns home at evening, there is a curious happiness and peace about him which a mere fishmonger would be at a loss to explain. Fish, as I said, were merely an excuse; and, as he vainly waited for fish, without knowing it, he was learning the rhythm of the stream, and the silence of ferns was entering into his soul, and the calm and patience of meadows were dreamily becoming a part of him. Suddenly, too, in the silence, maybe he caught sight of a strange, hairy, masterful presence, sitting by the stream, whittling reeds, and blowing his breath into them here and there, and finally binding them together with rushes, till he had made out of the empty reeds and rushes an instrument that sang everything that can be sung and told you everything that can be told.

> The sun on the hill forgot to die.
> And the lilies revived, and the dragon-fly
> Came back to dream on the river.

Do you really think that the huntsman hunts only the deer? He, himself, doubtless thinks that the trophy of the antlers was all he went out into the woods to win.   But there came a day to him when he missed the deer, and caught a glimpse instead of the divine huntress, Diana, high-bus-kined, short-kirtled, speeding with her hounds through the lonely woodland, and his thoughts ran no more on venison for that day.

The same truth is true of all men who go out into the green, blue-eyed wilderness, whether they go there in pursuit of game or butterflies. They find something stranger and better than what they went out to seek, and, if they come home disappointed in the day's bag or catch, there is yet something in their eyes, and across their brows, a light of peace, an enchanted calm, which tells those who understand that they, at all events, have seen the great god Pan, and heard the music he can make out of the pipy hemlocks or the lonely pines.

XIII

AN OLD AMERICAN TOW-PATH

THE charm of an old canal is one which every one seems to feel. Men who care nothing about ruined castles or Gothic cathedrals light up with romantic enthusiasm if you tell them of some old disused or seldom-used canal, grass-grown and tree-shaded, along which, hardly oftener than once a week, a leisurely barge—towed by an equally leisurely mule, with its fellow there on deck taking his rest, preparatory to his next eight-mile "shift"—sleepily dreams its way, presumably on some errand and to some destination, yet indeed hinting of no purpose or object other than its loitering passage through a summer afternoon. I have even heard millionaires express envy of the life lived by the little family hanging out its washing and smoking its pipe and cultivating its floating garden of nasturtiums and geraniums, with children playing and a house-dog to keep guard, all in that toy house of a dozen or so feet, whose foundations are played about by fishes, and whose sides are brushed by whispering reeds.

But the charm of an old canal is perhaps yet

more its own when even so tranquil a happening as the passage of a barge is no longer looked for, and the quiet water is called upon for no more arduous usefulness than the reflection of the willows or the ferrying across of summer clouds.   Nature herself seems to wield a new peculiar spell in such association—old quarries, the rusting tramways choked with fern; forgotten mines with the wild vine twining tenderly about the old iron of dismantled pit-tackle, grown as green as itself with the summer rains; roads once dusty with haste over which only the moss and the trailing arbutus now leisurely travel.   Wherever Nature is thus seen to be taking to herself, making her own, what man has first made and grown tired of, she is twice an enchantress, strangely combining in one charm the magic of a wistful, all but forgotten, past with her own sibyl-line mystery.

The symbol of that combined charm is that poppy of oblivion of which Sir Thomas Browne so movingly wrote: but, though along that old canal of which I am thinking and by which I walked a summer day, no poppies were growing, the freshest grass, the bluest flowers, the new-born rustling leafage of the innumerable trees, all alike seemed to whisper of forgetfulness, to be brooding, even thus in the very heyday of the mad young year, over time past.   And this eloquently retrospective air of Nature made me realize, with something of the sense of discovery, how much of what we call antiquity is really a trick of Nature.   She is as clever at the manufacture of antiques as some expert of "old masters." A little moss here and there, a network of ivy, a judicious use of ferns and grass, a careless display of weeds and wild flowers, and in twenty years Nature can make a modern building look as if it dated from the Norman Conquest. I came upon this reflection because, actually, my canal is not very old, though from the way it impressed me, and from the manner in which I have introduced it, the reader might well imagine it as old as Venice and no younger than Holland, and may find it as hard to believe as I did that its age is but some eighty years, and that it has its romantic being between Newark Bay and Phillipsburg, on the Delaware River.

One has always to be careful not to give too much importance to one's own associative fancies in regard to the names of places. To me, for instance, "Perth Amboy" has always had a romantic sound, and I believe that a certain majesty in the collocation of the two noble words would survive that visit to the place itself which I have been told is all that is necessary for disillusionment. On the other hand, for reasons less explainable, Hackensack, Paterson, Newark, and even Passaic are names that had touched me with no such romantic thrill. Wrongfully, no doubt, I had associated them with absurdity, anarchy, and railroads. Never having visited them, it was perhaps not surprising that I should not have associated them with such loveliness and luxury of Nature as I now unforgettably recall; and I cannot help feeling that in the case of places thus unfortunately named, Nature might well bring an action for damages, robbed as she thus undoubtedly is of a flock of worshippers.

At all events, I believe that my surprise and even incredulity will be understood when an artist friend of mine told me that by taking the Fort Lee ferry, and trolleying from the Palisades through Hackensack to Paterson, I might find—a dream canal.   It was as though he had said that I had but to cross over to Hoboken to find the Well at the World's End.   But it was true, for all that— quite fairy-tale true.   It was one of those surprises of peace, deep, ancient peace, in America, of which there are many, and of which more needs to be told.   I can conceive of no more suggestive and piquant contrast than that of the old canal gliding through water-lilies and spreading pastures, in the bosom of hills clothed with trees that scatter the sunshine or gather the darkness, the haunt of every bird that sings or flashes strange plumage and is gone, gliding past flowering rushes and blue dragon-flies, not

Flowing down to Camelot,

as one might well believe, but between Newark and Phillipsburg, touching Paterson midway with its dreaming hand.

Following my friend's directions, we had met at Paterson, and, desirous of finding our green pasture and still waters with the least possible delay, we took a trolley running in the Newark direction, and were presently dropped at a quaint, quiet little village called Little Falls, the last we were to see of the modern work-a-day world for several miles. A hundred yards or so beyond, and it is as though you had entered some secret green door into a pastoral dream-land. Great trees, like rustling walls of verdure, enclose an apparently endless roadway of gleaming water, a narrow strip of tow-path keeping it company, buttressed in from the surrounding fields with thickets of every species of bush and luxurious undergrowth, and starred with every summer flower.

Presently, by the side of the path, one comes to an object which seems romantically in keeping with the general character of the scene—a long block of stone, lying among the grasses and the wild geraniums, on which, as one nears it, one descries carved scroll-work and quaint, deep-cut lettering. Is it the tomb of dead lovers, the memorial of some great deed, or an altar to the *genius loci?* The willows whisper about it, and the great elms and maples sway and murmur no less impressively than if the inscription were in Latin of two thousand years ago. Nor is it in me to regret that the stone and its inscription, instead of celebrating the rural Pan, commemorate the men to whom I owe this lane of dreaming water and all its marginal green solitude: to wit —the "MORRIS CANAL AND BANKING CO., A.D. 1829," represented by its president, its cashier, its canal commissioner, and a score of other names of directors, engineers, and builders. Peace, therefore, to the souls of those dead directors, who, having only in mind their banking and engineering project, yet unconsciously wrought, nearly a century ago, so poetic a thing, and may their rest be lulled by such leafy murmurs and swaying of tendrilled shadows as all the day through stir and sway along the old canal!

A few yards beyond this monumental stone, there comes a great opening in the sky, a sense of depth and height and spacious freshness in the air, such as we feel on approaching the gorge of a great river; and in fact the canal has arrived at the Passaic and is about to be carried across it in a sort of long, wooden trough, supported by a noble bridge that might well pass for a genuine antique, owing to that collaborating hand of Nature which has filled the interstices of its massive masonry with fern, and so loosened it here and there that some of the canal escapes in long, ribbon-like cascades into the rocky bed of the river below. An aqueduct has always seemed to me, though it would be hard to say why, a most romantic thing. The idea of carrying running water across a bridge in this way—water which it is so hard to think of as imprisoned or controlled, and which, too, however shallow, one always associates with mysterious depth—the idea of thus carrying it across a valley high up in the air, so that one may look underneath it, underneath the bed in which it runs, and think of the fishes and the water-weeds and the waterbugs all being carried across with it, too—this, I confess, has always seemed to me engagingly marvellous. And I like, too, to think that the canal, whose daily business is to be a "common carrier" of others, thus occasionally tastes the luxury of being carried itself; as sometimes one sees on a freight car a new buggy, or automobile, or sometimes a locomotive, being luxuriously ridden along—as though out for a holiday—instead of riding others.

And talking of freight-cars, it came to me with a sense of illumination how different the word "Passaic" looks printed in white letters on the grey sides of grim produce-vans in begrimed procession, from the way it looks as it writes its name in wonderful white waterfalls, or murmurs it through corridors of that strange pillared and cake-shaped rock, amid the golden pomp of a perfect summer day. For a short distance the Passaic and the canal run side by side, but presently they part company, and mile after mile the canal seems to have the world to itself, once in a great while finding human companionship in a shingled cottage half hidden among willows, a sleepy brick-field run on principles as ancient as itself, shy little girls picking flowers on its banks, or saucy boys disporting themselves in the old swimming-hole; and

Sometimes an angler comes and drops his hook
Within its hidden depths, and 'gainst a tree
Leaning his rod, reads in some pleasant book,
Forgetting soon his pride of fishery;
   And dreams or falls asleep,
   While curious fishes peep
About his nibbled bait or scornfully
   Dart off and rise and leap.

Once a year, indeed, every one goes a-fishing along the old canal—men, women, boys, and girls. That is in spring, when the canal is emptied for repairs, the patching up of leaks, and so forth. Then the fish lie glittering in the shallow pools, as good as caught, and happy children go home with strings of sunfish,—"pumpkin-seeds" they call them,—cat-fish, and the like picturesque un-profitable spoils, while graver fisher-folk take count of pickerel and bream. This merry festival was over and gone, and the canal was all brimming with the lustral renewal of its waters, its depths flashing now and again with the passage of wary survivors of that spring *battue*.

It is essential to the appreciation of an old canal that one should not expect it to provide excitement, that it be understood between it and its fellow-pilgrim that there is very little to say and nothing to record. Along the old tow-path you must be content with a few simple, elemental, mysterious things. To enter into its spirit you must be somewhat of a monastic turn of mind, and have spiritual affiliations, above all, with La

Trappe. For the presiding muse of an old canal is Silence; yet, as at La Trappe, a silence far indeed from being a dumb silence, but a silence that contains all speech. My friend and I spoke hardly at all as we walked along, easily obedient to the spirit of the hour and the place. For there were so few of those little gossipy accidents and occurrences by the way that make those interruptions we call conversation, and such overwhelming golden-handed presences of sunlit woodlands, flashing water-meadows, shining, singing air, and distant purple hills—all the blowing, rippling, leafy glory and mighty laughter of a summer day —that we were glad enough to let the birds do such talking as Nature deemed necessary; and I seem never to have heard or seen so many birds, of so many varieties, as haunt that old canal.

As we chose our momentary camping-place under a buttonwood-tree, from out an exuberant swamp of yellow water-lilies and the rearing sword-blades of the coming cat-tail, a swamp blackbird, on his glossy black orange-tipped wings, flung us defiance with his long, keen, full, saucy note; and as we sat down under our buttonwood and spread upon the sward our pastoral meal, the veery-thrush—sadder and stranger than any nightingale —played for us, unseen, on an instrument like those old water-organs played on by the flow and ebb of the tide, a flute of silver in which some strange magician has somewhere hidden tears. I wondered, as he sang, if the veery was the thrush that, to Walt Whitman's fancy, "in the swamp in secluded recesses" mourned the death of Lincoln:

Solitary the thrush,
The hermit withdrawn to himself, avoiding the set-
    tlements,
Sings to himself a song.

But when the veery had flown with his heart-break to some distant copse, two song-sparrows came to persuade us with their blithe melody that life was worth living, after all; and cheerful little domestic birds, like the jenny-wren and the chip-ping-sparrow, pecked about and put in between whiles their little chit-chat across the boughs, while the bobolink called to us like a comrade, and the phœbe-bird gave us a series of imita-tions, and the scarlet tanager and the wild can-ary put in a vivid appearance, to show what can be done with colour, though they have no song.

Yet, while one was grateful for such long, green silence as we found along that old canal, one could not help feeling how hard it would be to put into words an experience so infinite and yet so un-dramatic. Birds and birds, and trees and trees, and the long, silent water! Prose has seldom been adequate for such moments. So, as my friend and I took up our walk again, I sang him this little song of the Silence of the Way:

Silence, whose drowsy eyelids are soft leaves,
   And whose half-sleeping eyes are the blue flowers,
On whose still breast the water-lily heaves,
   And all her speech the whisper of the showers.

Made of all things that in the water sway,
   The quiet reed kissing the arrowhead,
The willows murmuring, all a summer day,
   "Silence"—sweet word, and ne'er so softly said

As here along this path of brooding peace,
   Where all things dream, and nothing else is done
But all such gentle businesses as these
   Of leaves and rippling wind, and setting sun

Turning the stream to a long lane of gold,
   Where the young moon shall walk with feet of pearl,
And, framed in sleeping lilies, fold on fold,
   Gaze at herself like any mortal girl.

But, after all, trees are perhaps the best expression of silence, massed as they are with the merest hint of movement, and breathing the merest suggestion of a sigh; and seldom have I seen such abundance and variety of trees as along our old canal—cedars and hemlocks and hickory dominating green slopes of rocky pasture, with here and there a clump of silver birches bent over with the strain of last year's snow; and all along, near by the water, beech and basswood, blue-gum and pin-oak, ash, and even chestnut flourishing still, in defiance of blight. Nor have I ever seen such sheets of water-lilies as starred the swampy thickets, in which elder and hazels and every conceivable bush and shrub and giant grass and cane make wildernesses pathless indeed save to the mink and the water-snake, and the imagination that would fain explore their glimmering recesses.

No, nothing except birds and trees, water-lilies and such like happenings, ever happens along the old canal; and our nearest to a human event was our meeting with a lonely, melancholy man, sitting near a moss-grown water-wheel, smoking a corn-cob pipe, and gazing wistfully across at the Ramapo Hills, over which great sunlit clouds were billowing and casting slow-moving shadows. Stopping, we passed him the time of day and inquired when the next barge was due. For answer he took a long draw at his corn-cob, and, taking his eyes for a moment from the landscape, said in a far-away manner that it might be due any time now, as the spring had come and gone, and implying, with a sort of sad humour in his eyes, that spring makes all things possible, brings all things back, even an old slow-moving barge along the old canal.

"What do they carry on the canal?" I asked the melancholy man, the romantic green hush and the gleaming water not irrelevantly flashing on my fancy that far-away immortal picture of the lily-maid of Astolat on her strange journey, with a letter in her hand for Lancelot.

"Coal," was his answer; and, again drawing at his corn-cob, he added, with a sad and understanding smile, "once in a great while." Like most melancholy men, he seemed to have brains, in his way, and to have no particular work on hand, except, like ourselves, to dream.

"Suppose," said I, "that a barge should come along, and need to be drawn up this 'plane'— would the old machinery work?" and I pointed to six hundred feet of sloping grass, down which a tramway stretches and a cable runs on little wheels—technically known, it appeared, as a "plane."

Then the honour of the ancient company for which he had once worked seemed to stir his blood, and he awakened to something like enthusiasm as he explained the antique, picturesque device by which it is still really possible for a barge to climb six hundred feet of grass and fern —drawn up in a long "cradle," instead of being raised by locks in the customary way.

Then he took us into the old building where, in the mossed and dripping darkness, we could discern the great water-wheels that work this fascinating piece of ancient engineering; and added that there would probably be a barge coming along in three or four days, if we should happen to be in the neighbourhood. He might have added that the old canal is one of the few places where "time and tide" wait for any one and everybody —but alas! on this occasion we could not wait for them.

Our walk was nearing its end when we came

upon a pathetic reminder that, though the old canal is so far from being a stormy sea, there have been wrecks even in those quiet waters. In a backwater whispered over by willows and sung over by birds, a sort of water-side graveyard, eleven old barges were ingloriously rotting, unwept and unhonoured. The hulks of old men-of-war, forgotten as they may seem, have still their annual days of bunting and the salutes of cannon; but to these old servitors of peace come no such memorial recognitions.

"Unwept and unhonoured, may be," said I to my friend, "but they shall not go all unsung, though humble be the rhyme"; so here is the rhyme I affixed to an old nail on the mouldering side of the *Janita C. Williams:*

You who have done your work and asked no praise,
Mouldering in these unhonoured waterways,
Carrying but simple peace and quiet fire,
Doing a small day's work for a small hire—
You need not praise, nor guns, nor flags unfurled,
Nor all such cloudy glories of the world;
The laurel of a simple duty done
Is the best laurel underneath the sun,
Yet would two strangers passing by this spot
Whisper, "Old boat—you are not all forgot!"

XIV

A MODERN SAINT FRANCIS

WE were neither of us fox-hunting ourselves, but chanced both to be out on our morning walk and to be crossing a breezy Surrey common at the same moment, when the huntsmen and huntresses of the Slumberfold Hunt were blithely congregating for a day's run. A meet is always an attractive sight, and we had both come to a halt within a yard or two of each other, and stood watching the gallant company of fine ladies and gentlemen on their beautiful, impatient mounts, keeping up a prancing conversation, till the exciting moment should arrive when the cry would go up that the fox had been started, and the whole field would sweep away, a cataract of hounds, red-coats, riding habits, and dog-carts.

The moment came. The fox had been found in a spinney running down to Withy Brook, and his race for life had begun. With a happy shout, the hunt was up and off in a twinkling, and the stranger and I were left alone on the broad common.

I had scanned him furtively as he stood near

me; a tall, slightly built man of about fifty, with perfectly white hair, and strangely gentle blue eyes. There was a curious, sad distinction over him, and he had watched the scene with a smile of blended humour and pity.

Turning to me, as we were left alone, and speaking almost as though to himself: "It is a strange sight," he said with a sigh. "I wonder if it seems as strange to you? Think of all those grown-up, so-called civilized people being so ferociously intent on chasing one poor little animal for its life—and feeling, when at last the huntsman holds up his poor brush, with absurd pride (if indeed the fox is not too sly for them), that they have really done something clever, in that with so many horses and dogs and so much noise, they have actually contrived to catch and kill one fox!"

"It is strange!" I said, for I had been thinking just that very thing.

"Of course, they always tell you," he continued, as we took the road together, "that the fox really enjoys being hunted, and that he feels his occupation gone if there are no hounds to track him, and finally to tear him to pieces. What wonderful stories human nature will tell itself in its own justification! Can one imagine any created thing *enjoying* being pursued for its life, with all that loud terror of men and horses and savage dogs at its heels? No doubt—if we can imagine even a fox so self-conscious—it would take a certain pride in its own cunning and skill, if the whole thing were a game; but a race with death is too deadly in earnest for a fox even to relish his own stratagems. Happily for the fox, it is probable that he does not feel so much for himself as some of us feel for him; but any one who knows the wild things knows too what terror they are capable of feeling, and how the fear of death is always with them. No! you may be sure that a fox prefers a cosy hen-roost to the finest run with the hounds ever made."

"But even if he should enjoy being hunted," I added, "the even stranger thing to me is that civilized men and women should enjoy hunting him."

"Isn't it strange?" answered my companion eagerly, his face lighting up at finding a sympathizer. "When will people realize that there is so much more fun in studying wild things than in killing them! . . ."

He stopped suddenly in his walk, to gather a small weed which had caught his quick eye by the roadside, and which he examined for a moment through a little pocket microscope which I noticed, hanging like an eyeglass round his neck, and which I learned afterward quite affectionately to associate with him. Then, as we walked on, he remarked:

"But, of course, we are yet very imperfectly civilized. Humanity is a lesson learned very slowly by the human race. Yet we are learning it by degrees, yes! we are learning it," and he threw out his long stride more emphatically—the stride of one accustomed to long daily tramps on the hills.

"Strange, that principle of cruelty in the universe!" he resumed, after a pause in which he had walked on in silence. "Very strange. To me it is the most mysterious of all things—though, I suppose, after all, it is no more mysterious than pity. When, I wonder, did pity begin? Who was the first human being to pity another? How strange he must have seemed to the others, how incomprehensible and ridiculous—not to say dangerous! There can be little doubt that he was promptly dispatched with stone axes as an enemy of a respectable murderous society."

"I expect," said I "that our friends the foxhunters would take a similar view of our remarks on their sport."

"No doubt—and perhaps turn their hounds on us! A man hunt! 'Give me the hunting of man!' as a brutal young poet we know of recently sang."

"How different was the spirit of Emerson's old verse," I said:

"Hast thou named all the birds without a gun?
Loved the wood-rose, and left it on its stalk? . . .
O be my friend, and teach me to be thine!"

"That is one of my mottoes!" cried my companion with evident pleasure. "Let us go and quote it to our fox-hunters!"

"I wonder how the fox is getting on," I said.

"If he is any sort of fox, he is safe enough as yet, we may be sure. They are wonderful creatures. It is not surprising that mankind has always looked upon Reynard as almost a human being—if not more—for there is something quite uncanny in his instincts, and the cool, calculating way in which he uses them. He is come and gone like a ghost. One moment you were sure you saw him clearly close by and the next he is gone—who knows where? He can run almost as swiftly as light, and as softly as a shadow; and in his wildest dash, what a sure judgment he has for the lie of the ground, how unerringly—and at a moment when a mistake is death—he selects his cover! How learned, too, he is in his knowledge of the countryside! There is not a dry ditch, or a watercourse, or an old drain, or a hole in a bank for miles around that is not mysteriously set down in the map he carries in his graceful, clever head; and one need hardly say that all the suitable hiding-places in and around farm-yards are equally well known to him. Then withal he is so brave. How splendidly, when wearied out, and hopelessly tracked down, with the game quite up, he will turn on his pursuers, and die with his teeth fast in his enemy's throat!"

"I believe you are a fox-hunter in disguise," I laughed.

"Well, I have hunted as a boy," he said, "and I know something of what those red-coated gentlemen are feeling. But soon I got more interested in studying nature than killing it, and when I became a naturalist I ceased to be a hunter. You get to love the things so that it seems like killing little children. They come so close to you, are so beautiful and so clever; and sometimes there seems such a curious pathos about them. How any one can kill a deer with that woman's look in its eyes, I don't know. I should always expect the deer to change into a fairy princess, and die in my arms with the red blood running from her white breast. And pigeons, too, with their soft sunny coo all the summer afternoon, or the sudden lapping of sleepy wings round the chimneys—how can any one trap or shoot them with blood-curdling rapidity, and not expect to see ghosts!"

"Of course, there is this difference about the fox," I said, "that it is really in a sense born to be hunted. For not only is it a fierce hunter itself, but it would not be allowed to exist at all, so to say, unless it consented to being hunted. Like a gladiator it accepts a comfortable living for a certain time, on condition of its providing at last a spirited exhibition of dying. In other words, it is preserved entirely for the purpose of being hunted. It must accept life on that condition or be extirpated as destructive vermin by the plundered farmer. Life is sweet, after all, and to be a kind of protected highwayman of the poultry-yard, for a few sweet toothsome years, taking one's chances of being surely brought to book at last, may perhaps seem worth while."

"Yes! but how does your image of the protected gladiator reflect on those who protect him? There, of course, is the point. The gladiator, as you say, is willing to take his chances in exchange for fat living and idleness, as long as he lives. You may even say that his profession is good for him, develops fine qualities of mind even as well as body— but what of the people who crowd with blood-thirsty eagerness to watch those qualities exhibited in so tragic a fashion for their amusement? Do they gain any of his qualities of skill and courage, and strength and fearlessness in the face of death? No, they are merely brutalized by cruel excite-ment—and while they applaud his skill and admire his courage, they long most to watch him die. So—is it not?—with our friend the fox. The huntsman invariably compliments him on his spirit and his cunning, but what he wants is— the brush. He wants the excitement of hunting the living thing to its death; and, let huntsmen say what they will about the exhilaration of the horse exercise across country as being the main thing, they know better—and, if it be true, why don't they take it without the fox?"

"They do in America, as, of course, you know. There a man walks across country trailing a stick, at the end of which is a piece of cloth impregnated with some pungent scent which hounds love and mistake for the real thing."

"Hard on the poor hounds!" smiled my friend. "Even worse than a red herring. You could hardly blame the dogs if they mistook the man for Actæon and tore him to pieces."

"And I suspect that the huntsmen are no better satisfied."

"Yet, as we were saying, if the secret spring of their sport is not the cruel delight of pursuing a living thing to its death, that American plan should serve all the purposes, and give all the satisfaction for which they claim to follow the hounds: the keen pleasure of a gallop across country, the excitement of its danger, the pluck and pride of taking a bad fence, and equally, too, the pleasure of watching the hounds cleverly at work with their mysterious gift of scent. All the same, I suspect there are few sportsmen who would not vote it a tame substitute. Without something being killed, the zest, the 'snap,' is gone. It is as depressing as a sham fight."

"Yes, that mysterious shedding of blood! what a part it has played in human history! Even religion countenances it, and war glorifies it. Men are never in higher spirits than when they are going to kill, or be killed themselves, or see something else killed. Tennyson's 'ape and tiger' die very hard in the tamest of us."

"Alas, indeed they do!" said my friend with a sigh. "But I do believe that they are dying none the less. Just of late there has been a reaction in favour of brute force, and people like you and me have been ridiculed as old-fashioned sentimentalists. But reaction is one of the laws of advance.

Human progress always takes a step backwards after it has taken two forward. And so it must be here too. In the end, it is the highest type among men and nations that count, and the highest types among both today are those which show most humanity, shrink most from the infliction of pain. When one thinks of the horrible cruelties that were the legal punishment of criminals, even within the last two hundred years, and not merely brutal criminals, but also political offenders or so-called heretics—how every one thought it the natural and proper thing to break a man on the wheel for a difference of opinion, or torture him with hideous ingenuity into a better frame of mind, and how the pettiest larcenies were punished by death; it seems as if we of today, even the least sensitive of us, cannot belong to the same race—and it is impossible to deny that the heart of the world has grown softer and that pity is becoming more and more a natural instinct in human nature. I believe that some day it will have thrust out cruelty altogether, and that the voluntary infliction of pain upon another will be unknown. The idea of any one killing for pleasure will seem too preposterous to be believed, and soldiers and fox-hunters and pigeon-shooters will be spoken of as nowadays we speak of cannibals. But, of course, I am a dreamer," he concluded, his face shining with his gentle dream, as though he had been a veritable saint of the calendar.

"Yes, a dream," he added presently, "and yet——"

In that "and yet" there was a world of invincible faith that made it impossible not to share his dream, even see it building before one's eyes—such is the magnetic power of a passionate personal conviction.

"Of course," he went on again, "we all know that 'nature is one with rapine, a harm no preacher can heal.' But because the fox runs off with the goose, or the hawk swoops down on the chicken, and 'yon whole little wood is a world of plunder and prey'—is that any reason why we should be content to plunder and prey too? And after all, the cruelty of Nature is only one-sided. There is lots of pity in Nature too. These strange little wild lives around us are not entirely bent on killing and eating each other. They know the tenderness of motherhood, the sweetness of building a home together, and I believe there is far more comradeship and mutual help amongst them than we know of. Yes, even in wild Nature there is a principle of love working no less than a principle of hate. Nature is not all-devouring and destroying. She is loving and building too. Nature is more constructive than destructive, and she is ever at work evolving and evolving a higher dream. Surely it is not for man, to whom, so far as we know, Nature has entrusted the working out of her finest impulses, and whom she has endowed with all the fairy apparatus of the soul; it is not for him, whose

eyes—of all her children—Nature has opened,
the one child she has taken into her confidence
and to whom she has whispered her secret hopes
and purposes; surely it is not for man voluntarily
to deny his higher lot, and, because the wolf and
he have come from the same great mother, say:
'I am no better than the wolf. Why should I
not live the life of a wolf—and kill and devour like
my brother? '   Surely it is not for the cruel things
in Nature to teach man cruelty—rather, if it were
possible," and the saint smiled at his fancy,
"would it be the mission of man to teach them
kindness: rather should he preach pity to the
hawk and peace between the panther and the
bear. It is not the bad lessons of Nature, but
the good, that are meant for man—though, as
you must have noticed, man seldom appeals to
the precedents of Nature except to excuse that
in him which is Nature at her worst. When we
say, 'it is only natural,' we almost invariably refer
to that in Nature of which Nature herself has
entrusted the refinement or the elimination to man.
It is Nature's bad we copy, not Nature's good;
and always we forget that we ourselves are a part
of Nature—Nature's vicegerent, so to say, upon
the earth——"

As we talked, we had been approaching a house
built high among the heather, with windows looking over all the surrounding country. Presently,
the saint stopped in front of it.

"This is my house," he said. "Won't you

come in and see me some time?—and, by the way, I am going to talk to some of the village children about the wild things, bird's nesting, and so forth, up at the schoolhouse on Thursday. I wish you'd come and help me. One's only hope is with the children. The grown-up are too far gone. Mind you come."

So we parted, and, as I walked across the hill homeward, haunted by that gentle face, I thought of Melampus, that old philosopher who loved the wild things so and had made such friends with them, that they had taught him their language and told him all their secrets:

With love exceeding a simple love of the things
    That glide in grasses and rubble of woody wreck;
Or change their perch on a beat of quivering wings
    From branch to branch, only restful to pipe and
        peck;
Or, bridled, curl at a touch their snouts in a ball;
    Or cast their web between bramble and thorny
        hook;
The good physician, Melampus, loving them all,
    Among them walked, as a scholar who reads a
        book.

As I dipped into the little thick-set wood that surrounds my house, something stood for a second in one of the openings, then was gone like a shadow. I was glad to think how full of bracken and hollows, and mysterious holes and corners of mossed and lichened safety was our old wood—for the shadow was a fox. I like to think it was the very fox we had been talking about come to find shelter with me—and, if he stole a meal out of our hen-roost, I gave it him before he asked it, with all the will in the world. I hope he chose a good fat hen, and not one of your tough old capons that some-times come to table.

XV

THE LITTLE GHOST IN THE GARDEN

I DON'T know in what corner of the garden his busy little life now takes its everlasting rest. None of us had the courage to stand by, that summer morning, when Morris, our old negro man, buried him, and we felt sympathetic for Morris that the sad job should fall upon him, for Morris loved him just as we did. Perhaps if we had loved him less, more sentimentally than deeply, we should have indulged in some sort of appropriate ceremonial, and marked his grave with a little stone. But, as I have said, his grave, like that of the great prophet, is a secret to this day. None of us has ever asked Morris about it, and his grief has been as reticent as our own. I wondered the other night, as I walked the garden in a veiled moonlight, whether it was near the lotus-tanks he was lying—for I remembered how he would stand there, almost by the hour, watching the goldfish that we had engaged to protect us against mosquitoes, moving mysteriously under the shadows of the great flat leaves. In his short life he grew to understand much of this strange world, but he never got used to those goldfish; and often I have seen him, after a long wistful contemplation of them, turn away with a sort of half-frightened, puzzled bark, as though to say that he gave it up. Or, does he lie, I wonder, somewhere among the long grass of the salt-marsh, that borders our garden, and in perigee tides widens out into a lake. There indeed would be his appropriate country, for there was the happy hunting-ground through which in life he was never tired of roaming, in the inextinguishable hope of mink, and with the occasional certainty of a water-rat.

He had come to us almost as mysteriously as he went away; a fox-terrier puppy wandered out of the Infinite to the neighbourhood of our ice-box, one November morning, and now wandered back again. Technically, he was just graduating out of puppyhood, though, like the most charming human beings, he never really grew up, and re-mained, in behaviour and imagination, a puppy to the end. He was a dog of good breed and good manners, evidently with gentlemanly antecedents canine and human. There were those more learned in canine aristocracy than ourselves who said that his large leaf-like, but very becoming, ears meant a bar sinister somewhere in his pedigree, but to our eyes those only made him better-look-ing; and, for the rest of him, he was race—race nervous, sensitive, refined, and courageous—from the point of his all-searching nose to the end

of his stub of a tail, which the conventional dock-
ing had seemed but to make the more expressive.
We had already one dog in the family when he
arrived, and two Maltese cats. With the cats
he was never able to make friends, in spite of
persistent well-intentioned efforts. It was evident
to us that his advances were all made in the spirit
of play, and from a desire of comradeship, the two
crowning needs of his blithe sociable spirit. But
the cats received them in an attitude of invincible
distrust, of which his poor nose frequently bore
the sorry signature. Yet they had become friendly
enough with the other dog, an elderly setter, by
name Teddy, whose calm, lordly, slow-moving
ways were due to a combination of natural dignity,
vast experience of life, and some rheumatism. As
Teddy would sit philosophizing by the hearth of
an evening, immovable and plunged in memories,
yet alert on the instant to a footfall a quarter of
a mile away, they would rub their sinuous smoke-
grey bodies to and fro beneath his jaws, just as
though he were a piece of furniture; and he would
take as little notice of them as though he were the
leg of the piano; though sometimes he would wag
his tail gently to and fro, or rap it softly on the
floor, as though appreciating the delicate attention.

Of Teddy's reception of the newcomer we had
at first some slight misgiving, for, amiable as we
have just seen him with his Maltese companions,
and indeed as he is generally by nature, his is the

amiability that comes of conscious power, and is his, so to say, by right of conquest; for of all neighbouring dogs he is the acknowledged king. The reverse of quarrelsome, the peace of his declining years has been won by much historical fighting, and his reputation among the dogs of his acquaintance is such that it is seldom necessary for him to assert his position. It is only some hapless stranger ignorant of his standing that will occasionally provoke him to a display of those fighting qualities he grows more and more reluctant to employ. Even with such he is comparatively merciful; stern, but never brutal. Usually all that is necessary is for him to look at them steadfastly for a few moments in a peculiar way. This seems to convince them that, after all, discretion is the better part, and slowly and sadly they turn around in a curious cowed way, and walk off, apparently too scared to run, with Teddy, like Fate, grimly at their heels, steadily "pointing" them off the premises. We were a little anxious, therefore, as to how Teddy would take our little terrier, with his fussy, youthful self-importance, and eternal restless poking into other folks' affairs. But Teddy, as we might have told ourselves, had had a long and varied experience of terriers, and had nothing to learn from us. Yet I have no doubt that, with his instinctive courtesy, he divined the wishes of the family in regard to the newcomer, and was, therefore, predisposed in his favour. This, however, did not save the evidently much overawed youngster from a stern and searching examination, the most trying part of which seemed to be that long, silent, hypnotizing contemplation of him, which is Teddy's way of asserting his dignity. The little dog visibly trembled beneath the great one's gaze, his tongue hanging out of his mouth, and his eyes wandering helplessly from side to side; and he seemed to be saying, in his dog way: "O yes! I know you are a very great and important personage—and I am only a poor little puppy of no importance. Only please let me go on living—and you will see how well I will behave." Teddy seemed to be satisfied that some such recognition and submission had been tendered him; so presently he wagged his tail, that had up till then been rigid as a ramrod, and not only the little terrier, but all of us, breathed again. Yet it was some time before Teddy would admit him into anything like what one might call intimacy, and premature attempts at gamesome familiarity were checked by the gathering thunder of a lazy growl that unmistakably bade the youngster keep his place. But real friendship eventually grew between them, on Teddy's side a sort of big-brother affectionate tutelage and guardianship, and on Puppy's—for, though we tried many, we never found any other satisfactory name for him but "Puppy"—a reverent admiration and watchful worshipping imitation. No great man was ever more anxiously copied by some slavish flatterer than that old sleepy carelessly-great setter by that eager, ambitious little terrier. The occasions when to bark and when not to bark, for example. One could actually see Puppy studying the old dog's face on doubtful occasions of the kind. Boiling over, as he visibly was, with the desire to bark his soul out, yet he could be seen unmistakably restraining himself, till Teddy, after some preliminary soliloquizing in deep undertones, had made up his mind that the suspicious shuffling-by of probably some inoffensive Italian workman demanded investigation, and lumberingly risen to his feet and made for the door. Then, like a bunch of firecrackers, Puppy was at the heels, all officious assistance, and the two would disappear like an old and a young thunderbolt into the resounding distance.

Teddy's friendship had seemed to be definitely won on an occasion which brought home to one the quaint resemblance between the codes and ways of dogs and those of schoolboys. When the winter came on, a rather severe one, it soon became evident that the little short-haired fellow suffered considerably from the cold. Out on walks, he was visibly shivering, though he made no fuss about it. So one of the angels in the house knitted for him a sort of woollen sweater buttoned down his neck and under his belly, and trimmed it with some white fur that gave it an exceedingly smart appearance. Teddy did not happen to be there when it was first tried on, and, for the moment,

Puppy had to be content with our admiration, and his own vast sense of importance. Certainly, a more self-satisfied terrier never was than he who presently sped out, to air his new finery before an astonished neighbourhood. But alas! you should have seen him a few minutes afterwards. We had had the curiosity to stroll out to see how he had got on, and presently, in a bit of rocky woodland near by, we came upon a curious scene. In the midst of a clump of red cedars, three great dogs, our Teddy, a wicked old black retriever, and a bustling be-wigged and be-furred collie, stood in a circle round Puppy, seated on his haunches, trembling with fear, tongue lolling and eyes wandering, for all the world as though they were holding a court-martial, or, at all events, a hazing-party. The offence evidently lay with that dandified new sweater. One and another of the dogs smelt at it, then tugged at it in evident disgust; and, as each time Puppy made a move to get away, all girt him round with guttural thunder of disapproval, as much as to say: "Do you call that a thing for a manly dog to go around in? You ought to be ashamed of yourself, you miserable dandy."

We couldn't help reflecting that it was all very well for those great comfortable long-haired dogs to talk, naturally protected as they were from the cold. Yet that evidently cut no figure with them, and they went on sniffing and tugging and growling, till we thought our poor Puppy's eyes and tongue would drop out with fear. Yet, all the time, they seemed to be enjoying his plight, seemed to be smiling grimly together, wicked old experienced brutes as they were.

Presently the idea of the thing seemed to occur to Puppy, or out of his extremity a new soul was born within him, for suddenly an infinite disgust of his new foppery seemed to take possession of him too, and, regaining his courage, he turned savagely upon it, ripping it this way and that, and struggling with might and main to rid himself of the accursed thing. Presently he stood free, and barks of approval at once went up from his judges. He had come through his ordeal, and was once more a dog among dogs. Great was the rejoicing among his friends, and the occasion having been duly celebrated by joint destruction and contumely of the offending garment, Teddy and he returned home, friends for life.

It is to be feared that that friendship, deep and tender as it grew to be on both sides, perhaps particularly on Teddy's, was the indirect cause of Puppy's death. I have referred to Teddy's bark, and how he is not wont to waste it on trivial occasions, or without due thought. On the other hand, he is proud of it, and loves to practice it— just for its own sake, particularly on early mornings, when, however fine a bark it is, most of our neighbours would rather continue sleeping than wake up to listen to it. There is no doubt at all, for those who understand him, that it is a purely artistic bark. He means no harm to any one by it. When the milkman, his private enemy, comes at seven, the bark is quite different. This barking of Teddy's seems to be literally at nothing. Around five o'clock on summer mornings, he plants himself on a knob of rock overlooking the salt marsh and barks, possibly in honour of the rising sun, but with no other perceptible purpose. So have I heard men rise in the dawn to practice the cornet—but they were men, so they ran no risk of their lives. Teddy's practicing, however, has now been carried on for several years in the teeth of no little peril; and, had it not been for much human influence employed on his behalf, he would long since have antedated his little friend in Paradise. When that little friend, however, came to assist and emulate him in those morning recitals, adding to his bark an occasional—I am convinced purely playful—bite, I am inclined to think that a sentiment grew in the neighbourhood that one dog at a time was enough. At all events, Teddy still barks at dawn as of old, but our little Puppy barks no more.

Before the final quietus came to him, there were several occasions on which the Black dog, called Death, had almost caught him in his jaws. One there was in especial. He had, I believe, no hatred for any living thing save Italian workmen and automobiles. I have seen an Italian workman throw his pick-axe at him, and then take to his heels in grotesque flight. But the pick-axe missed him, as did many another clumsily hurled missile.

An automobile, however, on one occasion, came nearer its mark. Like every other dog that ever barked, particularly terriers, Puppy delighted to harass the feet of fast trotting horses, mockingly running ahead of them, barking with affected savagery, and by a miracle evading their on-coming hoofs—which to him, tiny thing as he was, must have seemed like trip-hammers pounding down from the sky. But horses understand such gaiety in terriers. They understand that it is only their foolish fun. Automobiles are different. They have no souls. They see nothing engaging in having their tires snapped at, as they whirl swiftly by; and, one day, after Puppy had flung himself in a fine fury at the tires of one of these soulless things, he gave a sharp yelp—"not cowardly!"— and lay a moment on the roadside. But only a moment; then he went limping off on his three sound legs, and hid himself away from all sympathy, in some unknown spot. It was in vain we called and sought him, and only after two days was he discovered, in the remotest corner of a great rocky cellar, determined apparently to die alone in an almost inaccessible privacy of wood and coal. Yet, when at last we persuaded him that life was still sweet and carried him upstairs into the great living-room, and the beautiful grandmother, who knows the sorrows of animals almost as the old Roman seer knew the languages of beasts and birds, had taken him in charge and made a cosy nest of comforters for him by the fire, and tempted his languid appetite—to which the very thought of bones was, of course, an offence—with warm, savory-smelling soup; then, he who had certainly been no coward—for his thigh was a cruel lump of pain which no human being would have kept so patiently to himself—became suddenly, like many human invalids, a perfect glutton of self-pity; and when we smoothed and patted him and told him how sorry we were, it was laughable, and almost uncanny, how he suddenly set up a sort of moaning talk to us, as much as to say that he certainly had had a pretty bad time, was really something of a hero, and deserved all the sympathy we would give him. So far as one can be sure about anything so mysterious as animals, I am sure that from then on he luxuriated in his little hospital by the fireside, and played upon the feelings of his beautiful nurse, and of his various solicitous visitors, with all the histrionic skill of the spoiled and petted convalescent. Suddenly, however, one day, he forgot his part. He heard some inspiring barking going on nearby—and, in a flash, his comforters were thrust aside, and he was off and away to join the fun. Then, of course, we knew that he was well again; though he still went briskly about his various business on three legs for several days.

His manner was quite different, however, the

afternoon he had so evidently come home to die. There was no pose about the little forlorn figure, which, after a mysterious absence of two days, suddenly appeared, as we were taking tea on the veranda, already the very ghost of himself. Wearily he sought the cave of the beautiful grandmother's skirts, where, whenever he had had a scolding, he was wont always to take refuge— barking, fiercely, as from an inaccessible fortress, at his enemies.

But, this afternoon, there was evidently no bark in him, poor little fellow; everything about him said that he had just managed to crawl home to die. His brisk white coat seemed dank with cold dews, and there was something shadowy about him and strangely quiet. His eyes, always so alert, were strangely heavy and indifferent, yet questioning and somehow accusing. He seemed to be asking us why a little dog should suffer so, and what was going to happen to him, and what did it all mean. Alas! We could not tell him; and none of us dare say to each other that our little comrade in the mystery of life was going to die. But a silence fell over us all, and the beautiful grandmother took him into her care, and so well did her great and wise heart nurse him through the night that next morning it almost seemed as though we had been wrong; for a flash of his old spirit was in him again, and, though his little legs shook under him, it was plain that he wanted to try and be up at his day's work on the veranda, warning off the passer-by, or in the garden carrying on his eternal investigations, or farther afield in the councils and expeditions of his fellows. So we let him have his way, and for a while he seemed happier and stronger for the sunshine, and the old familiar scents and sounds. But the one little tired husky bark he gave at his old enemy, the Italian workman, passing by, would have broken your heart; and the effort he made with a bone, as he visited the well-remembered neighbourhood of the ice-box for the last time, was piteous beyond telling. Those sharp, strong teeth that once could bite and grind through anything could do nothing with it now. To lick it sadly with tired lips, in a sort of hopeless way, was all that was left; and there was really a look in his face as though he accepted this mortal defeat, as he lay down, evidently exhausted with his exertions, on a bank nearby. But once more his spirit seemed to revive, and he scrambled to his legs again and wearily crawled to the back of the house, where the beautiful grandmother loves to sit and look over the glittering salt-marsh in the summer afternoons.

Of course, he knew that she was there. She had been his best friend in this strange world. His last effort was naturally to be near her again. Almost he reached that kind cave of her skirts. Only another yard or two and he had been there.

But the energy that had seemed irrepressible and everlasting had come to its end, and the little body had to give in at last, and lie down wearily once more with no life left but the love in its fading eyes.

There are some, I suppose, who may wonder how one can write about the death of a mere dog like this; and cannot understand how the death of a little terrier can make the world seem a lonelier place. But there are others, I know, who will scarce need telling, men and women with little ghosts of their own haunting their moonlit gardens; strange, appealing, faithful companions, kind little friendly beings that journeyed with them awhile the pilgrimage of the soul.

I often wonder if Teddy misses his little busy playfellow and disciple as we do; if, perhaps, as he barks over the marsh of a morning, he is sending him a message. He goes about the place with nonchalant greatness as of old, and the Maltese cats still rub their sinuous smoke-grey bodies to and fro beneath his jaws at evening. There is no sign of sorrow upon him. But he is old and very wise, and keeps strange knowledge to himself. So, who can say?

XVI

THE ENGLISH COUNTRYSIDE

FOR the genuine lover of nature, as distinct from the connoisseur of dainty or spectacular "scenery," nature has always and everywhere some charm or satisfaction. He will find it no less—some say more—in winter than in summer, and I have little doubt that the great Alkali Desert is not entirely without its enthusiasts. The nature among which we spent our childhood is apt to have a lasting hold on us, in defiance of showier competition, and I suppose there is no land with soul so dead that it does not boast itself the fairest under heaven.

I am writing this surrounded by a natural scene which I would not exchange for the Swiss lakes, yet I presume it is undeniable that Switzerland has a more universal reputation for natural beauty than Connecticut. It is, as we say, one of the show places of the earth. So Niagara Falls, the Grand Cañon, the Rockies, and California generally lord it over America. Italy has such a reputation for beauty that it is almost unfair to expect her to live up to it. I once ventured to say that the Alps must be greasy with being climbed, and it says much for such stock pieces in nature's repertoire, that, in spite of all the wear and tear of sentimental travellers, the mock-admiration of generations, the batteries of amateur cameras, the Riviera, the English lakes, the Welsh mountains, the Highlands of Scotland, and other tourist-trodden classics of the picturesque, still remain haunts of beauty and joys forever. God's master-pieces do not easily wear out.

Every country does something supremely well, and England may be said to have a patent for a certain kind of scenery which Americans are the first to admire. English scenery has no more passionate pilgrim than the traveller from the United States, as the visitors' books of its various show-places voluminously attest. Perhaps it is not difficult, when one has lived in both countries, to understand why.

While America, apart from its impressive natural splendours, is rich also in idyllic and pastoral landscape, it has, as yet, but little "countryside." I say, as yet, because "the countryside," I think I am right in feeling, is not entirely a thing of nature's making, but rather a collaboration resulting from nature and man living so long in partnership together. In England, with which the word is peculiarly, if not exclusively, associated, God is not entirely to be credited with making the country. Man has for generations also done his share.

It is perhaps not without significance that the word "countryside" was not to be found in Webster's dictionary, till a recent edition. Originally, doubtless, it was used with reference to those rural districts in the vicinity of a town; as one might say the country side of the town. Not wild or solitary nature was meant, but nature humanized, made companionable by the presence and occupations of man; a nature which had made the winding highway, the farm, and the pasture, even the hamlet, with its church tower and its ancient inn, one with herself.

The American, speeding up to London from his landing either at Liverpool or Southampton, always exclaims on the gardenlike aspect, the deep, rich greenness of the landscape. It is not so much the specific evidences of cultivation, though those, of course, are plentifully present, but a general air of ripeness and order. Even the land not visible under cultivation suggests immemorial care and fertility. We feel that this land has been fought over and ploughed over, nibbled over by sheep, sown and reaped, planted and drained, walked over, hunted over, and very much beloved, for centuries. It is not fanciful to see in it a land to which its people have been stubbornly and tenderly devoted—still "Shakespeare's England," still his favoured "isle set in the silver sea."

As seen from the railway-carriage window, one is struck, too, by the comparative tidiness of the English landscape. There are few loose ends, and the outskirts of villages are not those distressing dump-heaps which they too often are in America. Yet there is no excessive air of trimness. The order and grooming seem a part of nature's processes. There is, too, a casual charm about the villages themselves, the graceful, accidental grouping of houses and gardens, which suggests growth rather than premeditation. The general harmony does not preclude, but rather comes of, the greatest variety of individual character.

Herein the English village strikingly differs from the typical New England village, where the charm comes of a prim uniformity, and individuality is made to give place to a general parking of lawns and shade-trees in rectangular blocks and avenues. A New England village suggests some large institution disposed in separate uniform buildings, placed on one level carpet of green, each with a definite number of trees, and the very sunlight portioned out into gleaming allotments. The effect gained is for me one of great charm— the charm of a vivid, exquisitely ordered, green silence, with a touch of monastic, or Quakerish, decorum. I would not have it otherwise, and I speak of it only to suggest by contrast the different, desultory charm of an old English village, where beauty has not been so much planned, as has just "occurred."

Of course, this is the natural result of the long occupation of the land. Each century in succession has had a hand in shaping the countryside to its present aspect, and English history is literally a living visible part of English scenery. Here the thirteenth century has left a church, here the fourteenth a castle, here the sixteenth, with its suppression of the monasteries, a ruined abbey. Here is an inn where Chaucer's pilgrims stopped on the way to Canterbury. Here, in a field covered over by a cow-shed, is a piece of tessellated pavement which was once the floor of an old country house occupied by one of Cæsar's generals.

Those strange grassy mounds breaking the soft sky-line of the rolling South Downs are the tombs of Saxon chieftains, that rubble of stones at the top of yonder hill was once a British camp, and those curious ridges terracing yonder green slope mark the trenches of some prehistoric battlefield. All these in the process of time have become part and parcel of the English countryside, as necessary to its "English" character as its trees and its wild flowers.

How much, too, the English countryside owes for its beauty to the many old manor-houses, gabled and moated, with their quaint, mossy-walled gardens and great forestlike parks. Whatever we may think of the English territorial system as economics, its service to English scenery has been incalculable. Without English traditionalism we should hardly have had the English countryside.

The conservation of great estates, entailing a

certain conservatism in the treatment of farm lands from generation to generation, and the upholding, too, of game-preserves, however obnoxious to the land reformer, have been all to the good of the nature-lover. We owe no little of the beauty of the English woodland to the English pheasant; and with the coming of land nationalization we may expect to see considerable changes in the English countryside. Meanwhile, in spite of, or perhaps because of, the feudalistic character of English landlordism, the Englishman enjoys a right of walking over his native land of which no capitalist can rob him. Hence results another charming feature of the English countryside—the footpaths you see everywhere winding over hill and dale, through field and coppice. The ancient rights of these are safeguarded to the people forever by statute no wealth can defy; and, let any *nouveau riche* of a landlord try to close one of them, and he has to reckon with one of the pluckiest and most persistent organizations of English John Hampdens, the society that makes the protection of these traditional pathways its particular care. So the rich man cannot lock up his trees and his woodland glades all for himself, but is compelled to share them to the extent of allowing the poorest pedestrian to walk through them—which is about all the rich man can do with them himself.

These footpaths, in conjunction with English lanes, have made the charm of walking tours in England proverbial. Certain counties particu-

larly pride themselves on their lanes. Surrey
and Devonshire are the great rivals in this respect.
We say "Surrey lanes" or "Devonshire lanes,"
as we speak of "Italian skies" or "Southern
hospitality." Other counties—Warwickshire, for
example—doubtless have lanes no less lovely,
but Surrey and Devonshire have, so to say, got
the decision; and, if an American traveller wants
to see a typical English lane, he goes to Surrey or
Devonshire, just as, if he wants a typical English
pork-pie, he sends to Melton Mowbray.

And the English lane has come honestly by its
reputation. You may be disappointed in Venice,
but you will be hard to please if you are not caught
by the spell of an English lane. Of course, you
must not expect to feel that spell if you tear
through it in a motor-car. It was made for the
loiterer, as its whimsical twists and turns plainly
show. If you are in a hurry, you had better
keep to the king's highway, stretching swift and
white on the king's business. The English lane
was made for the leisurely meandering of cows to
and from pasture, for the dreamy snail-pace of
time-forgetting lovers, for children gathering
primroses or wild strawberries, or for the knap-
sacked wayfarer to whom time and space are no
objects, whose destination is anywhere and nowhere, whose only clocks are the rising sun and the
evening star, and to whom the way means more
than the goal.

I should not have spoken of it as "made," for,

when it is most characteristic, an English lane has no suggestion of ever having been man-made, like other roads. It seems as much a natural feature as the woods or meadows through which it passes; and sometimes, as in Surrey, when it runs between high banks, tunnelling its way under green boughs, it seems more like an old river-bed than a road, whose sides nature has tapestried with ferns and flowers. Of all roads in the world it is the dreamer's road, luring on the wayfarer with perpetual romantic promise and surprise, winding on and on, one can well believe, into the very heart of fairy-land. Everything beautiful seems to be waiting for us somewhere in the turnings of an English lane.

Had I sat down to write of the English countryside two years ago, I should have done so with a certain amount of cautious skepticism. I should have said to myself: "You have not visited England for over ten years. Are you quite sure that your impressions of its natural beauties are not the rose-coloured exaggerations of memory? Are not time and distance lending their proverbial enchantment?" In fact, as I set sail to revisit England, the spring before last, it was in some such mood of anticipatory disillusion.

After all, I had said to myself, is not the English countryside the work of the English poets—the English spring, the English wild flowers, the English lark, the English nightingale, and so forth? That longing of Browning expressed in the lines,

> O to be in England
> Now that April's there!

was, after all, the cry of a homesick versifier,
thinking "Home Thoughts, from Abroad"; and
are Herrick and Wordsworth quite to be trusted
on the subject of daffodils?

Well, I am glad to have to own that my revisit-
ing my native land resulted in an agreeable disappointment. With a critical American eye,
jealously on my guard against sentimental superstition, I surveyed the English landscape and
examined its various vaunted beauties and fasci-
nations, as though making their acquaintance for
the first time. No, my youthful raptures had
not been at fault, and the poets were once more
justified. The poets are seldom far wrong. If
they see anything, it is usually there. If we cannot see it, too, it is the fault of our eyes.

Take the English hawthorn, for instance. As
its fragrance is wafted to you from the bushes
where it hangs like the fairest of white linen, you
will hardly, I think, quarrel with its praises.
Yet, though it is, if I am not mistaken, of rare
occurrence in America, it is not absolutely necessary to go to England for the hawthorn. Any
one who cares to go a-Maying along the banks
of the Hudson, in the neighbourhood of Peekskill,
will find it there. But for the primrose and the
cowslip you must cross the sea; and, if you come
upon such a wood as I strayed into, my last visit,

you will count it worth the trip. It was literally carpeted with clumps of primroses and violets (violets that smell, too) so thickly massed together in the mossy turf that there was scarcely room to tread. There are no words rich or abundant enough to suggest the sense of innocent luxury brought one by such a natural Persian carpet of soft gold and dewy purple, at once so gorgeous and yet so gentle. In all this lavish loveliness of English wild flowers there is, indeed, a peculiar tenderness. The innocence of children seems to be in them, and the tenderness of lovers.

> A lover would not tread
> A cowslip on the head—

How appropriately such lines come to mind as one carefully picks one's way down a green hillside yellow with cowslips, and breathing perhaps the most delicate of all flowery fragrances. Yet again, as we pass into another stretch of woodland, another profusion and another fragrance await us, the winey perfume and the spectral blue sheen of the wild hyacinth. As one comes upon stretches of these hyacinths in the woods, they seem at first glance like pools of blue water or fallen pieces of the sky. Here, for once, the poets are left behind, and, of them all, Shakespeare and Milton alone have come near to suggesting the loveliness, at once so spiritual and so warmly and sweetly of the earth, that belongs to English wild flowers. I know not if Sheffield steel still keeps its position

13

among the eternal verities, but in an age when so many of one's cherished beliefs are threatened with the scrap-heap, I count it of no small importance to be able to retain one's faith in the English lark and English wild flowers.

But the English countryside is not all greenness and softness, blossomy lanes, moated granges, and idyllic villages. It by no means always suggests the gardener, the farmer, or the gamekeeper. It is rich, too, in wildness and solitude, in melancholy fens and lonely moorlands. To the American accustomed to the vast areas of his own enormous continent, it would come as a surprise to realize that a land far smaller than many of his States can in certain places give one so profound a sense of the wilderness. Yet I doubt if a man could feel lonelier anywhere in the world than on a Yorkshire moor or on Salisbury Plain.

After all, we are apt to forget that, even on the largest continent, we can see only a limited portion of the earth at once. When one is in the middle of Lake Erie we are as much out of sight of land, as impressed by the illusion of boundless water, as if we were in the middle of the Pacific Ocean. So, on Salisbury Plain, with nothing but rolling billows of close-cropped turf, springy and noiseless to the tread, as far as the eye can see, one feels as alone with the universe as in the middle of some Asian desert. In addition to the actual loneliness of the scene, and a silence broken only by the occasional tinkle of sheep-bells, as a flock moves like a fleecy cloud across the grass, is an imaginative loneliness induced by the overwhelming sense of boundless unrecorded time, the "dim-grey-grown ages," of which the mysterious boulders of Stonehenge are the voiceless witnesses. To experience this feeling to the full one should come upon an old Roman road in the twilight, grass-grown, choked with underbrush, but still running straight and clearly defined as when it shook to the tread of Roman legions. It is eery to follow one of these haunted roads, filled with the far-off thoughts and fancies it naturally evokes, and then suddenly to come out again into the world of to-day, as it joins the highway once more, and the lights of a wayside inn welcome us back to humanity, with perhaps a touring car standing at the door.

One need hardly say that the English wayside inn is as much a feature of the English countryside as the English hawthorn. Its praises have been the theme of essayists and poets for generations, and at its best there is a cosiness and cheer about it which warm the heart, as its quaintness and savour of past days keep alive the sense of romantic travel. There the spirit of ancient hospitality still survives, and, though the motor-car has replaced the stage-coach, that is, after all, but a detail, and the old, low-ceilinged rooms, the bay windows with their leaded panes, the tap-room with its shining vessels, the great kitchen, the solid English fare, the brass candlesticks at bedtime, and the lavendered sheets, still preserve the atmosphere of a novel by Fielding or an essay by Addison.

There still, as in Shakespeare's day, one can take one's ease at one's inn, as perhaps in the hostelries of no other land.   It is the frequency and excellence of these English inns that make it charmingly possible to see England, as it is best seen, on foot or on a bicycle.   It is not a country of isolated wonders, with long stretches of mere road between.   Every mile counts for something. But, if the luxury of walking it with stick and knapsack is denied us, and we must needs see it by motor-car, we cannot fail to make one observation, that of the surprising variety of natural scenery packed in so small a space.   Between Land's End and the Tweed the eye and the imagination have encountered every form of the picturesque.   In an area some three hundred and fifty miles long by three hundred broad are contained the ruggedness of Cornwall, the idyllic softness of Devon, the dreamy solitudes of the South Downs, with their billowy, chalky contours, the agricultural fertility of Kent and Middlesex, the romantic woodlands and hilly pastures of Surrey, the melancholy fens of Lincolnshire, the broad, bosky levels of the midlands, the sudden wildness of Wales, with her mountains and glens, Yorkshire, with its grim, heather-clad moors, Westmoreland, with its fells and Wordsworthian "Lakes"; every note in the gamut of natural

beauty has been struck, from honeysuckle pretti-
ness to savage grandeur.

Yet, although all these contrasts are included
in the English scene, it is not of solitude or grandeur that we think when we speak of the English
countryside.   They are the exceptions to the rule
of a gentler, more humanized natural beauty, in
which the village church and the ivy-clad ruin play
their part.   Perhaps some such formula as this
would represent the typical scene that springs to
the mind's eye with the phrase "the English
countryside": a village green, with some geese
stringing out across it.   A straggle of quaint
thatched cottages, roses climbing about the windows, and in front little, carefully kept gardens,
with hollyhocks standing in rows, stocks and sweet-
williams and such old-fashioned flowers.   At one
end of the village, rising out of a clump of yews,
the mouldering church-tower, with mossy grave-
stones on one side and a trim rectory on the other.
At the other end of the village a gabled inn, with a
great stable-yard, busy with horses and waggons.
Above the village, the slopes of gently rising pastures, intersected with footpaths and shadowed
with woodlands.   A little way out of the village,
an old mill with a lilied mill-pond, a great, dripping
water-wheel, and the murmur of the escaping
stream.   And winding on into the green, sun-
steeped distance, the blossom-hung English lanes.

XVII

LONDON—CHANGING AND UNCHANGING

I FIND it an unexpectedly strange experience to be in London again after ten years in New York. I had no idea it could be so strange. Of course, there are men to whom one great city is as another—commercial travellers, impresarios, globe-trotting millionaires. Being none of these, I am not as much at home in St. Petersburg·as in Buda-Pesth, in Berlin as in Paris, and, while once I might have envied such plastic cosmopolitanism, I am realizing, this last day or two in London, that, were such an accomplishment mine, it had been impossible for me to feel as deeply as I do my brief reincarnation into a city and a country with which I was once so intimate, and which now seems so romantically strange, while remaining so poignantly familiar. The man who is at home everywhere has nowhere any home. My home was once this London—this England—in which I am writing; but nothing so much as being in London again could make me realize that my home now is New York, and how long and how instinctively, without knowing it, I have been an

American. It is not indeed that I love New York and America more than I love London and England. In fact, London has never seemed so wonderful to me in the past as she has seemed during these days of my wistful momentary return to her strange great heart. But this very freshness of her marvel to one who once deemed that he knew her so well proves but the completeness of my spiritual acclimatization into another land. I seem to be seeing her face, hearing her voice, for the first time; while, all the while, my heart is full with unforgotten memories, and my eyes have scarce the hardihood to gaze with the decorum befitting the public streets on many a landmark of vanished hours. To find London almost as new and strange to me as New York once seemed when I first sighted her soaring morning towers, and yet to know her for an enchanted Ghost-Land; to be able to find my way through her streets—in spite of the new Kingsway and Aldwych!—with closed eyes, and yet to see her, it almost seems, for the first time: surely it is a curious, almost uncanny, experience.

Do I find London changed?—I am asked. I have been so busy in rediscovering what I had half-forgotten, in finding engaging novelties in things anciently familiar, that the question is one which I feel hardly competent to answer. For instance, I had all but forgotten that there was so noble a thing in the world as an old-fashioned English pork-pie. Yesterday I saw one in a window, with a thrill of recognition, that made a friend with whom I was walking think for a moment that I had seen a ghost. He knows nothing of the human heart who cannot realize how tremulous with ancient heart-break may seem an old-fashioned English pork-pie—after ten years in America.

And, again, how curiously novel and charming seemed the soft and courteous English voices—with or without aitches—all about one in the streets and in the shops—I had almost said the "stores." I am enamoured of the American accent, these many years, and—the calumny of superficial observation to the contrary—I will maintain, so far as my own experience goes, that there is as much courtesy broadcast in America as in any land; more, I am inclined to think than in France. Yet, for all that, that something or other in the English voice which I had heard long since and lost awhile smote me with a peculiar pleasure, and, though I like the comradely American "Cap" or "Professor," and am hoping soon to hear it again—yet the novelty of being addressed once more as "Sir" has had, I must own, a certain antiquarian charm.

Wandering in a quaint by-street near my hotel, and reading the names and signs on one or two of the neat old-world "places of business," I came on the word "sweep." I believe it was on a brass-plate. For a moment, I wondered what it meant; and then I realized, with a great gratitude, that

London had not changed so much, after all, since the days of Charles Lamb. As I emerged into a broader thoroughfare, my ears were smitten with the sound of minstrelsy. It is true that the tune was changed. It was unmistakably rag-time. Yet, there was the old piano-organ, and in a broad circle of spectators, suspended awhile from their various wayfaring, a young man in tennis flannels was performing a spirited Apache dance with a quite comely short-skirted young woman, who rightly enough felt that she had no need to be ashamed of her legs. Across the extemporized stage, every now and then, taxicabs tooted cautiously, longing in their hearts to stay; and once a motor coal-waggon, like a sort of amateur freight-train, thundered across; but not even these could break the spell that held that ring of enchanted loiterers, from which presently the pennies fell like rain—the eternal spell—still operating, I was glad to see, under the protection of the only human police in the world—of the strolling player in London town. Just before the players turned to seek fresh squares and alleys new, I noticed on the edge of the crowd what seemed, in the gathering twilight, to be a group of uplifted spears. Spears or halberds, were they? It was a little company of the ancient brotherhood of lamplighters, seduced, like the rest of us, from the strict pursuance of duty by the vagabond music.

To me this thought is full of reassurance, whatever be the murmurs of change: London has still hèr sweeps, her strolling minstrels, and her lamp-lighters.

Of course, I missed at once the old busses, yet there are far more horses left than I had dared to hope, and the hansom is far from extinct. In fact, there seems to be some promise of its renaissance, and even yet, in the words of the ancient bard, despite the competition of taxis—

> Like dragon-flies,
>   The hansoms hover
> With jewelled eyes,
>   To catch the lover.

Further,—the quietude of the Temple remains undisturbed, the lawns of Gray's Inn are green as of old, the Elizabethanism of Staple Inn is unchanged, about the cornices of the British Museum the pigeons still flutter and coo, and the old clocks chime sweetly as of old from their mysterious stations aloft somewhere in the morning and the evening sky.

Changes, of course, there are. It is easier to telephone in London today than it was ten years ago—almost as easy as in some little provincial town in Connecticut. Various minor human conveniences have been improved. The electric lighting is better. Some of the elevators—I mean the "lifts"—almost remind one of New York. The problem of "rapid transit" has been simplified. All which things, however, have nothing to do with national characteristics, but are now the common property of the civilized, or rather, I should say, the commercialized, world, and are probably to be found no less in full swing in Timbuctoo. No one—save, maybe, the citizens of some small imitative nation—confounds these things with change, or calls them "progress." The soul of a great old nation adopts all such contrivances as in the past it has adopted new weapons, or new modes of conveyance. Only a Hottentot or a Cook's Tourist can consider such superficial developments as evidences of "change."

There are, of course, some new theatres—though I have heard of no new great actor or actress. The old "favourites" still seem to dominate the play-bills, as they did ten years ago. There is Mr. Hammerstein's Opera House in the Kingsway. I looked upon it with pathos. Yet, surely, it is a monument not so much of changing London as of that London which sees no necessity of change.

In regard to the great new roadways, Kingsway, Aldwych, and the broadening of the Strand, I have been grateful for the temper which seems to have presided over their making—a temper combining the necessary readjustment of past and present, with a spirit of sensitive conservation for those buildings which more and more England will realize as having a lasting value for her spirit.

So far as I have observed, London has been guilty of no such vandalism as is responsible for the new Boulevard Raspail in Paris, and similar heartless destructiveness, in a city which belongs less to France than to the human soul. Such cities as London and Paris are among the eternal spiritual possessions of mankind. If only those temporarily in charge of them could be forced somehow to remember that, when their brief mayoral, or otherwise official, lives are past, there will be found those who will need to look upon what they have destroyed, and who will curse them in their graves.

Putting aside such merely superficial "changes" as new streets, new theatres, and new conveniences, there does seem to me one change of a far higher importance for which I have no direct evidence, and which I can only hint at, even to myself, as "something in the air." It is, of course, nothing new either to London or to England. It is rather the reawakening of an old temper to which England's history has so often and so momentously given expression. I seem to find it in a new alertness in the way men and women walk and talk in the streets, a braced-up expectancy and readiness for some approaching development in England's destiny, a new quickening of that old indomitable spirit that has faced not merely external dangers, but grappled with and resolved her own internal problems. London seems to me like a city that has heard a voice crying "Arise, thou that sleepest!" and is answering to the cry with girt loins and sloth-purged heart and blithe readiness for some new unknown summons of a future that can but develop the glory of her past.

England seems to be no more sleepily resting on her laurels, as she was some twenty years ago. Nor does she seem, on the other hand, to show the least anxiety that she could ever lose them. She is merely realizing that the time is at hand when she is to win others—that one more of those many re-births of England, so to speak, out of her own womb, approaches, and that once more she is about to prove herself eternally young.

New countries are apt to speak of old countries as though they are dying, merely because they have lived so long. Yet there is a longevity which is one of the surest evidences of youth. Such I seem to feel once more is England's—as from my window I watch the same old English May weather: the falling rain and the rich gloom, within which moves always, shouldering the darkest hour, an oceanic radiance, a deathless principle of celestial fire.

LONDON, May, 1913.

XVIII

THE HAUNTED RESTAURANT

WERE one to tell the proprietors of the very prosperous and flamboyant restaurant of which I am thinking that it is haunted—yea, that ghosts sit at its well appointed tables, and lost voices laugh and wail and sing low to themselves through its halls—they would probably take one for a lunatic—a servant of the moon.

Certainly, to all appearance, few places would seem less to suggest the word "haunted" than that restaurant, as one comes upon it, in one of the busiest of London thoroughfares, spreading as it does for blocks around, like a conflagration, the festive glare of its electrically emblazoned façade. Yet no ruined mansion, with the moon shining in through its shattered roof, the owl nesting in its banqueting hall, and the snake gliding through its bed chambers, was ever more peopled with phantoms than this radiant palace of prandial gaiety, apparently filled with the festive murmur of happy diners, the jocund strains of its vigorous orchestra, the subdued clash of knives and forks and delicate dishes, the rustle of women's gowns and the fairy music of women's voices. For me its portico, flaming like a vortex of dizzy engulfing light, upon which, as upon a swift current, gay men and women, alighting from motor and hansom, are swept inward to glittering tables of snow-white napery, fair with flowers—for me the mouth of the grave is not less dread, and the walls of a sepulchre are not so painted with dead faces or so inscribed with elegiac memories. I could spend a night in Père-la-Chaise, and still be less aware of the presence of the dead than I was a short time ago, when, greatly daring, I crossed with a shudder that once so familiar threshold.

It was twelve years since I had been in London, so I felt no little of a ghost myself, and I knew too well that it would be vain to look for the old faces. Yes, gone was the huge good-natured commissionaire, who so often in the past, on my arrival in company with some human flower, had flung open the apron of our cab with such reverential alacrity, and on our departure had so gently tucked in the petals of her skirts, smiling the while a respectfully knowing benediction on the prospective continuance of our evening's adventure. Another stood in his place, and watched my lonely arrival with careless indifference. Glancing through the window of the treasurer's office to the right of the hall, I could see that an unfamiliar figure sat at the desk, where in the past so many a cheque had been cashed for me with eager *bonhomie*. Now I reflected that considerable identification would be necessary for that once light-hearted transaction. It is true that I was welcomed with courtesy by a bowing majordomo, but alas, my welcome was that of a stranger; and when I mounted the ornate, marble-walled staircase leading to the gallery where I had always preferred to sit, I realized that my hat and cane must pass into alien keeping, and that no waiter's face would light up as he saw me threading my way to the sacred table, withdrawn in a nook of the balcony, where one could see and hear all, participate in the general human stir and atmosphere, and yet remain apart.

Ah! no; for the friendly Cockney that once greeted me with an enfolding paternal kindness was substituted broken English of a less companionable accent. A polite young Greek it was who stood waiting respectfully for my order, knowing nothing of all it meant for me—*me*—to be seated at that table again—whereas, had he been one of half a dozen of the waiters of yesteryear, he would have known almost as much as I of the "secret memoirs" of that historic table.

In ordering my meal I made no attempt at sentiment, for my mood went far deeper than sentiment. Indeed, though, every second of the time, I was living so vividly, so cruelly, in the past, I made one heartbroken acknowledgment of the present by beginning with the anachronism of a dry Martini cocktail, which, twelve years previous, was unknown and unattainable in that haunted gallery. That cocktail was a sort of desperate epitaph. It meant that I was alone—alone with my ghosts. Yet it had a certain resurrecting influence, and as I sat there proceeding dreamily with my meal, one face and another would flash before me, and memory after memory re-enact itself in the theatre of my fancy. So much in my actual surroundings brought back the past with an aching distinctness—particularly the entrance of two charming young people, making rainbows all about them, as, ushered by a smiling waiter, who was evidently no stranger to their felicity, they seated themselves at a neighbouring table with a happy sigh, and neglected the menu for a moment or two while they gazed, rapt and lost, into each other's eyes. How well I knew it all; how easily I could have taken the young man's place, and played the part for which this evening he was so fortunately cast! As I looked at them, I instinctively summoned to my side the radiant shade of Aurea, for indeed she had seemed made of gold—gold and water lilies. And, as of old, when I had called to her, she came swiftly with a luxurious rustle of fragrant skirts, like the sound of the west wind among the summer trees, or the swish and sway of the foam about the feet of Aphrodite. There she sat facing me once more, "a feasting presence made of light"— her hair like a golden wheat sheaf, her eyes like blue flowers amid the wheat, and her bosom, by no means parsimoniously concealed, literally suggesting that the loveliness of all the water lilies in the world was amassed there within her corset as in some precious casket. Ours was not one of the great tragic loves, but I know I shall think of Aurea's bosom on my death-bed. At her coming I had ordered champagne—we always drank champagne together, because, as we said, it matched so well with her hair—champagne of a no longer fashionable brand. The waiter seemed a little surprised to hear it asked for, but it had been the only *chic* brand in 19—.

"Look at those two yonder," I said presently, after we had drunk to each other, smiling long into each other's eyes over the brims of our glasses. "You and I were once as they. It is their first wonderful dinner together. Watch them—the poor darlings; it is enough to break one's heart."

"Do you remember ours?" asked Aurea quite needlessly.

"I wonder what else I was thinking of—dear idiot!" said I, with tender elegance, as in the old days.

As I said before, Aurea and I had not been tragic in our love. It was more a matter of life—than death; warm, pagan, light-hearted life. Ours was perhaps that most satisfactory of relationships between men and women, which contrives to enjoy the happiness, the fun, even the ecstasy, of loving, while evading its heartache. It was, I suppose, what one would call a healthy physical enchantment, with lots of tenderness and kindness in it, but no possibility of hurt to each other. There was nothing Aurea would not have done for me, or I for Aurea, except—marry each other; and, as a matter of fact, there were certain difficulties on both sides in the way of our doing that, difficulties, however, which I am sure neither of us regretted.

Yes, Aurea and I understood thoroughly what was going on in those young hearts, as we watched them, our eyes starry with remembrance. Who better than we should know that hush and wonder, that sense of enchanted intimacy, which belongs of all moments perhaps in the progress of a passion to that moment when two standing tiptoe on the brink of golden surrender, sit down to their first ambrosial meal together—delicious adventure!—with all the world to watch them, if it choose, and yet aloof in a magic lonéliness, as of youthful divinities wrapped in a roseate cloud! Hours of divine expectancy, at once promise and fulfilment. Happy were it for you, lovers, could you thus sit forever, nor pass beyond this moment, touched by some immortalizing wand as those lovers on the Grecian Urn:

Bold Lover, never, never canst thou kiss,
    Though winning near the goal—yet, do not grieve;
She cannot fade, though thou hast not thy bliss.
    Forever wilt thou love, and she be fair!

"See," said Aurea presently, "they are getting ready to go. The waiter has brought the bill, and is looking away, suddenly lost in profound meditation.   Let us see how he pays the bill.   I am sure she is anxious."

"Your old test!" said I.   "Do you remember?"

"Yes! And it's one that never fails," said Aurea with decision.   "When a woman goes out to dinner with a man for the first time, he little knows how much is going to depend on his way of paying the bill.   If, as with some men one meets, he studies it through a microscope and adds it up with anxious brow—meanwhile quite evidently forgetting your presence—how your heart sinks, sinks and hardens—but you are glad all the same, and next day you congratulate yourself on your narrow escape!"

"Was I like that?" said I.

"Did we escape?" asked Aurea. Then she added, touching my arm as with a touch of honeyed fire: " O I'm so glad! He did it delightfully—quite *en prince*. Just the right nonchalance—and perhaps, poor dear, he's as poor——"

"As we often were," I added.

And then through the corners of our eyes we saw the young lovers rise from the table, and the man enfold his treasure in her opera cloak, O so reverently, O so tenderly, as though he were wrapping up some holy flower. And O those deep eyes she gave him, half turning her head as he did so!

"That look," whispered Aurea, quoting Tennyson, "'had been a clinging kiss but for the street.'"

Then suddenly they were gone, caught up like Enoch, into heaven—some little heaven, maybe, like one that Aurea and I remember, high up under the ancient London roofs.

But, with their going, alas, Aurea had vanished too, and I was left alone with my Greek waiter, who was asking me what cheese I would prefer.

With the coming of coffee and cognac, I lit my cigar and settled down to deliberate reverie, as an opium smoker gives himself up to his dream. I savoured the bitter-sweetness of my memories; I took a strange pleasure in stimulating the ache of my heart with vividly recalled pictures of innumerable dead hours. I systematically passed from table to table all around that spacious peristyle. There was scarcely one at which I had not sat with some vanished companion in those years of ardent, irresponsible living which could never come again. Not always a woman had been the companion whose form I thus conjured out of the past, too often out of the grave; for the noble friendship of youth haunted those tables as well, with its generous starry-eyed enthusiasms and passionate loyalties. Poets of whom but their songs remain, themselves by tragic pathways descended into the hollow land, had read their verses to me there, still glittering with the dawn dew of their creation, as we sat together over the wine and talked of the only matters then—and perhaps even yet—worth talking of: love and literature. Of these but one can still be met in

London streets, but all now wear crowns of varying brightness—

> Where the oldest bard is as the young,
>   And the pipe is ever dropping honey,
> And the lyre's strings are ever strung.

Dear boon fellows of life as well as literature, how often have we risen from those tables, to pursue together the not too swiftly flying petticoat, through the terrestrial firmament of shining streets, aglow with the midnight sun of pleasure, a-dazzle with eyes brighter far than the city lamps—passionate pilgrims of the morning star! Ah! we go on such quests no more—"another race hath been and other palms are won."

No, not always women—but naturally women nearly always, for it was the time of rosebuds, and we were wisely gathering them while **we** might—

> Through the many to the one—
>   O so many!
> Kissing all and missing none,
>   Loving any.

Every man who has lived a life worthy the name of living has his own private dream of fair women, the memory of whom is as a provision laid up against the lean years that must come at last, however long they may be postponed by some special grace of the gods, which is, it is good to remember, granted to some—the years when one has reluctantly to accept that the lovely game is almost, if not quite at an end, and to watch the bloom and abundance of fragrant young creatures pass us, unregarding, by. And, indeed, it may happen that a man who has won what is for him the fairest of all fair faces, and has it still by his side, may enter sometimes, without disloyalty, that secret gallery of those other fair faces that were his before hers, in whom they are all summed up and surpassed, had dawned upon his life. We shall hardly be loyal to the present if we are coldly disloyal to the past. In the lover's calendar, while there is but one Madonna, there must still be minor saints, to whom it is meet, at certain times and seasons, to offer retrospective candles—saints that, after the manner of many saints, were once such charming sinners for our sakes, that utter forgetfulness of them were an impious boorishness surely unacceptable to the most jealous of Madonnas. Public worship of them is not, of course, desirable, but occasional private celebrations are surely more than permissible—such celebrations as that "night of memory and tears" which Landor consecrated to Rose Aylmer, or that song which Thackeray consecrated to certain loves of the long ago—

> Gillian's dead, God rest her bier,
>> How I loved her twenty years syne!
> Marian's married, but I sit here,
> Alone and merry at forty year,
>> Dipping my nose in the Gascon wine.

So I, seated in my haunted restaurant, brought the burnt offerings of several cigars, and poured out various libations to my own private Gillians and Marians, and in fancy sat and looked into Angelica's eyes at this table, and caressed Myrtle's opaled hand at that, and read Sylvia a poem I had just written for her at still another. "Whose names are five sweet symphonies," wrote Rossetti. Yes, symphonies, indeed, in the ears of memory are the names of the lightest loves that flittered butterfly-like across our path in the golden summer of our lives, each name calling up its human counterpart, with her own endearing personality distinguishing her from all other girls, her way of smiling, her way of talking, her way of being serious, all the little originalities on which she prided herself, her so solemnly held differentia of tastes and manners—all, in a word, that made you realize that you were dining with Corinna and not with Chloe. What a service of contrast each —all unwittingly, need one say—did the other, just in the same fashion as contrasting colours accentuate the special quality one of the other. To have dined last night with Amaryllis, with her Titian red hair and green eyes, her tropic languor and honey-drowsy ways, was to feel all the keener zest in the presence of Callithoe on the following evening, with her delicate soul-lit face, and eager responsiveness of look and gesture— *blonde cendré*, and *fausse maigre*—a being one of the hot noon, the other a creature of the starlight.

But I disclaim the sultanesque savour of thus writing of these dear bearers of symphonic names. To talk of them as flowers and fruit, as colour and perfume, as ivory and velvet, is to seem to forget the best of them, and the best part of loving them and being loved again; for that consisted in their comradeship, their enchanted comradeship, the sense of shared adventure, the snatching of a fearful joy together. For a little while we had escaped from the drab and songless world, and, cost what it might, we were determined to take possession, for a while at least, of that paradise which sprang into existence at the moment when "male and female created He them." Such divine foolishness, let discretion warn, or morality frown, or society play the censorious hypocrite, "were wisdom in the scorn of consequence."

"Ah, then," says every man to himself of such hours, as I said to myself in my haunted restaurant —"ah, then came in the sweet o' the year."

But lovely and pleasant as were the memories over which I thus sat musing, there was one face immeasurably beyond all others that I had come there hoping and yet fearing to meet again, hers of whom for years that seem past counting all the awe and wonder and loveliness of the world have seemed but the metaphor. Endless years ago she and I had sat at this table where I was now sitting and had risen from it with breaking hearts, never to see each other's face, hear each other's voice again. Voluntarily, for another's sake, we were breaking our hearts, renouncing each other, putting from us all the rapture and religion of our loving, dying then and there that another might live—vain sacrifice! Once and again, long silences apart, a word or two would wing its way across lands and seas and tell us both that we were still under the same sky and were still what nature had made us from the beginning—each other's. But long since that veil of darkness unpierced of my star has fallen between us, and no longer do I hear the rustle of her gown in the autumn woods, nor do the spring winds carry me the sweetness of her faithful thoughts any more. So I dreamed maybe that, after the manner of phantoms, we might meet again on the spot where we had both died— but alas, though the wraiths of lighter loving came gaily to my call, she of the starlit silence and the tragic eyes came not, though I sat long awaiting her—sat on till the tables began to be deserted, and the interregnum between dinner and after-theatre supper had arrived. No, I began to understand that she could no longer come to me: we must both wait till I could go to her.

And with this thought in my mind, I set about preparing to take my leave, but at that moment I was startled—almost superstitiously—startled by a touch on my shoulder. I was not to leave those once familiar halls without one recognition, after all. It was our old waiter of all those years ago, who, with an almost paternal gladness, was telling me how good it was to see me again, and, with consolatory mendacity, was assuring me that I had hardly changed a bit. God bless him—he will never know what good it did me to have his honest recognition. The whole world was not yet quite dead and buried, after all, nor was I quite such an unremembered ghost as I had seemed. Dear old Jim Lewis! So some of the old guard were still on deck, after all! And, I was thinking as I looked at him: "He, too, has looked upon her face. He it was who poured out our wine, that last time together." Then I had a whim. My waiter had been used to them in the old days.

"Jim," I said, "I want you to give this half-sovereign to the bandmaster and ask him to play Chopin's *Funeral March*. There are not many people in the place, so perhaps he won't mind. Tell him it's for an old friend of yours, and in memory of all the happy dinners he had here long ago."

So to the strains of that death music, which so strangely blends the piercing pathos of lost things with a springlike sense of resurrection, a spheral melody of immortal promise, I passed once more through the radiant portals of my necropolitan restaurant into the resounding thoroughfares of still living and still loving humanity.

XIX

THE NEW PYRAMUS AND THISBE

THERE never was a shallower or more short-sighted criticism than that which has held that science is the enemy of romance. Ruskin, with all the April showers of his rhetoric, discredited himself as an authoritative thinker when he screamed his old-maidish diatribes against that pioneer of modern romantic communication, the railroad. Just as surely his idol Turner proved himself a romantic painter, not by his rainbows, or his Italian sunsets, but by that picture of *Storm, Rain, and Speed*—an old-fashioned express fighting its way through wind, rain, and of course rainbows—in the English National Gallery.

With all his love of that light that never was on sea or land, Turner was yet able to see the romance of that new thing of iron and steam so affrighting to other men of his generation. A lover of light in all its swift prismatic changes, he was naturally a lover of speed. He realized that speed was one of the two most romantic things in the world. The other is immobility. At present the two extremes of romantic expression are the Sphinx and—the

automobile.   Unless you can realize that an automobile is more romantic than a stage-coach, you
know nothing about romance.   Soon the automobile will have its nose put out by the air-ship,
and we shall not need to be long-lived to see the day
when we shall hear old-timers lamenting the good
old easy-going past of the seventy-miles-an-hour
automobile—just as we have heard our grand-
fathers talk of postilions and the Bath "flyer."

Romance is made of two opposites: Change, and
That Which Changeth Not.   In spite of foolish
sentimentalism, who needs be told that love is one
of those forces of the universe that is the same
yesterday, today, and forever—the same today
as when Dido broke her heart, as when Leander
swam the Hellespont?   Gravitation is not more
inherent in the cosmic scheme, nor fire nor water
more unchangeable in their qualities.

But Love, contrary to the old notion that he is
unpractical, is a business-like god, and is ever on
the lookout for the latest modern appliances that
can in anyway serve his purposes.   True love is
far from being old-fashioned.   On the contrary,
true love is always up-to-date.   True love has its
telephone, its phonograph, its automobile, and
soon it will have its air-ship.   In the telephone
alone what a debt love owes to its supposed
enemy, modern science!   One wonders how lovers
in the old days managed to live at all without the
telephone.

We often hear how our modern appliances wear

upon our nerves. But think how the lack of modern appliances must have worn upon the nerves of our forefathers, and particularly our fore-mothers! Think what distance meant in the Middle Ages, when the news of a battle took days to travel, though carried by the swiftest horses. Horses! Think again of news being carried by—horses! And once more think, with a prayer of gratitude to two magicians named Edison and Bell, and with a due sense of your being the spoiled and petted offspring of the painful ages, that should your love be in Omaha this night and you in New York City, you can say good-night to her through the wall of your apartment, and hear her sigh back her good-night to you across two thousand miles of the American flag. Or should your love be on the sea, you can interrupt her flirtations all the way across with your persistent wireless conversation. Contrast your luxurious communicativeness with the case of the lovers of old-time. Say that you have just married a young woman, and you are happy together in your castle in the heart of the forest. Suddenly the courier of war is at your gates, and you must up and arm and away with your men to the distant danger. You must follow the Cross into the savage King-dom of the Crescent. The husband must become the crusader, and the Lord Christ alone knows when he shall look on the child's face of his wife again. Through goblin-haunted wildernesses he must go, through unmapped no-man's lands, and vacuum solitudes of the world's end, and peril and pestilence meet in every form, the face of his foe the friendliest thing in all his mysterious travel. Not a pay-station as yet in all the wide world, and fully five hundred years to the nearest telegraph office!

And think of the young wife meanwhile, alone with her maids and her tapestry in the dank isolation of her lonely, listening castle. Not a leaf falls in the wood, but she hears it. Not a footstep snaps the silence, but her eyes are at the sleepless slit of light which is her window in the armoured stone of her fortified bridal tower. The only news of her husband she can hope for in a full year or more will be the pleasing lies of some flattering minstrel, or broken soldier, or imaginative pilgrim. On such rumours she must feed her famishing heart—and all the time her husband's bones may be whitening unepitaphed outside the walls of Ascalon or Joppa.

There is an old Danish ballad which quaintly tells the tale of such old long-distance days, with that blending of humour and pathos that forever goes to the heart of man. A certain Danish lord had but yesterday taken unto himself a young wife, and on the morrow of his marriage there came to him the summons to war. Then, as now, there was no arguing with the trumpets of martial duty. The soldier's trumpet heeds not the soldier's tears. The war was far away and likely to be long. Months, even years, might go by before that Danish lord would look on the face of his bride again.

So much might happen meanwhile! A little boy, or a little girl, might be born to the castle, and the father, fighting far away, know nothing of the beautiful news. And there was no telephone in the castle, and it was five hundred years to the nearest telegraph office.

So the husband and wife agreed upon a facetious signal of their own. The castle stood upon a ridge of hills which could be seen fifty miles away, and on the ridge the bride promised to build a church. If the child that was to be born proved to be a boy, the church would be builded with a tower; if a girl, with a steeple. So the husband went his way, and three years passed, and at length he returned with his pennons and his men-at-arms to his own country. Scanning the horizon line, he hurried impatiently toward the heliographic ridge. And lo! when at last it came in sight against the rising sun, there was a new church builded stately there —with two towers.

So it was with the most important of all news in the Middle Ages; and yet today, as I said, you in New York City have only to knock good-night on your wall, to be heard by your true love in Omaha, and hear her knock back three times the length of France; Pyramus and Thisbe—with this difference: that the wall is no longer a barrier, but a sensitive messenger. It has become, indeed, in the words of Demetrius in *A Midsummer Night's Dream,* the wittiest of partitions, and the modern Pyramus may apostrophize it in grateful earnest:

"Thou wall, O wall, O sweet and lovely wall . . .
   Thanks, courteous wall.   Jove shield thee well for
      this!"

So at least I always feel toward the wall of my
apartment every time I call up her whom my soul
loveth that dwelleth far away in Massachusetts.
She being a Capulet and I a Montague, it would go
hard with us for communication, were it not for
this long-distance wall; and any one who knows
anything of love knows that the primal need of
lovers is communication.   Lovers have so deep a
distrust of each other's love that they need to be
assured of it from hour to hour.   To the philosopher it may well seem strange that this certitude
should thus be in need of progressive corroboration.
But so it is, and the pampered modern lover may
well wonder how his great-grandfather and great-
grandmother supported the days, or even kept
their love alive, on such famine rations as a letter
once a month.   A letter once a month!   They
must have had enormous faith in each other, those
lovers of old-time, or they must have suffered as we
can hardly bear to think of—we, who write to each
other twice a day, telegraph three times, telephone
six, and transmit a phonographic record of our
sighs to each other night and morn.   The telephone
has made a toy of distance and made of absence,
in many cases, a sufficient presence.   It is almost
worth while to be apart on occasion just for the
sake of bringing each other so magically near.   It
is the Arabian Nights come true.   As in them, you

15

have only to say a word, and the jinn of the electric fire is waiting for your commands. The word has changed. Once it was "Abracadabra." Now it is "Central." But the miracle is just the same.

One might almost venture upon the generalization that most tragedies have come about from lack of a telephone. Of course, there are exceptions, but as a rule tragedies happen through delays in communication.

If there had been a telephone in Mantua, Romeo would never have bought poison of the apothecary. Instead, he would have asked leave to use his long-distance telephone. Calling up Verona, he would first cautiously disguise his voice. If, as usual, the old nurse answered, all well; but if a bearded voice set all the wires a-trembling, he would, of course, hastily ring off, and abuse "Central" for giving him the wrong number. And "Central" would understand. Then Romeo would wait an hour or two till he was sure that Lord Capulet had gone to the Council, and ring up again. This time he would probably get the nurse and confide to her his number in Mantua. Next morning Juliet and her nurse had only to drop in at the nearest drug store, and confide to Romeo the whole plot which Balthazar so sadly bungled. All that was needed was a telephone, and Romeo would have understood that Juliet was only feigning death for the sake of life with him.

But, as in the case of our Danish knight, there

was not a pay-station as yet in all the wide world, and it was fully five hundred years to the nearest telegraph office. Another point in this tragedy is worth considering by the modern mind: that not only would the final catastrophe have been averted by the telephone, but that those beautiful speeches to and from Juliet's balcony, made at such desperate risk to both lovers, had the telephone only been in existence, could have been made in complete security from the seclusion of their distant apartments.

Seriously speaking, there are few love tragedies, few serious historic crises of any kind, that might not have been averted by the telephone. Strange indeed, when one considers a little, is that fallacy of sentimentalism which calls science the enemy of love.

Far from being its enemy, science is easily seen to be its most romantic servant; for all its strenuous and delicate learning it brings to the feet of love for a plaything. Not only will it carry the voice of love across space and time, but it will even bring it back to you from eternity. It will not only carry to your ears the voices of the living, but it will also keep safe for you the sweeter voices of the dead. In fact, it would almost seem as though science had made all its discoveries for the sake of love.

XX

TWO WONDERFUL OLD LADIES

IT is a pity that our language has no other word to indicate that one has lived seventy, eighty, or ninety years, than the word "old"; for the word "old" carries with it implications of "senility" and decrepitude, which many merely chronologically "old" people very properly resent. The word "young," similarly, needs the assistance of another word, for we all know individuals of thirty and forty, sometimes even only twenty, whom it is as absurd to call "young" as it is to call those others of seventy, eighty, or ninety, "old."

"Youth" is too large and rich a word to serve the limited purpose of numbering the years of undeveloped boys and girls. It should stand rather for the vital principle in men and women, ever expanding, and rebuilding, and refreshing the human organism, partly a physical, but perhaps in a greater degree a spiritual energy.

I am not writing this out of any compliment to two wonderful "old" ladies of whom I am particularly thinking. They would consider me a dunce

Two Wonderful Old Ladies

were they to suspect me of any such commonplace intent. No! I am not going to call them "eighty years young," or employ any of those banal euphemisms with which would-be "tactful" but really club-footed sentimentalists insult the intelligence of the so-called "old." Of course, I know that they are both eighty or thereabouts, and they know very well that I know. We make no secret of it. Why should we? Actually though the number of my years falls short of eighty, I feel so much older than either of them, that it never occurs to me to think of them as "old," and often as I contemplate their really glowing energetic youth, I grow melancholy for myself, and wonder what has become of my own.

They were schoolgirls together. Luceia married Irene's brother—for they allow me the privilege of calling them by their Christian names—and they have been friends all their lives. Sometimes I see them together, though oftener apart, for Luceia and her white-haired poet husband—no "older" than herself,—are neighbours of mine in the country, and Irene lives for the most part in New York—as much in love with its giant developments as though she did not also cherish memories of that quaint, almost vanished, New York of her girlhood days; for she is nothing if not progressive.

But I will tell about Luceia first, and the first thing it is natural to speak of—so every one else finds too—is her beauty. They say that she was beautiful when she was young (I am compelled sometimes, under protest, to use the words "young" and "old" thus chronologically) and, of course, she must have been.   I have, however, seen some of her early portraits, before her hair was its present beautiful colour, and I must confess that the Luceia of an earlier day does not compare with the Luceia of today.   I don't think I should have fallen in love with her then, whereas now it is impossible to take one's eyes off her.   She seems to have grown more flower-like with the years, and while her lovely indestructible profile has gathered distinction, and a lifelong habit of think- ing beautiful thoughts, and contemplating beauti- ful things, has drawn honeyed lines as in silver point about her eyes and mouth, the wild-roses of her cheeks still go on blooming—like wild-roses in moonlight.   And over all glow her great clear witty eyes, the eyes of a *grand dame* who has still remained a girl.   Her humour, no doubt, has much to do with her youth, and I have seen strangers no little surprised, even disconcerted, at finding so keen a humour in one so beautiful; for beauty and humour are seldom found together in so irresistible a combination.   Is it to be wondered at that often on summer days when I feel the need of a companion, I go in search of Luccia, and take tea with her on the veranda?   Sometimes I will find her in the garden seated in front of her easel, making one of her delicate water-colour sketches— for she was once a student in Paris and has roman- tic Latin-quarter memories.   Or I will find her with her magnifying glass, trying to classify some weed she has come upon in the garden, for she is a learned botanist; and sometimes we will turn over the pages of books in which she hoards the pressed flowers gathered by her and her husband in Italy and Switzerland up till but a year or two ago, memorials of a life together that has been that flawless romance which love sometimes grants to his faithful servants.

At other times we will talk politics, and I wish you could hear the advanced views of this "old" lady of eighty. Indeed, generally speaking, I find that nowadays the only real progressives are the "old" people. It seems to be the fashion with the "young" to be reactionary. Luceia, however, has been a radical and a rebel since her girlhood, and years before the word "feminist" was invented, was fighting the battle of the freedom of woman. And what a splendid Democrat she is, and how thoroughly she understands and fearlessly faces the problems and developments of the moment! She is of the stuff the old Chartist women and the women of the French Revolution were made of, and in her heart the old faith in Liberty and the people burns as brightly as though she were some young Russian student ready to give her life for the cause. When the revolution comes to America, stern masculine authority will be needed to keep her—her friend Irene too—from the barricades.

"Stern masculine authority"! As I write that

phrase, how plainly I can hear her mocking laughter; for she is never more delightful than when pouring out her raillery on the magisterial pretensions of man. To hear her talk! The idea of a mere man daring to assume any authority or direction over a woman! Yet we who know her smile and whisper to ourselves that, for all her witty tirades, she is perhaps of all women the most feminine, and really the most "obedient" of wives —a rebel in all else save to the mild tyranny of the poet she has loved, honoured, and yes! obeyed, all these wonderful years.

Perhaps in nothing is the reality of her youthfulness so expressive as in her adorable gaiety. Like a clear fresh spring, it is ever brimming up from the heart into her mischief-loving eyes. By her side merely technically young people seem heavy and serious. And nothing amuses her more than gravely to mystify, or even bewilderingly shock, some proper acquaintance, or some respectable strangers, with her carefully designed mock improprieties of speech or action. To look at the loveliest of grandmothers, it is naturally somewhat perplexing to the uninitiated visitor to hear her talk, with her rarely distinguished manner, of frivolous matters with which they assume she has long since done.

A short while ago, when I was taking tea with her, she had for visitor a staid old-maidish lady, little more than half her age, whom she had known as a girl, but had not seen for some years. In the course of conversation, she turned to her guest, with her grand air:

"Have you done much dancing this season?" she asked.

"O indeed no," answered the other unsuspiciously, "my dancing days are over."

"At your age!" commented Luceia with surprise. "Nonsense! You must let me teach you to dance the tango. I have enjoyed it immensely this winter."

"Really?" gasped the other in astonishment, with that intonation in the voice naturally so gratifying to the "old" suggesting that the person talking with them really regards them as dead and buried.

"Of course, why not?" asks Luceia with perfect seriousness. "I dance it with my grandsons. My husband doesn't care to dance it. He prefers the polka."

Not knowing what to think, the poor old maid—actually "old" compared with Luceia—looked from her to the beautiful venerable figure of her polka-dancing husband seemingly meditating over his pipe, a little withdrawn from them on the veranda, but inwardly shaken with mirth at the darling nonsense of her who is still the same madcap girl he first fell in love with so many years ago.

When the guest had departed, with a puzzled, questioning look still lingering on her face, Luceia turned to me, her eyes bright pools of merriment:

"It was quite true, wasn't it? Come, let us try it."

And, nimble as a girl, she was on her feet, and we executed quite a passable tango up and down the veranda, to the accompaniment of her husband's—"Luceia! Luceia! what a wild thing you are!"

A certain reputation for "wildness," a savour of innocent Bohemianism, has clung to Luceia, and Irene too, all through their lives, as a legacy from that far-off legendary time when, scarcely out of their girlhood, they were fellow art-students together in Paris. Belonging both to aristocratic, rather straitlaced New England families, I have often wondered how they contrived to accomplish that adventure in a day when such independent action on the part of two pretty young ladies was an adventure indeed. But it was the time when the first vigorous spring of feminine revolt was in the air. Rosa Bonheur, George Eliot, Elizabeth Cady Stanton, and other leaders were setting the pace for the advanced women, and George Sand was still a popular romancer. As a reminiscence of George Sand, Luceia to this day pretends that she prefers to smoke cigars to cigarettes, though, as a matter of fact, she has never smoked either, and has, indeed, an ultra-feminine detestation of tobacco—even in the form of her husband's pipe. She only says it, of course, for the fun of seeming "naughty"; which recalls to my mind her shocking behaviour one day when I went with her to call on some very prim cousins in New York.   It was a household of an excessively brown-stone respectability, just the atmosphere to rouse the wickedness in Luceia. As we sat together in an upright conversation that sounded like the rustling of dried leaves in a cemetery, why! Luceia, for all her eighty years, seemed like a young wild-rose bush filling the tomb-like room with living light and fragrance.   I could see the wickedness in her surging for an out-burst.   She was well aware that those respectable connections of hers had always looked upon her as a sort of "artistic" black sheep in the family. Presently her opportunity came.   As our visit dragged mournfully towards its end, the butler entered, in pursuance of the early Victorian ritual on such occasions, bearing a tray on which was a decanter of sherry, some tiny wine-glasses, and some dry biscuits of a truly early Victorian dryness.   This ghostly hospitality was duly dispensed, and Luceia, who seldom drinks anything but tea, instead of sipping her sherry with a lady-like aloofness, drained her glass with a sudden devil-may-care abandon, and, to the evident amazement even of the furniture, held it out to be refilled.   Such pagan behaviour had never disgraced that scandalized drawing-room before. And when to her action she added words, the room absolutely refused to believe its ears.   "I feel," she said, with a deep-down mirth in her eyes which only I could suspect rather than see, "I feel

today as if I should like to go on a real spree.   Do
you ever feel that way?"

A palpable shudder passed through the room.

"Cousin Luccia!" cried out the three outraged
mummies; the brother with actual sternness, and
the sisters in plain fear.   Had their eccentric
cousin really gone out of her mind at last?

"Never feel that way?" she added, delighting
in the havoc she was making.   "You should.   It's
a wonderful feeling."

Then she drained her second glass, and to
the evident relief of all three, rose to go.   How
we laughed together, as we sped away in our taxi-
cab.   "It's as well to live up to one's reputation
with such people," she said, that dear, fantastic
Luceia.

À propos that early Parisian adventure, Rosa
Bonheur had been one of Luccia's and Irene's great
exemplars, and one might say, in one particular
connection,—heroes.   I refer to the great painter's
adoption of masculine costume.   Why two unusually pretty young women should burn to discard
the traditional flower-furniture of their sex, in
exchange for the uncouth envelopes of man, is hard
to understand.   But it was the day of Mrs.
Bloomer, as well as Rosa Bonheur; and earnest
young "intellectuals" among women had a notion,
I fancy, that to shake off their silks and laces was,
symbolically, at all events, to shake off the general
disabilities of their sex, and was somehow an
assertion of a mental equality with man.   At all

events, it was a form of defiance against their sex's immemorial tyrant, which seems to have appealed to the imaginations of some young women of the period.   Another woman's weakness to be sternly discarded was that scriptural "glory" of her hair. That must be ruthlessly lopped.   So it is easy to imagine the horror of such relatives as I have hinted at when our two beautiful adventuresses returned from Paris, and appeared before their families in great Spanish cloaks, picturesque, coquettish enough you may be sure, veiling with some show of discretion those hideous compromises with trousers invented and worn by the strong-minded Mrs. Bloomer, and wearing their hair after the manner of Florentine boys.   To face one's family, and to walk New York streets so garbed, must have needed real courage in those days; yet the two friends did both, and even for a while accepted persecution for vagaries which for them had the dead-seriousness of youth.

Passionate young propagandists as they were, they even preferred to abandon their homes for a while—rather than their bloomers—and, taking a studio together in New York, started out to earn their own living by the teaching of art.   Those were the days of the really brave women.

But to return to the less abstract topic of the bloomers, I often tease Luceia and Irene about them, seeking for further information as to why they ever came to retrograde from a position so heroically taken, one of such serious import to human progress, and to condescend once more to don the livery of feminine servitude, and appear, as they do today, in delicate draperies which the eye searches in vain for any hint of sanguinary revolution.   Luccia always looks shamefaced at the question.   She still feels guilty, I can see, of a traitorous backsliding and occasionally threatens to make up for it by a return to masculine costume—looking the most exquisite piece of Dresden, china as she says it.   I have seen that masculine tyrant of hers smiling knowingly to himself on such occasions, and it has not been difficult to guess why and when those historic bloomers disappeared into the limbo of lost causes.   There is little doubt that when Love came in by the door, the bloomers went out, so to speak, by the window.

Irene seems to have held out longer, and, doubtless, scornful of her more frivolous comrade's defection, steadfastly kept the faith awhile unsupported, walking the world in bloomered loneliness—till a like event overtook her.   Such is the end of every maid's revolt!   But Irene, to this day, retains more of her student seriousness than her more worldly-minded friend.   Her face is of the round cherubic type, and her large heavy-lidded eyes have a touch of demureness veiling humour no less deep than Luccia's, but more reflective, chuckling quietly to itself, though on occasion I know no one better to laugh with, even giggle with, than Irene.   But, whereas Luccia will talk gaily of revolution and even anarchy for the fun of it, and in the next breath talk hats with real seriousness, Irene still remains the purposeful revolutionary student she was as a girl; while Luccia contents herself with flashing generalizations, Irene seriously studies the latest developments of thought and society, reads all the new books, sees all the new plays and pictures, and has all the new movements of whatever kind—art, philosophy, and sociology—at her finger ends; and I may add that her favourite writer is Anatole France. Whenever I need light on the latest artistic or philosophic nonsense calling itself a movement (cubism, futurism, Bergsonism, syndicalism, or the like) I go to her, certain that she will know all about it. Nothing is too "modern" for this wonderful "old" lady of seventy-nine; and, whenever I am in town, we always go together to the most "advanced" play in the newest of new theatres.

À propos our theatre-going together, I must not forget a story about her which goes back to that bloomer period. A little while ago, calling to take tea with her, I found her seated with a fine soldierly white-haired "old" man, and they were in such merry talk that I felt that perhaps I was interrupting old memories. But they generously took me into the circle of their reminiscence. They had been laughing as I came in— "Shall I tell him, General?" she said, "what we were laughing about?" Then she did. She and the General had been girl and boy together, and as they came to eighteen and nineteen had been semi-serious sweethearts. The embryo General—no doubt because of her pretty face—had taken all her student vagaries with lover-like seriousness, and had, on one ocasion, assisted in a notable enterprise. The bloomers had not been definitely donned at that time, but they were on the way, glimmering ahead as a discussed ideal. Whether it was as a preliminary experiment, or only in consequence of a "dare," I am not quite sure. I think it was a little of both, and that the General had dared Irene to go with him to the opera (in the gallery) dressed in boy's clothes. She accepted the challenge, borrowing a suit of clothes from her brother for the purpose. Her figure, according to the General's account, had looked anything but masculine, and her hair, tucked up under her boy's hat as best she could, was a peculiar peril. How her heart had almost stopped beating as a policeman had turned upon the youthful pair a suspicious scrutiny, how they had taken to their heels at his glance, how she had crimsoned at the box-office, and hid her face behind a fat man as they had scurried past the ticket-attendant, and how during the whole performance a keen-faced woman had glanced at her with a knowing persistency that seemed to threaten her with imminent exposure and arrest, and how wonderful the whole thing had been—just to be in boy's clothes and go in them to the theatre with one's sweetheart. O youth! youth! youth!

As I looked at the General with his white hair, and Irene with her quaint little old lady's cap over her girlish face, and visualized for myself those two figures before me as they had appeared on the night of that escapade, I realized that the real romance of life is made by memory, and that for these two old friends to be able thus to recall together across all those years that laughing freak of their young blood was still more romantic than the original escapade. But as I went on looking at Irene, with the bloom of her immortal youth upon her, I grew jealous of the General's share in that historic night. Well, never mind, it is I who take her to the theatre nowadays—and, after all, I think I prefer her to go dressed just as she is.

16

XXI

A CHRISTMAS MEDITATION

CHRISTMAS already! However welcome its coming, Christmas always seems to take us by surprise. Is the year really so soon at the end of its journey? Why, it seems only yesterday that it needed a special effort of remembrance to date our letters with the new *"anno domini."* And have you noticed that one always does that reluctantly, with something almost of misgiving? The figures of the old year have a warm human look, but those of the new wear a chill, unfamiliar, almost menacing expression. Nineteen hundred and——we know. It is nearly "all in." It has done its best—and its worst. Between Christmas Day and New-Year it has hardly time to change its character. Good or bad, as it may have been, we feel at home with it, and we are fain to keep the old almanac a little longer on the wall. But the last leaves are falling, the days are shortening. There is a smell of coming snow in the air, and for weeks past it has already been Christmas in the shops.

Yes, however it strikes us, we are a year older.

On the first of January last we had twelve brand-new months of a brand-new year to spend, and now the last of them is all but spent. We had a new spring to look out for, like the coming of one's sweetheart, a new summer bounteous in prospect with inexhaustible wealth of royal sunshine, a new autumn, with ruddy orchards and the glory of the tapestried woods; and now of the four new seasons that were to be ours but one remains:

And here is but December left and I,
    To wonder if the hawthorn bloomed in May,
And if the wild rose with so fine a flush
    Mantled the cheek of June, and if the way
The stream went singing foamed with meadow sweet,
    And if the throstle sang in yonder bush,
And if the lark dizzied with song the sky.
    I watched and listened—yet so sweet, so fleet,
The mad young year went by!

Strange, that feeling at the end of the year that somehow we have missed it, have failed to experience it all to the full, taken it too carelessly, not dwelt sufficiently on its rich, expressive hours. Each year we feel the same, and however intent we may have been, however we have watched and listened, sensitively eager to hold and exhaust each passing moment, when the year-end has come, we seem somehow to have been cheated after all. Who, at the beginning of each year, has not promised himself a stricter attentiveness to his experience? This year he will "load every rift with ore."

This year, I said, when first along the lane
   With tiny nipples of the tender green
The winter-blackened hedge grew bright again,
   This year I watch and listen; I have seen
So many springs steal profitless away,
   This year I garner every sound and sweet.
And you, young year, make not such haste to bring
   Hawthorn and rose; nor jumble, indiscreet,
Treasure on treasure of the precious spring;
   But bring all softly forth upon the air,
Unhasting to be fair. . . .

Yet, for all our watchfulness, the year seems to have escaped us. We know that the birds sang, that the flowers bloomed, that the grass was green, but it seems to us that we did not take our joy of them with sufficient keenness; our sweetheart came, but we did not look deep enough into her eyes. If only we live to see the wild rose again! But meanwhile here is the snow.

Unless we are still numbered among those happy people for whom Christmas-trees are laden and lit, this annual prematurity of Christmas cannot but make us a little meditative amid our mirth, and if, while Santa Claus is dispensing his glittering treasures, our thoughts grow a little wistful, they will not necessarily be mournful thoughts, or on that account less seasonable in character; for Christmas is essentially a retrospective feast, and we may, with fitness, with indeed a proper piety of unforgetfulness, bring even our sad memories, as it were to cheer themselves, within the glow of its festivity. Ghosts have always been invited to Christmas parties, and whether they are seen or not, they always come; nor is any form of story so popular by the Christmas fire as the ghost-story—which, when one thinks of it, is rather odd, considering the mirthful character of the time. Yet, after all, what are our memories but ghost-stories? Ah! the beautiful ghosts that come to the Christmas fire!

Christmas too is pre-eminently the Feast of the Absent, the Festival of the Far-Away, for the most prosperous ingathering of beloved faces about the Christmas fire can but include a small number of those we would fain have there; and have you ever realized that the absent are ghosts? That is, they live with us sheerly as spiritual presences, dependent upon our faithful remembrance for their embodiment. We may not, with our physical eyes, see them once a year; we may not even have so seen them for twenty years; it may be decreed that we shall never see them again; we seldom, perhaps never, write to each other; all we know of each other is that we are alive and love each other across space and time. Alive—but how? Scarce otherwise, surely, than the unforgotten dead are alive—alive in unforgetting love.

It is rather strange, if you will give it a thought, how much of our real life is thus literally a ghost-

story.   Probably it happens with the majority of
us that those who mean most to us, by the necessities of existence, must be far away, met but now
and then in brief flashes of meeting that often seem
to say so much less than absence; our intercourse
is an intercourse of the imagination—yet how real!
They belong to the unseen in our lives, and have
all its power over us.   The intercourse of a mother
and a son—is it not often like that in a world
which sends its men on the four winds, to build and
fight, while the mother must stay in the old nest?
Seldom at Christmas can a mother gather all her
children beneath the wing of her smile.   Her big
boys are seven seas away, and even her girls have
Christmas-trees of their own.   But motherhood
is in its very nature a ghostly, a spiritual, thing,
and the big boys and the old mother are not really
divided.   They meet unseen by the Christmas
fire, as they meet all the year round in that mysterious ether of the soul, where space and time are
not.

Yes, it is strange to think how small a proportion of our lives we spend with those we love;
even when we say that we spend all our time with
them.   Husband and wife even—how much of the
nearness of the closest of human relations is, and
must be, what Rossetti has called "parted presence!"   The man must go forth to his labour until
the evening.   How few of the twenty-four hours
can these two beings who have given their whole
lives to each other really give!   Husband and wife

even must be content to be ghosts to each other for
the greater part of each day. As Rossetti says in
his poem, eyes, hands, voice, lips, can meet so
strangely seldom in the happiest marriage; only
in the invisible home of the heart can the most
fortunate husband and wife be always together:

> Your heart is never away,
>   But ever with mine, forever,
>   Forever without endeavour,
> Tomorrow, love, as today;
> Two blent hearts never astray,
>   Two souls no power may sever,
>   Together, O my love, forever!

When I said that the absent were ghosts, I don't
think you quite liked the saying. It gave you a
little shiver. It seemed rather grimly fantastic.
But do you not begin to see what I meant? Begin
to see the comfort in the thought? begin to see the
inner connection between Christmas and the
ghost-story? Yes, the real lesson of Christmas is
the ever presence of the absent through love;
the ghostly, that is to say the spiritual, nature of
all human intercourse. Our realities can exist
only in and through our imaginations, and the most
important part of our lives is lived in a dream with
dream-faces, the faces of the absent and the dead—
who, in the consolation of this thought, are alike
brought near.

I have a friend who is dead—but I say to myself
that he is in New Zealand; for, if he were really in

New Zealand, we should hardly seem less distant, or be in more frequent communication. We should say that we were both busy men, that the mails were infrequent, but that between us there was no need of words, that we both "understood." That is what I say now. It is just as appropriate. Perhaps he says it too. And—we shall meet by the Christmas fire.

I have a friend who is alive. He is alive in England. We have not met for twelve years. He never writes, and I never write. Perhaps we shall never meet, never even write to each other, again. It is our way, the way of many a friendship, none the less real for its silence—friendship by faith, one might say, rather than by correspondence. My dead friend is not more dumb, not more invisible. When these two friends meet me by the Christmas fire, will they not both alike be ghosts—both, in a sense, dead, but both, in a truer sense, alive?

It is so that, without our thinking of it, our simple human feelings one for another at Christmas-time corroborate the mystical message which it is the church's meaning to convey by this festival of "peace and good-will to men"—the power of the Invisible Love; from the mystical love of God for His world, to the no less mystical love of mother and child, of lover and lover, of friend and friend.

And, when you think of it, is not this festival founded upon what, without irreverence, we may call the Divine Ghost-Story of Christmas? Was there ever another ghost-story so strange, so full of marvels, a story with so thrilling a message from the unseen? Taken just as a story, is there anything in the *Arabian Nights* so marvellous as this ghost-story of Christmas? The world was all marble and blood and bronze, against a pitiless sky of pitiless gods. The world was Rome. No rule ever stood builded so impregnably from earth to stars—a merciless wall of power. Strength never planted upon the earth so stern a foot. Never was tyranny so invincibly bastioned to the cowed and conquered eye.

And against all this marble and blood and bronze, what frail fantastic attack is this? What quaint expedition from fairy-land that comes so insignificantly against these battlements on which the Roman helmets catch the setting sun?

A Star in the Sky. Some Shepherds from Judea. Three Wise Men from the East. Some Frankincense and Myrrh. A Mother and Child.

Yes, a fairy-tale procession—but these are to conquer Rome, and that child at his mother's breast has but to speak three words, for all that marble and bronze to melt away: "Love One Another."

It may well have seemed an almost ludicrous weapon—three gentle words. So one might attack a fortress with a flower. But Rome fell before them, for all that, and cruel as the world still is, so cruel a world can never be again. The history of Christianity from Christ to Tolstoi is the history of a ghost-story; and as Rome fell before the men

it martyred, so Russia has been compelled at last
to open its prison doors by the passive imperative
of the three gentle words. Stone and iron are
terribly strong to the eye and even to the arm of
man, but they are as vapour before the breath of the
soul. Many enthroned and magisterial authorities
seem so much more important and powerful than
the simple human heart, but let the trial of strength
come, and we see the might of the delicate invisible
energy that wells up out of the infinite mystery to
support the dreams of man.

Christmas is the friendly human announcement
of this ghostly truth; its holly and boar's-head are
but a rough-and-tumble emblazonment of that
mystic gospel of—The Three Words; the Gospel
of the Unseen Love.

And how well has the church chosen this particular season of the year for this most subtly
spiritual of all its festivals, so subtle because its
ghostly message is so ruddily disguised in human
mirth, and thus the more unconsciously operative
in human hearts!

Winter, itself so ghostly a thing, so spiritual
in its beauty, was indeed the season to catch our
ears with this ghost-story of the Invisible and
Invincible Love. The other seasons are full of
sensuous charm and seductiveness. With endless
variety of form and colour and fragrance, they
weave "a flowery band to bind us to the earth."
They are running over with the pride of sap, the
luxury of green leaves, and the intoxicating fulness

of life. The summer earth is like some voluptuous enchantress, all ardour and perfume, and soft dazzle of moted sunshine. But the beauty of winter seems a spiritual, almost a supernatural, thing, austere and forbidding at first, but on a nearer approach found to be rich in exquisite exhilaration, in rare and lofty discoveries and satisfactions of the soul. Winter naturally has found less favour with the poets than the other seasons. Praise of it has usually a strained air, as though the poet were making the best of a barren theme, like a portrait-painter reluctantly flattering some unattractive sitter. But one poet has seen and seized the mysterious beauty of winter with unforced sympathy—Coventry Patmore, whose "Odes," in particular, containing as they do some of the most rarely spiritual meditation in English poetry, are all too little known. In one of these he has these beautiful lines, which I quote, I hope correctly, from memory:

I, singularly moved
To love the lovely that are not beloved,
Of all the seasons, most love winter, and to trace
The sense of the Trophonian pallor of her face.
It is not death, but plenitude of peace;
And this dim cloud which doth the earth enfold
Hath less the characters of dark and cold
Than light and warmth asleep,
And intermittent breathing still doth keep
With the infant harvest heaving soft below
Its eider coverlet of snow.

The beauty of winter is like the beauty of certain austere classics of literature and art, and as with them, also, it demands a certain almost moral strenuousness of application before it reveals itself. The loftiest masterpieces have something aloof and cheerless about them at our first approach, something of the cold breath of those starry spaces into which they soar, and to which they uplift our spirits.   When we first open Dante or Milton, we miss the flowers and the birds and the human glow of the more sensuous and earth-dwelling poets.   But after awhile, after our first rather bleak introduction to them, we grow aware that these apparently undecorated and unmusical masterpieces are radiant and resounding with a beauty and a music which "eye hath not seen nor ear heard."   For flowers we are given stars, for the song of birds the music of the spheres, and for that human glow a spiritual ecstasy.

Similarly with winter.   It has indeed a strange beauty peculiar to itself, but it is a beauty we must be at some pains to enjoy.   The beauty of the other seasons comes to us, offers itself to us, without effort.   To study the beauty of summer, it is enough to lie under green boughs with half-closed eyes, and listen to the running stream and the murmur of a million wings.   But winter's is no such idle lesson.   In summer we can hardly stay indoors, but in winter we can hardly be persuaded to go out.   We must gird ourselves to overcome that first disinclination, else we shall know nothing of winter but its churlish wind and its ice-in-the-pail. But, the effort made, and once out of doors on a sunlit winter's morning, how soon are we finding out the mistake we were making, coddling ourselves in the steam-heat! Indoors, indeed, the prospect had its Christmas-card picturesqueness; snow-clad roofs, snow-laden boughs, silhouetted tracery of leafless trees; but we said that it was a soulless spectacular display, the beauty of death, and the abhorred coldness thereof. We have hardly walked a hundred yards, however, before impressions very different are crowding upon us, among which the impression of cold is forgotten, or only retained as pleasantly heightening the rest.

Far from the world's being dead, as it had seemed indoors, we are presently, in some strange indefinable way, made intensely conscious of a curious overwhelming sense of life in the air, as though the crystal atmosphere was, so to say, ecstatically charged with the invisible energy of spiritual forces. In the enchanted stillness of the snow, we seem to hear the very breathing of the spirit of life. The cessation of all the myriad little sounds that rise so merrily and so musically from the summer surface of the earth seems to allow us to hear the solemn beat of the very heart of earth itself. We seem very near to the sacred mystery of being, nearer than at any other season of the year, for in other seasons we are distracted by its pleasurable phenomena, but in winter we seem close to the very mystery itself; for the world seems to have put on robes of pure spirit and ascended into a diviner ether.

The very phenomena of winter have a spiritual air which those of summer lack, a phantom-like strangeness. How mysterious this ice, how ghostly this snow, and all the beautiful fantastic shapes taken by both; the dream-like foliage, and feathers and furs of the snow, the Gothic diablerie of icicled eaves, all the fairy fancies of the frost, the fretted crystal shapes that hang the brook-side with rarer than Venetian glass, the strange flowers that stealthily overlay the windows, even while we watch in vain for the unseen hand! No flowers of summer seem so strange as these, make us feel so weirdly conscious of the mystery of life. As the ghostly artist covers the pane, is it not as though a spirit passed?

As we walk on through the shining morning, we ourselves seem to grow rarefied as the air. Our senses seem to grow finer, purged to a keener sensitiveness. Our eyes and ears seem to become spiritual rather than physical organs, and an exquisite elation, as though we were walking on shining air, or winging through celestial space, fills all our being. The material earth and our material selves seem to grow joyously transparent, and while we are conscious of our earthly shoe-leather ringing out on the iron-bound highway, we seem, nevertheless, to be spirits moving without effort, in a world of spirit. Seldom, if ever, in summer are we thus made conscious of, so to say, our own ghosts, thus lifted up out of our material selves with a happy sense of disembodiment.

There would, indeed, seem to be some relation between temperature and the soul, and something literally purifying about cold. Certain it is that we return from our winter's walk with something sacred in our hearts and something shining in our faces, which we seldom, if ever, bring back with us in summer. Without understanding the process, we seem to have been brought nearer to the invisible mystery, and a solemn peace of happy insight seems for a little while at least to possess our souls. Our white walk in the snow-bright air has in some way quickened the half-torpid immortal within us, revived awhile our sluggish sense of our spiritual significance and destiny, made us once more, if only for a little, attractively mysterious to ourselves. Yes! there is what one might call a certain monastic discipline about winter which impels the least spiritual minded to meditation on his mortal lot and its immortal meanings; and thus, as I said, the Church has done wisely to choose winter for its most Christian festival. The heart of man, thus prepared by the very elements, is the more open to the message of the miraculous love, and the more ready to translate it into terms of human goodness. And thus, I hope, the ghostly significance of mince-pie is made clear.

But enough of ghostly, grown-up thoughts.
Let us end with a song for the children:

> O the big red sun,
>   And the wide white world,
> And the nursery window
>   Mother-of-pearled;
>
> And the houses all
>   In hoods of snow,
> And the mince-pies,
>   And the mistletoe;
>
> And Christmas pudding,
>   And berries red,
> And stockings hung
>   At the foot of the bed;
>
> And carol-singers,
>   And nothing but play—
> O baby, this is
>   Christmas Day!

XXII

ON RE-READING WALTER PATER

IT is with no small satisfaction, and with a sense of reassurance of which one may, in moods of misgiving, have felt the need during two decades of the Literature of Noise, that one sees a writer so pre-eminently a master of the Literature of Meditation coming, for all the captains and the shouting, so surely into his own. The acceptance of Walter Pater is not merely widening all the time, but it is more and more becoming an acceptance such as he himself would have most valued, an acceptance in accordance with the full significance of his work rather than a one-sided appreciation of some of its Corinthian characteristics. The Doric qualities of his work are becoming recognized also, and he is being read, as he has always been read by his true disciples—so not inappropriately to name those who have come under his graver spell—not merely as a *prosateur* of purple patches, or a sophist of honeyed counsels tragically easy to misapply, but as an artist of the interpretative imagination of rare insight and magic, a writer of deep humanity as well as æs-

17 257

thetic beauty, and the teacher of a way of life at once ennobling and exquisite.   It is no longer possible to parody him—after the fashion of Mr. Mallock's brilliancy in *The New Republic*—as a writer of "all manner and no matter," nor is it possible any longer to confuse his philosophy with those gospels of unrestrained libertinism which have taken in vain the name of Epicurus.   His highly wrought, sensitively coloured, and musically expressive style is seen to be what it is because of its truth to a matter profound and delicate and intensely meditated, and such faults as it has come rather of too much matter than too little; while his teaching, far from being that of a facile "Epicureanism," is seen, properly understood, to involve something like the austerity of a fastidious Puritanism, and to result in a jealous asceticism of the senses rather than in their indulgence.   "Slight as was the burden of positive moral obligation with which he had entered Rome," he writes of Marius, as on his first evening in Rome the murmur comes to him of "the lively, reckless call to 'play,' from the sons and daughters of foolishness," "it was to no wasteful and vagrant affections, such as these, that his Epicureanism had committed him." Such warnings against misunderstanding Pater is careful to place, at, so to say, all the cross-roads in his books, so scrupulously concerned is he lest any reader should take the wrong turning.   Few writers, indeed, manifest so constant a consideration for, and, in minor matters, such a sensitive courtesy toward, their readers, while in matters of conscience Pater seems to feel for them an actual pastoral responsibility. His well-known withdrawal of the "Conclusion" to *The Renaissance* from its second edition, from a fear that "it might possibly mislead some of those young men into whose hands it might fall," is but one of many examples of his solicitude; and surely such as have gone astray after such painstaking guidance have but their own natures to blame. As he justly says, again of Marius, "in the reception of metaphysical *formulæ*, all depends, as regards their actual and ulterior result, on the pre-existent qualities of that soil of human nature into which they fall—the company they find already present there, on their admission into the house of thought."

That Pater's philosophy could ever have been misunderstood is not to be entertained with patience by any one who has read him with even ordinary attention; that it may have been misapplied, in spite of all his care, is, of course, possible; but if a writer is to be called to account for all the misapplications, or distortions, of his philosophy, writing may as well come to an end. Yet, inconceivable as it may sound, a critic very properly held in popular esteem recently gave it as his opinion that the teaching of Walter Pater was responsible for the tragic career of the author of *The Picture of Dorian Gray*. Certainly that remarkable man was an "epicurean"—but one, to quote Meredith, "whom Epicurus would have scourged out of his garden"; and the statement made by the critic in question that *The Renaissance* is the book referred to in *The Picture of Dorian Gray* as having had a sinister influence over its hero is so easily disposed of by a reference to that romance itself that it is hard to understand its ever having been made. Here is the passage describing the demoralizing book in question:

His eye fell on the yellow book that Lord Henry had sent him. . . . It was the strangest book he had ever read. It seemed to him that in exquisite raiment, and to the delicate sound of flutes, the sins of the world were passing in dumb show before him. Things that he had dimly dreamed of were suddenly made real to him. Things of which he had never dreamed were gradually revealed.

It was a novel without a plot, and with only one character, being, indeed, simply a psychological study of a certain young Parisian who spent his life trying to realize in the nineteenth century all the passions and modes of thought that belonged to every century except his own, and to sum up, as it were, in himself the various moods through which the world-spirit had ever passed, loving for their mere artificiality those renunciations that men have unwisely called virtue, as much as those natural rebellions that wise men still call sin. The style in which it was written was that curious jewelled style, vivid and obscure at once, full of *argot* and of archaisms, of technical expressions and of elaborate paraphrases, that characterizes the work of some of the finest artists of the French school of *Décadents*. There were in it metaphors as monstrous as orchids, and as evil in colour. The life of the senses was described in the terms of mystical philosophy. One hardly knew at times whether one was reading the spiritual ecstasies of some medieval saint or the morbid confessions of a modern sinner. It was a poisonous book. The heavy odour of incense seemed to cling about its pages and to trouble the brain. The mere cadence of the sentences, the subtle monotony of their music, so full as it was of complex refrains and movements elaborately repeated, produced in the mind of the lad, as he passed from chapter to chapter, a form of reverie, a malady of dreaming, that made him unconscious of the falling day and the creeping shadows. . . .

For years Dorian Gray could not free himself from the memory of this book. Or perhaps it would be more accurate to say that he never sought to free himself from it. He procured from Paris no less than five large paper copies of the first edition, and had them bound in different colours, so that they might suit his various moods and the changing fancies of a nature over which he seemed, at times, to have almost entirely lost control.

The book thus characterized is obviously by a French writer—I have good reason for thinking that it was *À Rebours* by Huysmans—and how any responsible reader can have imagined that Walter Pater's *The Renaissance* answers to this description passes all understanding. A critic guilty of so patent a misstatement must either never have read *The Picture of Dorian Gray*, or never have read *The Renaissance.* On the other hand, if on other more reliable evidence it can be found that Oscar Wilde was one of those "young men" misled by Pater's book, for whose spiritual safety Pater, as we have seen, was so solicitous, one can only remind oneself again of the phrase quoted above in regard to "that soil of human nature" into which a writer casts his seed. If that which was sown a lily comes up a toadstool, there is evidently something wrong with the soil.

Let us briefly recall what this apparently so "dangerous" philosophy of Pater's is, and we cannot do better than examine it in its most concentrated and famous utterance, this oft-quoted passage from that once-suppressed "Conclusion" to *The Renaissance:*

Not the fruit of experience, but experience itself, is the end. A counted number of pulses only is given to us of a variegated dramatic life. How may we see in them all that there is to be seen in them by the finest senses? How shall we pass most swiftly from point to point, and be present always at the focus where the greatest number of vital forces unite in their purest energy? To burn always with this hard, gem-like flame, to maintain this ecstasy, is success in life. . . . While all melts under our feet, we may well grasp at any exquisite passion, or any contribution to knowledge that seems by a lifted horizon to set the spirit free for a moment, or any stirring of the senses, strange dyes, strange colours, and curious odours, or work of the artist's hands, or the face of one's friend.

With this sense of the splendour of our experience and of its awful brevity, gathering all we are into one desperate effort to see and touch, we shall hardly have time to make theories about the things we see and touch. . .   Well! we are all *condamnés*, as Victor Hugo says; we are all under sentence of death, but with a sort of indefinite reprieve—*les hommes sont tous condamnés à mort avec des sursis indéfinis:* we have an interval, and then our place knows us no more. Some spend this interval in listlessness, some in high passions, the wisest, at least among "the children of this world," in art and song.   For our one chance lies in expanding that interval, in getting as many pulsations as possible into the given time.   Great passions may give us this quickened sense of life, ecstasy and sorrow of love, the various forms of enthusiastic activity, disinterested or otherwise, which come naturally to many of us.   Only be sure it is passion—that it does yield you this fruit of a quickened, multiplied consciousness.   Of such wisdom, the poetic passion, the desire of beauty, the love of art for its own sake, has most.   For art comes to you proposing frankly to give nothing but the highest quality to your moments as they pass, and simply for those moments' sake.

Now, if it be true that the application, or rather the misapplication, of this philosophy led Oscar Wilde to Reading Gaol, it is none the less true that another application of it led Marius to something like Christian martyrdom, and Walter Pater himself along an ever loftier and serener path of spiritual vision.

Nothing short of wilful misconstruction can
make of the counsel thus offered, with so priestly
a concern that the writer's exact meaning be
brought home to his reader, other than an inspiration toward a noble employment of that mysterious opportunity we call life. For those of us,
perhaps more than a few, who have no assurance
of the leisure of an eternity for idleness or experiment, this expansion and elevation of the doctrine
of the moment, carrying a merely sensual and
trivial moral in the Horatian maxim of *carpe diem*,
is one thrillingly charged with exhilaration and
sounding a solemn and yet seductive challenge
to us to make the most indeed, but also to make
the best, of our little day.   To make the most, and
to make the best of life!   Those who misinterpret
or misapply Pater forget his constant insistence
on the second half of that precept.   We are to get
"as many pulsations as possible into the given
time," but we are to be very careful that our use
of those pulsations shall be the finest.   Whether
or not it is "simply for those moments' sake,"
our attempt must be to give *"the highest quality,"*
remember, to those "moments as they pass."
And who can fail to remark the fastidious care
with which Pater selects various typical interests
which he deems most worthy of dignifying the
moment? The senses are, indeed, of natural
right, to have their part; but those interests on
which the accent of Pater's pleading most persuasively falls are not so much the "strange dyes,

strange colours, and curious odours," but rather
"the face of one's friend," ending his subtly musical sentence with a characteristic shock of simplicity, almost incongruity—or "some mood of
passion or insight or intellectual excitement," or
"any contribution to knowledge that seems by a
lifted horizon to set the spirit free for a moment."
There is surely a great gulf fixed between this
lofty preoccupation with great human emotions
and high spiritual and intellectual excitements,
and a vulgar gospel of "eat, drink, for tomorrow
we die," whether or not both counsels start out
from a realization of "the awful brevity" of our
mortal day.   That realization may prompt certain
natures   to   unbridled   sensuality.   Doomed   to
perish as the beasts, they choose, it would seem
with no marked reluctance, to live the life of the
beast, a life apparently not without its satisfactions.   But it is as stupid as it is infamous to
pretend that such natures as these find any warrant for their tragic libertinism in Walter Pater.
They may, indeed, have found æsthetic pleasure in
the reading of his prose, but the truth of which
that prose is but the beautiful garment has passed
them by.   For such it can hardly be claimed that
they have translated into action the aspiration of
this tenderly religious passage:

Given the hardest terms, supposing our days are
indeed but a shadow, even so we may well adorn and
beautify, in scrupulous self-respect, our souls and
whatever   our   souls   touch   upon—these   wonderful

bodies, these material dwelling-places through which the shadows pass together for a while, the very raiment we wear, our very pastimes, and the intercourse of society.

Here in this passage from *Marius* we find, to use Pater's own words once more, "the spectacle of one of the happiest temperaments coming, so to speak, to an understanding with the most depressing of theories." That theory, of course, was the doctrine of the perpetual flux of things as taught by Aristippus of Cyrene, making a man of the world's practical application of the old Heraclitean formula, his influence depending on this, "that in him an abstract doctrine, originally somewhat acrid, had fallen upon a rich and genial nature well fitted to transform it into a theory of practice of considerable stimulative power toward a fair life." Such, too, was Pater's nature, and such his practical usefulness as what one might call a philosophical artist. Meredith, Emerson, Browning, and even Carlyle were artists so far related to him and each other in that each of them wrought a certain optimism, or, at all events, a courageous and even blithe working theory of life and conduct, out of the unrelenting facts of existence unflinchingly faced, rather than ecclesiastically smoothed over—the facts of death and pain and struggle, and even the cruel mystery that surrounds with darkness and terror our mortal lot. Each one of them deliberately faced the worst, and with each, after his own nature, the worst returned to laughter. The force of all these men was in their artistic or poetic embodiment of philosophical conceptions, but, had they not been artists and poets, their philosophical conceptions would have made but little way. And it is time to recall, what critics preoccupied with his "message" leave unduly in the background, that Pater was an artist of remarkable power and fascination, a maker of beautiful things, which, whatever their philosophical content, have for our spirits the refreshment and edification which all beauty mysteriously brings us, merely because it is beauty. *Marius the Epicurean* is a great and wonderful book, not merely on account of its teaching, but because it is simply one of the most *beautiful* books, perhaps the most beautiful book, written in English. It is beautiful in many ways. It is beautiful, first of all, in the uniquely personal quality of its prose, prose which is at once austere and sensuous, simple at once and elaborate, scientifically exact and yet mystically suggestive, cool and hushed as sanctuary marble, sweet-smelling as sanctuary incense; prose that has at once the qualities of painting and of music, rich in firmly visualized pictures, yet moving to subtle, half-submerged rhythms, and expressive with every delicate accent and cadence; prose highly wrought, and yet singularly surprising one at times with, so to say, sudden innocencies, artless and instinctive beneath all its sedulous art. It is no longer necessary, as I hinted above, to fight the battle of this prose. Whether it appeal to one or not, no critic worth attention any longer disparages it as mere ornate and perfumed verbiage, the elaborate mannerism of a writer hiding the poverty of his thought beneath a pretentious raiment of decorated expression. It is understood to be the organic utterance of one with a vision of the world all his own striving through words, as he best can, to make that vision visible to others as nearly as possible as he himself sees it. Pater himself has expounded his theory and practice of prose, doubtless with a side-thought of self-justification, in various places up and down his writings, notably in his pregnant essay on "Style," and perhaps even more persuasively in the chapter called "Euphuism" in *Marius*. In this last he thus goes to the root of the matter:

That preoccupation of the *dilettante* with what might seem mere details of form, after all, did but serve the purpose of bringing to the surface, sincerely and in their integrity, certain strong personal intuitions, a certain vision or apprehension of things as really being, with important results, thus, rather than thus—intuitions which the artistic or literary faculty was called upon to follow, with the exactness of wax or clay, clothing the model within.

This striving to express the truth that is in him has resulted in a beauty of prose which for individual quality must be ranked with the prose of such masters as De Quincey and Lamb, and, to make a not irrelevant comparison, above the very fine prose of his contemporary Stevenson, by virtue of its greater personal sincerity.

There is neither space here, nor need, to illustrate this opinion by quotation, though it may not be amiss, the musical and decorative qualities of Pater's prose having been so generally dwelt upon, to remind the reader of the magical simplicities by which it is no less frequently characterized. Some of his quietest, simplest phrases have a wonderful evocative power: "the long reign of these quiet Antonines," for example; "the thunder which had sounded all day among the hills"; "far into the night, when heavy rain-drops had driven the last lingerers home"; "Flavian was no more. The little marble chest with its dust and tears lay cold among the faded flowers." What could be simpler than these brief sentences, yet how peculiarly suggestive they are; what immediate pictures they make! And this magical simplicity is particularly successful in his descriptive passages, notably of natural effects, effects caught with an instinctively selected touch or two, an expressive detail, a grey or coloured word. How lightly sketched, and yet how clearly realized in the imagination, is the ancestral country-house of Marius's boyhood, "White-Nights," "that exquisite fragment of a once large and sumptuous villa"—"Two centuries of the play of the sea-wind were in the velvet of the mosses which lay along its inaccessible ledges and angles." Take again this picture:

The cottagers still lingered at their doors for a few minutes as the shadows grew larger, and went to rest early; though there was still a glow along the road through the shorn corn-fields, and the birds were still awake about the crumbling grey heights of an old temple.

And again this picture of a wayside inn:

The room in which he sat down to supper, unlike the ordinary Roman inns at that day, was trim and sweet. The firelight danced cheerfully upon the polished three-wicked *lucernæ* burning cleanly with the best oil, upon the whitewashed walls, and the bunches of scarlet carnations set in glass goblets. The white wine of the place put before him, of the true colour and flavour of the grape, and with a ring of delicate foam as it mounted in the cup, had a reviving edge or freshness he had found in no other wine.

Those who judge of Pater's writing by a few purple passages such as the famous rhapsody on the *Mona Lisa*, conceiving it as always thus heavy with narcotic perfume, know but one side of him, and miss his gift for conveying freshness, his constant happiness in light and air and particularly running water, "green fields—or children's faces." His lovely chapter on the temple of Æsculapius seems to be made entirely of morning light, bubbling· springs, and pure mountain air; and the religious

influence of these lustral elements is his constant
theme. For him they have a natural sacramental
value, and it is through them and such other influences that Pater seeks for his hero the sancti-
fication of the senses and the evolution of the spirit.
In his preoccupation with them, and all things
lovely to the eye and to the intelligence, it is that
the secret lies of the singular purity of atmosphere
which pervades his *Marius*, an atmosphere which
might be termed the soul-beauty of the book, as
distinct from its, so to say, body-beauty as beautiful prose.

Considering *Marius* as a story, a work of imagination, one finds the same evocative method used in
the telling of it, and in the portrayal of character,
as Pater employs in its descriptive passages.
Owing to certain violent, cinematographic methods
of story-telling and character-drawing to which we
have become accustomed, it is too often assumed
that stories cannot be told or characters drawn
in any other way. Actually, of course, as many
an old masterpiece admonishes us, there is no one
canon in this matter, but, on the contrary, no
limit to the variety of method and manner a creative artist is at liberty to employ in his imaginative
treatment of human life. All one asks is that the
work should live, the characters and scenes appear
real to us, and the story be told. And Pater's
Marius entirely satisfies this demand for those to
whom such a pilgrimage of the soul will alone
appeal. It is a real story, no mere German

scholar's attempt to animate the dry bones of his erudition; and the personages and the scenes do actually live for us, as by some delicate magic of hint and suggestion; and, though at first they may seem shadowy, they have a curious way of persisting, and, as it were, growing more and more alive in our memories.   The figure of Marcus Aurelius, for example, though so delicately sketched, is a masterpiece of historical portraiture, as the pictures of Roman life, done with so little, seem to me far more convincing than the like over-elaborated pictures of antiquity, so choked with learned detail, of Flaubert and of Gautier.   Swinburne's famous praise of Gautier's *Mademoiselle de Maupin* applies with far greater fitness to Pater's masterpiece; for, if ever a book deserved to be described as

> The golden book of spirit and sense,
> The holy writ of beauty,

it is *Marius the Epicurean.*

It has been natural to dwell so long on this "golden book," because Pater's various gifts are concentrated in it, to make what is, of course, his masterpiece; though some one or other of these gifts is to be found employed with greater mastery in other of his writings, notably that delicate dramatic gift of embodying in a symbolic story certain subtle states of mind and refinements of temperament which reaches its perfection in

Imaginary Portraits, to which the later "Apollo in Picardy" and "Hippolytus Veiled" properly belong. It is only necessary to recall the exquisitely austere "Sebastian Van Storck" and the strangely contrasting Dionysiac "Denys L'Auxerrois" to justify one's claim for Pater as a creative artist of a rare kind, with a singular and fascinating power of incarnating a philosophic formula, a formula no less dry than Spinoza's, or a mood of the human spirit, in living, breathing types and persuasive tragic fables.

This genius for creative interpretation is the soul and significance of all his criticism. It gives their value to the studies of *The Renaissance*, but perhaps its finest flower is to be found in the later *Greek Studies*. To Flavian, Pater had said in *Marius*, "old mythology seemed as full of untried, unexpressed motives and interest as human life itself," and with what marvellous skill and evocative application of learning, he himself later developed sundry of those "untried, unexpressed motives," as in his studies of the myths of Dionysus—"The spirit of fire and dew, alive and leaping in a thousand vines"—and Demeter and Persephone—"the peculiar creation of country people of a high impressibility, dreaming over their work in spring or autumn, half consciously touched by a sense of its sacredness, and a sort of mystery about it"—no reader of Pater needs to be told. This same creative interpretation gives a like value to his studies of Plato; and so by virtue of this gift, active throughout the ten volumes which

18

constitute his collected work, Pater proved himself to be of the company of the great humanists.

Along with all the other constituents of his work, its sacerdotalism, its subtle reverie, its sensuous colour and perfume, its marmoreal austerity, its honeyed music, its frequent pre-occupation with the haunted recesses of thought, there go an endearing homeliness and simplicity, a deep human tenderness, a gentle friendliness, a something childlike. He has written of her, "the presence that rose thus so strangely beside the waters," to whom all experience had been "but as the sound of lyres and flutes," and he has written of "The Child in the House." Among all "the strange dyes, strange colours, and curious odours, and work of the artist's hands," one never misses "the face of one's friend"; and, in all its wanderings, the soul never strays far from the white temples of the gods and the sound of running water.

It is by virtue of this combination of humanity, edification, and æsthetic delight that Walter Pater is unique among the great teachers and artists of our time.

XXIII

.THE MYSTERY OF "FIONA MACLEOD"[1]

IN the fascinating memoir of her husband, which Mrs. William Sharp has written with so much dignity and tact, and general biographic skill, she dwells with particular fondness of recollection on the two years of their life at Phenice Croft, a charming cottage they had taken in the summer of 1892 at Rudgwick in Sussex, seven miles from Horsham, the birthplace of Shelley. Still fresh in my memory is a delightful visit I paid them there, and I was soon afterwards to recall with special significance a conversation I had with Mrs. Sharp, as four of us walked out one evening after dinner in a somewhat melancholy twilight, the glow-worms here and there trimming their ghostly lamps by the wayside, and the nightjar churring its hoarse lovesong somewhere in the thickening dusk.

"Will," Mrs. Sharp confided to me, was soon to

[1] *William Sharp* (*Fiona Macleod*). A Memoir, compiled by his wife, Elizabeth A. Sharp. (Duffield & Co)

The Writings of Fiona Macleod. Uniform edition. Arranged by Mrs. William Sharp. (Duffield & Co.)

have a surprise for his friends in a fuller and truer expression of himself than his work had so far attained, but the nature of that expression Mrs. Sharp did not confide—more than to hint that there were powers and qualities in her husband's make-up that had hitherto lain dormant, or had, at all events, been but little drawn upon.

Mrs. Sharp was thus vaguely hinting at the future "Fiona Macleod," for it was at Rudgwick, we learn, that that so long mysterious literary entity sprang into imaginative being with *Pharais*. *Pharais* was published in 1894, and I remember that early copies of it came simultaneously to myself and Grant Allen, with whom I was then staying, and how we were both somewhat *intrigué* by a certain air of mystery which seemed to attach to the little volume. We were both intimate friends of William Sharp, but I was better acquainted with Sharp's earlier poetry than Grant Allen, and it was my detection in *Pharais* of one or two subtly observed natural images, the use of which had previously struck me in one of his *Romantic Ballads and Poems of Phantasy*, that brought to my mind in a flash of understanding that Rudgwick conversation with Mrs. Sharp, and thus made me doubly certain that "Fiona Macleod"and William Sharp were one, if not the same. Conceiving no reason for secrecy, and only too happy to find that my friend had fulfilled his wife's prophecy by such fuller and finer expression of himself, I stated my belief as to its authorship in a review I wrote for the London *Star*. My review brought me an urgent telegram from Sharp, begging me, for God's sake, to shut my mouth—or words to that effect. Needless to say, I did my best to atone for having thus put my foot in it, by a subsequent severe silence till now unbroken; though I was often hard driven by curious inquirers to preserve the secret which my friend afterwards confided to me.

When I say "confided to me," I must add that in the many confidences William Sharp made to me on the matter, I was always aware of a reserve of fanciful mystification, and I am by no means sure, even now, that I, or any of us—with the possible exception of Mrs. Sharp—know the whole truth about "Fiona Macleod." Indeed it is clear from Mrs. Sharp's interesting revelations of her husband's temperament that "the whole truth" could hardly be known even to William Sharp himself; for, very evidently in "Fiona Macleod" we have to deal not merely with a literary mystification, but with a psychological mystery. Here it is pertinent to quote the message written to be delivered to certain of his friends after his death: "This will reach you," he says, "after my death. You will think I have wholly deceived you about Fiona Macleod. But, in an intimate sense this is not so, though (and inevitably) in certain details I have misled you. Only, it is a mystery. I cannot explain. Perhaps you will intuitively understand or may come to understand. 'The rest is silence.' Farewell. WILLIAM SHARP."

"It is only right, however, to add that I, and I only, was the author—in the literal and literary sense—of all written under the name of 'Fiona Macleod.'"

"Only, it is a mystery. I cannot explain." Does "I cannot explain" mean "I must not explain," or merely just what it says? I am inclined to think it means both; but, if so, the "must not" would refer to the purely personal mystification on which, of course, none would desire to intrude, and the "cannot" would refer to that psychological mystery which we are at liberty to investigate.

William Sharp's explanation to myself—as I believe to others of his friends—was to the same tenor as this posthumous statement. He and he only had actually *written* the "Fiona Macleod" fantasies and poems, but—yes! there was a real "Fiona Macleod" as well. She was a beautiful cousin of his, living much in solitude and dreams, and seldom visiting cities. Between her and him there was a singular spiritual kinship, which by some inexplicable process, so to say, of psychic collaboration, had resulted in the writings to which he had given her name. They were hers as well as his, his as well as hers. Several times he even went so far as to say that Miss Macleod was contemplating a visit to London, but that her visit was to be kept a profound secret, and that he intended introducing her to three of his friends and no more —George Meredith, W. B. Yeats, and myself.

Probably he made the same mock-confidence to other friends, as a part of his general scheme of mystification. On one occasion, when I was sitting with him in his study, he pointed to the framed portrait of a beautiful woman which stood on top of a revolving book-case, and said "That is Fiona!" I affected belief, but, rightly or wrongly, it was my strong impression that the portrait thus labelled was that of a well-known Irish lady prominently identified with Home Rule politics, and I smiled to myself at the audacious white lie. Mrs. Sharp, whose remembrance of her husband goes back to "a merry, mischievous little boy in his eighth year, with light-brown curly hair, blue-grey eyes, and a laughing face, and dressed in a tweed kilt," tells us that this "love not only of mystery for its own sake, but of mystification also," was a marked characteristic of his nature—a · characteristic developed even in childhood by the necessity he always felt of hiding away from his companions that visionary side of his life which was almost painfully vivid with him, and the sacredness of which in late years he felt compelled to screen under his pseudonym.

That William Sharp's affirmation of an actual living and breathing "Fiona Macleod" was, however, virtually true is confided by this significant and illuminating passage in Mrs. Sharp's biography. Mrs. Sharp is speaking of a sojourn together in Rome during the spring of 1891, in which her husband had experienced an unusual

exaltation and exuberance of vital and creative
energy.

There, at last [she says], he had found the desired
incentive towards a true expression of himself, in the
stimulus and sympathetic understanding of the friend
to whom he dedicated the first of the books published
under his pseudonym. This friendship began in Rome
and lasted throughout the remainder of his life.
And though this new phase of his work was at no time
the result of collaboration, as certain of his critics
have suggested, he was deeply conscious of his indebt-
edness to this friend, for—as he stated to me in a
letter of instructions, written before he went to America in 1896, concerning his wishes in the event of
his death—he realized that it was "to her I owe my development as 'Fiona Macleod,' though in a sense of
course that began long before I knew her, and indeed
while I was still a child," and that, as he believed,
"without her there would have been no 'Fiona Macleod.'" Because of her beauty, her strong sense of
life and of the joy of life; because of her keen intuitions
and mental alertness, her personality stood for him as
a symbol of the heroic women of Greek and Celtic
days, a symbol that, as he expressed it, unlocked
new doors in his mind and put him "in touch with
ancestral memories" of his race. So, for a time, he
stilled the critical, intellectual mood of William Sharp,
to give play to the development of this new-found
expression of subtle emotions, towards which he had
been moving with all the ardour of his nature.

From this statement of Mrs. Sharp one naturally turns to the dedication of *Pharais* to which she

refers, finding a dedicatory letter to "E. W. R." dealing for the most part with "Celtic" matters, but containing these more personal passages:

Dear friend [the letter begins], while you gratify me by your pleasure in this inscription, you modestly deprecate the dedication to you of this study of alien life—of that unfamiliar island-life so alien in all ways from the life of cities, and, let me add, from that of the great mass of the nation to which, in the communal sense, we both belong. But in the Domhan-Tòir of friendship there are resting-places where all barriers of race, training, and circumstances fall away in dust. At one of these places we met, a long while ago, and found that we loved the same things, and in the same way."

The letter ends with this: "There is another Pàras (Paradise) than that seen of Alastair of Innisròn—the Tir-Nan-Oigh of friendship. Therein we both have seen beautiful visions and dreamed dreams. Take, then, out of my heart, this book of vision and dream."

"Fiona Macleod," then, would appear to be the collective name given to a sort of collaborative Three-in-One mysteriously working together: an inspiring Muse with the initials E. W. R.; that psychical "other self" of whose existence and struggle for expression William Sharp had been conscious all his life; and William Sharp, general *littérateur*, as known to his friends and reading public. "Fiona Macleod" would seem to have

always existed as a sort of spiritual prisoner within
that comely and magnetic earthly tenement
of clay known as William Sharp, but whom William Sharp had been powerless to free in words,
till, at the wand-like touch of E. W. R.—the
creative stimulus of a profound imaginative
friendship—a new power of expression had been
given to him—a power of expression strangely
missing from William Sharp's previous acknowledged writings.

To speak faithfully, it was the comparative
mediocrity, and occasional even positive badness,
of the work done over his own name that formed
one of the stumbling-blocks to the acceptance of
the theory that William Sharp *could* be "Fiona
Macleod." Of course, his work had been that of
an accomplished widely-read man of letters, his
life of Heine being perhaps his most notable
achievement in prose; and his verse had not been
without intermittent flashes and felicities, suggestive of smouldering poetic fires, particularly
in his *Sospiri di Roma;* but, for the most part, it
had lacked any personal force or savour, and was
entirely devoid of that magnetism with which William Sharp, the man, was so generously endowed.
In fact, its disappointing inadequacy was a secret
source of distress to the innumerable friends who
loved him with a deep attachment, to which the
many letters making one of the delightful features
of Mrs. Sharp's biography bear witness. In himself William Sharp was so prodigiously a person-

ality, so conquering in the romantic flamboyance of his sun-like vitality, so overflowing with the charm of a finely sensitive, richly nurtured temperament, so essentially a poet in all he felt and did and said, that it was impossible patiently to accept his writings as any fair expression of himself. He was, as we say, so much more than his books—so immeasurably and delightfully more— that, compared with himself, his books practically amounted to nothing; and one was inclined to say of him in one's heart, as one does sometimes say of such imperfectly articulate artistic natures: "What a pity he troubles to write at all! Why not be satisfied with being William Sharp? Why spoil 'William Sharp' by this inadequate and misleading translation?"

The curious thing, too, was that the work he did over his own name, after "Fiona Macleod" had escaped into the freedom of her own beautiful individual utterance, showed no improvement in quality, no marks of having sprung from the same mental womb where it had lain side by side with so fair a sister. But, of course, one can readily understand that such work would naturally lack spontaneity of impulse, having to be done, more or less, against the grain, from reasons of expediency: so long as "Fiona Macleod" must remain a secret, William Sharp must produce something to show for himself, in order to go on protecting that secret, which would, also, be all the better kept by William Sharp continuing in his original mediocrity. Of this dual activity, Mrs. Sharp thus writes with much insight:

From then till the end of his life [she says] there was a continual play of the two forces in him, or of the two sides of his nature: of the intellectually observant, reasoning mind—the actor, and of the intuitively observant, spiritual mind—the dreamer, which differentiated more and more one from the other, and required different conditions, different environment, different stimuli, until he seemed to be two personalities in one. It was a development which, as it proceeded, produced a tremendous strain on his physical and mental resources, and at one time between 1897–8 threatened him with a complete nervous collapse. And there was for a time distinct opposition between those two natures which made it extremely difficult for him to adjust his life, for the two conditions were equally imperative in their demands upon him.

His preference, naturally, was for the intimate creative work which he knew grew out of his inner self; though the exigencies of life, his dependence on his pen for his livelihood, and, moreover, the keen active interest "William Sharp" took in all the movements of the day, literary and political, at home and abroad, required of him a great amount of applied study and work.

The strain must indeed have been enormous, and one cannot but feel that much of it was a needless, even trival "expense of spirit," and regret that, when "Fiona Macleod" had so manifestly come into her own, William Sharp should have continued to keep up the mystification, entailing as it did such an elaborate machinery of concealment, not the least taxing of which must have been the necessity of keeping up "Fiona Macleod's" correspondence as well as his own. Better, so to say, to have thrown William Sharp overboard, and to have reserved the energies of a temperament almost abnormally active, but physically delusive and precarious, for the finer productiveness of "Fiona Macleod." But William Sharp deemed otherwise. He was wont to say, "Should the secret be found out, Fiona dies," and in a letter to Mrs. Thomas A. Janvier—she and her husband being among the earliest confidants of his secret— he makes this interesting statement: "I can write out of my heart in a way I could not do as William Sharp, and indeed I could not do so if I were the woman Fiona Macleod is supposed to be, unless veiled in scrupulous anonymity. . . . This rapt sense of oneness with nature, this *cosmic ecstasy* and elation, this wayfaring along the extreme verges of the common world, all this is so wrought up with the romance of life that I could not bring myself to expression by my outer self, insistent and tyrannical as that need is. . . . My truest self, the self who is below all other selves, and my most intimate life and joys and sufferings, thoughts, emotions, and dreams, *must* find expression, yet I cannot save in this hidden way. . . ."

Later he wrote: "Sometimes I am tempted to believe I am half a woman, and so far saved as I am by the hazard of chance from what a woman can be made to suffer if one let the light of the common day illuminate the avenues and vistas of her heart. . . ."

At one time, I thought that William Sharp's assumption of a feminine pseudonym was a quite legitimate device to steal a march on his critics, and to win from them, thus disguised, that recognition which he must have been aware he had failed to win in his own person. Indeed, it is doubtful whether, if he had published the "Fiona Macleod" writings under his own name, they would have received fair critical treatment. I am very sure that they would not; for there is quite a considerable amount of so-called "criticism" which is really foregone conclusion based on personal prejudice, or biassed preconception, and the refusal to admit (employing a homely image) that an old dog does occasionally learn new tricks. Many well-known writers have resorted to this device, sometimes with considerable success. Since reading Mrs. Sharp's biography, however, I conclude that this motive had but little, if any, influence on William Sharp, and that his statement to Mrs. Janvier must be taken as virtually sincere.

A certain histrionism, which was one of his charms, and is perhaps inseparable from imaginative temperaments, doubtless had its share in his consciousness of that "dual nature" of which we hear so much, and which it is difficult sometimes to take with Sharp's "Celtic" seriousness.

Take, for example, this letter to his wife, when, having left London, precipitately, in response to the call of the Isles, he wrote: "The following morning we (for a kinswoman was with me) stood on the Greenock pier waiting for the Hebridean steamer, and before long were landed on an island, almost the nearest we could reach, that I loved so well." Mrs. Sharp dutifully comments: "The 'we' who stood on the pier at Greenock is himself in his dual capacity; his 'kinswoman' is his other self." Later he writes, on his arrival in the Isle of Arran: "There is something of a strange excitement in the knowledge that two people are here: so intimate and yet so far off. For it is with me as though Fiona were asleep in another room. I catch myself listening for her step sometimes, for the sudden opening of a door. It is unawaredly that she whispers to me. I am eager to see what she will do—particularly in *The Mountain Lovers*. It seems passing strange to be here with her alone at last. . . ." I confess that this strikes me disagreeably. It is one thing to be conscious of a "dual personality"—after all, consciousness of dual personality is by no means uncommon, and it is a commonplace that, spiritually, men of genius are largely feminine—but it is another to dramatize one's consciousness in this rather childish fashion. There seems more than a suspicion of pose in such writing: though one cannot but feel that William Sharp was right in thinking that the real "Fiona Macleod" was asleep at the moment.　At the same time, William Sharp seems unmistakably to have been endowed with what I suppose one has to call "psychic" powers—though the word has been "soiled with all ignoble use"—and to be the possessor in a considerable degree of that mysterious "sight" or sixth sense attributed to men and women of Gaelic blood. Mrs. Sharp tells a curious story of his mood immediately preceding that flight to the Isles of which I have been writing.　He had been haunted the night before by the sound of the sea.　It seemed to him that he heard it splashing in the night against the walls of his London dwelling.　So real it had seemed that he had risen from his bed and looked out of the window, and even in the following afternoon, in his study, he could still hear the waves dashing against the house.　"A telegram had come for him that morning," writes Mrs. Sharp, "and I took it to his study.　I could get no answer. I knocked, louder, then louder,—at last he opened the door with a curiously dazed look in his face. I explained.　He answered: 'Ah, I could not hear you for the sound of the waves!'"

His last spoken words have an eerie suggestiveness in this connection.　Writing of his death on the 12th of December, 1905, Mrs. Sharp says: "About three o'clock, with his devoted friend Alec Hood by his side, he suddenly leant forward with shining eyes and exclaimed in a tone of joyous recognition, 'Oh, the beautiful "Green Life," again!' and the next moment sank back in my arms with the contented sigh, 'Ah, all is well!'"

"The green life" was a phrase often on Sharp's lips, and stood for him for that mysterious life of elemental things to which he was almost uncannily sensitive, and into which he seemed able strangely to merge himself, of which too his writings as "Fiona Macleod" prove him to have had "invisible keys." It is this, so to say, conscious pantheism, this kinship with the secret forces and subtle moods of nature, this responsiveness to her mystic spiritual "intimations," that give to those writings their peculiar significance and value. In the external lore of nature William Sharp was exceptionally learned. Probably no writer in English, with the exceptions of George Meredith and Grant Allen, was his equal here, and his knowledge had been gained, as such knowledge can only be gained, in that receptive period of an adventurous boyhood of which he has thus written: "From fifteen to eighteen I sailed up every loch, fjord, and inlet in the Western Highlands and islands, from Arran and Colonsay to Skye and the Northern Hebrides, from the Rhinns of Galloway to the Ord of Sutherland. Wherever I went I eagerly associated myself with fishermen, sailors, shepherds, gamekeepers, poachers, gypsies, wandering pipers, and other musicians." For two months he had "taken the heather" with, and had been "star-brother" and "sun-brother" to, a tribe of gypsies, and in later years he had wandered variously in many lands, absorbing the wonder and the beauty of the world. Well might he write to Mrs. Janvier: "I have had a very varied, and, to use a much abused word, a very romantic life in its internal as well as in its external aspects." Few men have drunk so deep of the cup of life, and from such pure sky-reflecting springs, and if it be true, in the words of his friend Walter Pater, that "to burn ever with this hard gem-like flame, to maintain this ecstasy, is success in life," then indeed the life of William Sharp was a nobly joyous success.

And to those who loved him it is a great happiness to know that he was able to crown this ecstasy of living with that victory of expression for which his soul had so long travailed, and to leave behind him not only a lovely monument of star-lit words, but a spiritual legacy of perennial refreshment, a fragrant treasure-house of recaptured dreams, and hallowed secrets of the winds of time: for such are *The Writings of "Fiona Macleod."*

XXIV

FORBES-ROBERTSON : AN APPRECIATION

THE voluntary abdication of power in its zenith has always fascinated and "intrigued" the imagination of mankind. We are so accustomed to kings and other gifted persons holding on to their sceptres with a desperate tenacity, even through those waning years when younger men, beholding their present feebleness, wonder whether their previous might was not a fancy of their fathers, whether, in fact, they were ever really kings or gifted persons at all. In so many cases we have to rely on a legend of past accomplishment to preserve our reverence. Therefore, when a Sulla or a Charles V. or a Mary Anderson, leave their thrones at the moment when their sway over us is most assured and brilliant, we wonder—wonder at a phenomenon rare in humanity, and suggestive of romantic reserves of power which seal not only our allegiance to them, but that of posterity. The mystery which resides in all greatness, in all charm, is not violated by the cynical explanations of decay. They remain fortunate as those whom the gods loved, wearing the aureoles of immortal promise.

Few artists have been wise in this respect; poets, for example, very seldom. Thus we find the works of most of them encumbered with the débris of their senility. Coventry Patmore was a rare example of a poet who laid down his pen deliberately, not merely as an artist in words, but as an artist in life, having, as he said in the memorable preface to the collected edition of his poems, completed that work which in his youth he had set before him. His readers, therefore, are not saddened by any pathetic gleanings from a once-rich harvest-field, or the carefully picked-up shakings of November boughs.

Forbes-Roberston is one of those artists who has chosen to bid farewell to his art while he is still indisputably its master. One or two other distinguished actors before him have thus chosen, and a greater number have bade us those professional "farewells" that remind one of that dream of De Quincey in which he heard reverberated "Everlasting farewells! and again and yet again reverberated—everlasting farewells!" In Forbes-Robertson's case, however, apart from our courteous taking the word of his management, we know that the news is sadly true. There is a curious personal honour and sincerity breathing through all his impersonations that make us feel, so to say, that not only would we take the ghost's word for a thousand pounds, but that between him and his art is such an austere compact that he would be incapable of humiliating it by any mere advertising devices; and beyond that, those who have seen him play this time (1914) in New York must have been aware that in the very texture of all his performances was woven like a sigh the word "farewell." His very art, as I shall have later to emphasize, is an art of farewell; but, apart from that general quality, it seemed to me, though, indeed, it may have been mere sympathetic fancy, that in these last New York performances, as in the performances last spring in London, I heard a personal valedictory note. Forbes-Robertson seemed to be saying good-by at once to his audience and to his art.

In doing this, along with the inevitable sadness that must accompany such a step, one cannot but think there will be a certain private whimsical satisfaction for him in being able to go about the world in after years with his great gift still his, hidden away, but still his to use at any moment, and to know not only that he has been, but still is, as it were, in secret, the supreme Hamlet of his time. Something like that, one may imagine, must be the private fun of abdication. Forbes-Robertson, as he himself has told us, lays down one art only to take up another to which he has long been devoted, and of his early affiliation to which the figure of Love Kissing Beatrice in Rossetti's "Dante's Dream" bears illustrious and significant witness. As, one recalls that he was the model for that figure one realizes that even then he was the young lord

Hamlet, born to be *par excellence* the actor of sorrow and renunciation.

It is not my province to write here of Forbes-Robertson from the point of view of the reminiscent playgoer or of the technical critic of acting. Others, obviously, are far better qualified to undertake those offices for his fame. I would merely offer him the tribute of one to whom for many years his acting has been something more than acting, as usually understood, something to class with great poetry, and all the spiritual exaltation which "great poetry" implies. From first to last, however associated with that whimsical comedy of which, too, he is appropriately a master, he has struck for me that note of almost heartbreaking spiritual intensity which, under all its superficial materialism and cynicism, is the keynote of the modern world.

When I say "first," I am thinking of the first time I saw him, on the first night of *The Profligate* by Pinero, in its day one of the plays that blazed the trail for that social, or, rather, I should say, sociological, drama since become even more deadly in earnest, though perhaps less deadly in skill. Incidentally, I remember that Miss Olga Nethersole, then quite unknown, made a striking impression of evil, though playing only a small part. It was Forbes-Robertson, however, for me, and I think for all the playgoing London of the time, that gave the play its chief value by making us startlingly aware, through the poignancy of his personality, of what one might call the voice of the modern conscience. To associate that thrillingly beautiful and profound voice of his with anything that sounds so prosaic as a "modern conscience" may seem unkind, but actually our modern conscience is anything but prosaic, and combines within it something at once poetic and prophetic, of which that something ghostly in Forbes-Robertson's acting is peculiarly expressive. That quality of other-worldliness which at once scared and fascinated the lodgers in *The Passing of the Third Floor Back* is present in all Forbes-Robertson's acting. It was that which strangely stirred us, that first night of *The Profligate*. We meet it again with the blind Dick Heldar in *The Light That Failed*, and of course we meet it supremely in *Hamlet*. In fact, it is that quality which, chief among others, makes Forbes-Robertson's Hamlet the classical Hamlet of his time.

Forbes-Robertson has of course played innumerable parts. Years before *The Profligate*, he had won distinction as the colleague of Irving and Mary Anderson. He may be said to have played everything under the sun. His merely theatric experience has thus enriched and equipped his temperament with a superb technique. It would probably be impossible for him to play any part badly, and of the various successes he has made, to which his present repertoire bears insufficient witness, others, as I have said, can point out the excellences. My concern here is with his art in its fullest and finest expression, in its essence; and therefore it is unnecessary for me to dwell upon any other of his impersonations than that of Hamlet. When a man can play *Hamlet* so supremely, it may be taken for granted, I presume, that he can play *Mice and Men*, or even that masterpiece of all masterpieces, *Cæsar and Cleopatra*. I trust that it is no disrespect to the distinguished authors of these two plays to say that such plays in a great actor's repertoire represent less his versatility than his responsibilities, that pot-boiling necessity which hampers every art, and that of the actor, perhaps, most of all.

To my thinking, the chief interest of all Forbes-Robertson's other parts is that they have "fed" his Hamlet; and, indeed, many of his best parts may be said to be studies for various sides of Hamlet, his fine *Romeo*, for example, which, unfortunately, he no longer plays. In *Hamlet* all his qualities converge, and in him the tradition of the stage that all an ambitious actor's experience is only to fit him to play Hamlet is for once justified. But, of course, the chief reason of that success is that nature meant Forbes-Robertson to play Hamlet. Temperament, personality, experience, and training have so worked together that he does not merely play, but *is*, Hamlet. Such, at all events, is the complete illusion he is able to produce.

Of course, one has heard from them of old time that an actor's personality must have nothing to do with the part he is playing; that he only is an actor who can most successfully play the exact opposite of himself. That is the academic theory of "character-acting," and of course the half-truth of it is obvious. It represents the weariness induced in audiences by handsome persons who merely, in the stage phrase, "bring their bodies on"; yet it would go hard with some of our most delightful comedians were it the whole truth about acting. As a matter of fact, of course, a great actor includes a multiplicity of selves, so that he may play many parts, yet always be playing himself. Beyond himself no artist, whatever his art, has ever gone.

What reduplication of personality is necessary for the man who plays Hamlet need hardly be said, what wide range of humanity and variety of accomplishment; for, as Anatole France has finely said of Hamlet, "He is a man, he is man, he is the whole of man."

Time was when *Hamlet* was little more than an opportunity for some robustious periwig-pated fellow, or it gave the semi-learned actor the chance to conceal his imaginative incapacity by a display of "new readings." For example, instead of saying:

The air bites shrewdly; it is very cold,

you diverted attention from your acting by an appeal to the literary antiquarianism of your audience, and, out of one or other of the quartos, read the line:

The air bites shrewdly; *is* it very cold?

with the implication that there was a whole world of suggestion in the difference.

One has known actors, far from unillustrious, who staked their whole performance on some such learned triviality or some trifling novelty of business, when, for example, in Hamlet's scene with his mother, the prince comes to:

Look here upon this picture, and on this.

An actor who deserves better than he has yet received in the tradition of the acted *Hamlet*— I mean Wilson Barrett—used to make much of taking a miniature of his father from his bosom to point the contrast.

But all such things in the end are of no account. New readings, new business, avail less and less. Nor does painstaking archæology of scenery or dresses any longer throw dust in our eyes. We are for the play, the living soul of the play. Give us that, and your properties may be no more elaborate than those of a *guignol* in the Champs-Elysées.

Forbes-Robertson's acting is so imaginative, creating the scene about him as he plays, that one almost resents any stage-settings for him at all, however learnedly accurate and beautifully painted.

His soul seems to do so much for us that we almost wish it could be left to do it all, and he act for us as they acted in Elizabeth's day, with only a curtain for scenery, and a placard at the side of the stage saying, "This is Elsinore."

One could hardly say more for one's sense of the reality of Forbes-Robertson's acting, as, naturally, one is not unaware that distressing experiments have been made to reproduce the Elizabethan theatre by actors who, on the other hand, were sadly in need of all that scenery, archæology, or orchestra could do for them.

With a world overcrowded with treatises on the theme, from, and before, Gervinus, with the commentary of *Wilhelm Meister* in our minds, not to speak of the starlit text ever there for our reading, there is surely no need to traverse the character of Hamlet. He has meant so much to our fathers—though he can never have meant so much to them as he does to us of today—that he is, so to say, in our blood. He is strangely near to our hearts by sheer inheritance. And perhaps the most beautiful thing Forbes-Robertson's Hamlet does for us is that it commands our love for a great gentleman doing his gentlest and bravest and noblest with a sad smile and a gay humour, in not merely a complicated, wicked, absurd, and tiresome, but, also, a ghostly world.

When we think of Hamlet, we think of him as two who knew him very well thought of him,— Ophelia and Horatio,—and as one who saw him only as he sat at last on his throne, dead, with the crown of Denmark on his knees.

Ophelia's

Courtier's, soldier's, scholar's eye, tongue, sword,
The expectancy and rose of the fair state;

the "sweet prince" of Horatio's "good-night"—the soldier for whose passage Fortinbras commanded

The soldier's music and the rites of war.

We think of him, too, as the haunted son of a dear father murdered, a philosophic spectator of the grotesque brutality of life, suddenly by a ghostly summons called on to take part in it; a prince, a philosopher, a lover, a soldier, a sad humourist.

Were one asked what aspects of Hamlet does Forbes-Robertson specially embody, I should say, in the first place, his princeliness, his ghostliness, then his cynical and occasionally madcap humour, as where, at the end of the play-scene, he capers behind the throne in a terrible boyish glee. No actor that I have seen expresses so well that scholarly irony of the Renaissance permeating the whole play. His scene with Rosencrantz and Guildenstern and the recorders is masterly: the silken sternness of it, the fine hauteur, the half-appeal as of lost ideals still pleading with the vulgarity of life, the fierce humour of its disillusion, and behind, as always, the heartbreak—that side of it which comes of the recognition of what it is to be a gentleman in such a world.

In this scene, too, as in others, Forbes-Robertson makes it clear that that final tribute of Fortinbras was fairly won.

The soldier—if necessary, the fighter—is there as supple and strong as a Damascus blade. One is always aware of the "something dangerous," for all his princely manners and scholarly ways. One is never left in doubt as to how this Hamlet will play the man. It is all too easy for him to draw his sword and make an end of the whole fantastic business. Because this philosophic swordsman holds the sword, let no one think that he knows not how to wield it. All this gentleness —have a care!—is that of an unusually masculine restraint.

In the scene with Ophelia, Forbes-Robertson's tenderness was almost terrible. It came from such a height of pity upon that little uncomprehending flower!

"I never gave you aught," as Forbes-Robertson said it, seemed to mean: "I gave you all—all that you could not understand." "Yet are not you and I in the toils of that destiny there that moves the arras. *Is* it your father?"

Along with Forbes-Robertson's spiritual interpretation of Shakespeare goes pre-eminently, and doubtless as a contributive part of it, his imaginative revitalization of the great old lines—lines worn like a highway with the passage of the genera-

tions.   As a friend of mine graphically phrased **it,**
"How he revives for us the splendour **of the**
text!"

The splendour of the text! It is a good phrase,
and how splendid the text is we, of course, all know
—know so well that we take it for granted, and so
fall into forgetfulness of its significance; forgetting what central fires of soul and intellect must
have gone to the creation of such a world of tran-
scendent words.

Yet how living the lines still are, though the
generations have almost quoted the life out of
them, no man who has spoken them on the stage in
our day, except Forbes-Robertson, has had the gift
to show.

It is more than elocution, masterly elocution as
it is, more than the superbly modulated voice: the
power comes of spiritual springs welling up beneath
the voice—springs fed from those infinite sources
which "lie beyond the reaches of our souls."

Merely to take the phrase I have just quoted,
how few actors—or readers of Shakespeare, or
members of any Shakespearian audience, for that
matter—have any personal conception of what it
means!   They may make a fine crescendo with it,
but that is all.   They have never stood, shrinking
and appalled, yet drawn with a divine temptation,
upon the brink of that vastness along the margin
of which, it is evident, that Hamlet often wandered.   It is in vain they tell their audiences and
Horatio:

There are more things in heaven and earth, Horatio,
Than are dreamt of in your philosophy.

We are quite sure that they know nothing of what
they are saying; and that, as a matter of fact, there
are few things for them in heaven or earth except
the theatre they are playing in, their actors' club,
and, generally, their genial mundane lives; and,
of course, one rather congratulates them on the
simplicity of their lives, congratulates them on
their ignorance of such haunted regions of the
mind.   Yet, all the same, that simplicity seems
to disqualify them from playing *Hamlet*.

Few Shakespearian actors seem to remember
what they are playing—Shakespeare.   One would
think that to be held a worthy interpreter of so
great a dramatist, so mysterious a mind, and so
golden a poet, were enough distinction.   Oscar
Wilde, in a fine sonnet, addressed Henry Irving as

Thou trumpet set for Shakespeare's lips to blow,

and we may be sure that Irving appreciated the
honour thus paid him, he who so wonderfully
interpreted so many of Shakespeare's moods, so well
understood the irony of his intellect, even the
breadth of his humanity, yet in *Hamlet*, at all
events, so strangely missed his soul.

Most of us have seen many Hamlets die.   We
have watched them squirming through those
scientific contortions of dissolution, to copy which
they had very evidently walked the hospitals in a
businesslike quest of death-agonies, as certain

histrionic connoisseurs of madness **in France**
lovingly haunt the Saltpétrière.   As I look back,
I wonder how we tolerated their wriggling absurdity.   I suppose it was that the hand of tradition
was still upon us, as upon them.   And, let us not
forget, the words were there, the immortal words,
and an atmosphere of tragic death and immortality
that only such words could create:

> Absent thee from felicity awhile,
> And in the harsh world draw thy breath **in pain**
> To hear my story . . .
> The rest is silence. . . .

How different it is when **Forbes-Robertson's**
Hamlet dies!   All my life I seem to have been asking my friends, those I loved best, those who
valued the dearest, the kindest, the greatest, and
the strongest in our strange human life, to come
with me and see **Forbes-Robertson** die in *Hamlet*.
I asked them because, as that strange young dead
king sat upon his throne, there was something,
whatever it meant—death, life, immortality, what
you will—of a surpassing loveliness, something
transfiguring the poor passing moment of trivial,
brutal murder into a beauty to which it was quite
natural that that stern Northern warrior, with
his winged helmet, should bend the knee.   I
would not exchange anything I have ever read or
seen for **Forbes-Robertson** as he sits there so still
and starlit upon the throne of Denmark.
   Forbes-Robertson is not merely a great Shake-

spearian actor; he is a great spiritual actor. The
one doubtless implies the other, though the implication has not always appeared to be obvious.

He is prophetic of what the stage will some
day be, and what we can see it here and there
preparing to become. In all the welter of the dramatic conditions of the moment there emerges
one fact, that of the growing importance of the
stage as a vehicle for what one may term general
culture. The stage, with its half-sister, the cinema,
is strangely, by how long and circuitous a route,
returning of course, with an immeasurably developed equipment, to its starting-point, ending
curiously where it began as the handmaid of the
church. As with the old moralities or miracle-
plays, it is becoming once more our teacher. The
lessons of truth and beauty, as those of plain gaiety
and delight, are relying more and more upon the
actor for their expression, and less on the accredited
doctors of divinity or literature. Even the dancers
are doing much for our souls. Our duties as
citizens are being taught us by well-advertised
plays, and if we wish to abolish Tammany or
change our police commissioner, we enforce our
desire by the object-lesson of a play. The great
new plays may not yet be here, but the public
once more is going to the theatre, as it went
long ago in Athens, to be delighted and amused,
of course, but also to be instructed in national
and civic affairs, and, most important of all, to be
purified by pity and terror.

XXV

A MEMORY OF FRÉDÉRIC MISTRAL

THERE are many signs that poetry is coming into its own again—even here in America, which, while actually one of the most romantic and sentimental of countries, fondly imagines itself the most prosaic.

Kipling, to name but one instance, has, by his clarion-tongued quickening of the British Empire, shown so convincingly what dynamic force still belongs to the right kind of singing, and the poet in general seems to be winning back some of that serious respect from his fellow-citizens which, under a misapprehension of his effeminacy and general uselessness, he had lost awhile. The poet is not so much a joke to the multitude as he was a few years ago, and the term "minor poet" seems to have fallen into desuetude.

Still for all this, I doubt if it is in the Anglo-Saxon blood, nowadays at all events, to make a national hero of a poet, one might say a veritable king, such as Frédéric Mistral is today in Provence. In our time, Björnson in Norway was perhaps the only parallel figure, and he held his position as actual "father of his people" for very much the same reasons. At once a commanding and lovable personality, he and his work were absolutely identified with his country and his countrymen. He was simply Norway incarnate.

So, today in Provence, it is with Frédéric Mistral. He is not only a poet of Provence. He is Provence incarnate, and, apart from the noble quality of his work, his position as the foremost representative of his compatriots is romantically unique. No other country today, pointing to its greatest man, would point out—a poet; whereas Mistral, were he not as unspoiled as he is laurelled, might, with literal truth, say:

"*Provence—c'est moi!*"

We had hardly set foot in Provence this last spring, my wife and I, before we realized, with grateful wonder, that we had come to a country that has a poet for a king.

On arriving at Marseilles almost the first word we heard was "Mistral"—not the bitter wind of the same name, but the name of the honey-tongued "Master." Our innkeeper—O the delightful innkeepers of France!—on our consulting him as to our project of a walking trip through the Midi— as Frenchmen usually speak of Provence—said, for his first aid to the traveller: " Then, of course, you will see our great poet, Mistral." And he promptly produced a copy of *Mirèio*, which he begged me to use till I had bought a copy for myself.

"Ah! Mistral," he cried, with Gallic enthusiasm, using the words I have borrowed from his lips, "Mistral is the King of Provence!"

Marseilles had not always been so enthusiastic over Mistral and his fellows. And Mistral, in his memoirs, gives an amusing account of a philological battle fought over the letter "s" in a room behind one of the Marseilles bookshops between "the amateurs of trivialities, the rhymers of the white beard, the jealous, the grumblers," and the young innovators of the "félibrige."

But that was over fifty years ago, and the battle of those young enthusiasts has long since been won. What that battle was and what an extraordinary victory came of it must needs be told for the significance of Mistral in Provence to be properly understood.

The story is one of the most romantic in the history of literature. Briefly, it is this:

The Provençal language, the "langue d'oc," was, of course, once the courtly and lettered language of Europe, the language of the great troubadours, and through them the vehicle of the culture and refinement of the thirteenth and fourteenth centuries. From it may be said to have sprung the beginnings of Italian literature.

But, owing to various historical vicissitudes, the language of Northern France, the "langue d'oil," gradually took its place, and when Mistral was born, in 1830, Provençal had long been regarded as little more than a *patois*.

Now it was the young Mistral's dream, as a

school-boy in the old convent school of Saint
Michael de Frigolet, at Avignon, to restore his
native tongue to its former high estate, to make it
once more a literary language, and it chanced
that one of his masters, Joseph Roumanille, was
secretly cherishing the same dream.

The master, looking over his pupil's shoulder one
day, found that, instead of working at his prescribed
task, he was busily engaged in translating the
Penitential Psalms into Provençal. Instead of
punishing him, the master gratefully hailed a
kindred spirit, and presently confided Provençal
verses of his own making. From that moment,
though there was a dozen years' difference between
their ages, Mistral and Roumanille began a friendship which was to last till Roumanille's death, a
friendship of half a century.

Soon their dream attracted other recruits, and
presently seven friends, whose names are all
famous now, and most of whom have statues in
Arles or in Avignon—Roumanille, Mistral, Au-
banel, Mathieu, Giéra, Brunet, and Tavan—after
the manner of Ronsard's "Pléiade," and Rossetti's
"P. R. B."—formed themselves into a brotherhood
to carry on the great work of regeneration.

They needed a name to call themselves by.
They had all met together to talk things over in the
old castle of Font-Ségugne, or, as Mistral more
picturesquely puts it: "It was written in heaven
that one blossoming Sunday, the twenty-first of
May, 1854, in the full springtide of life and of the

year, seven poets should come to meet together in the castle of Font-Ségugne." Several suggestions were made for a name for this brotherhood, but presently Mistral announced that in an old folk-story he had collected at his birthplace, Maillane, he believed that he had found the word they were in search of. In this folk-story the boy Christ is represented as discoursing in the temple with "the seven félibres of the Law."

"Why, that is us!" exclaimed the enthusiastic young men as Mistral finished, and there on the spot "félibre" was adopted as the password of their order, Mistral coining the word "félibrige" to represent the work they aimed to do, and also their association. The name stuck, and has now for many years been the banner-word for the vigorous school of Provençal literature and the allied arts of painting and sculpture which has responded with such eager vitality to Mistral's rallying cry.

But, excellent as are the other poets which the school has produced—and one need only glance through a recent *Anthologie du Félibrige* to realize what a wealth of true poetry the word "félibrige" now stands for—there can be no question that its greatest asset still remains Mistral's own work, as it was his first great poem, *Mirèio*, which first drew the eyes of literary Paris, more than inclined to be contemptuous, to the Provençal renaissance.

Adolphe Dumas had been sent to Provence in

the year 1856 by the Minister of Public Instruction to collect the folk-songs of the people, and calling on Mistral (then twenty-six), living quietly with his widowed mother at Maillane, he had found him at work on *Mirèio*. Mistral read some passages to him, with the result that the generous Dumas returned to Paris excitedly to proclaim the advent of a new poet. Presently, Mistral accepted his invitation to visit Paris, was introduced to the great Lamartine—who has left some charming pages descriptive of his visit,—read some of *Mirèio* to him, and was hailed by him as "the Homer of Provence."

The press, however, had its little fling at the new-comer. "The Mistral it appears," said one pitiful punster, "has been incarnated in a poem. We shall soon see whether it is anything else but wind." Such has been the invariable welcome of·great men in a small world.

But Mistral had no taste for Paris, either as a lion or a butt, and, after a few days' stay, we find him once more quietly at home at Maillane. Yet he had brought back with him one precious trophy —the praise of Lamartine; and when, in the course of a year or two (1859), *Mirèio* came to be published at Avignon, it bore, as it still bears, this heart-felt dedication to Lamartine:

"To thee I dedicate *Mirèio*; it is my heart and my soul; it is the flower of my years; it is a bunch of grapes from Crau with all its leaves—a rustic's offering."

With the publication of *Mirèio* Mistral instantly "arrived," instantly found himself on that throne which, as year has followed year, has become more securely his own. Since then he has written much noble poetry, all embodying and vitalizing the legendary lore of his native land, a land richer in momentous history, perhaps, than any other section of Europe. But in addition to his poetry he has, single-handed, carried through the tremendous scholarly task of compiling a dictionary of the Provençal language—a *Thesaurus of the Félibrige*, for which work the Institute awarded him a prize of ten thousand francs.

In 1904, he was awarded the Nobel prize of 100,000 francs, but such is his devotion to his fellow-countrymen that he did not keep that prize for himself, but used it to found the Musée Arlésien at Arles, a museum designed as a treasure house of anything and everything pertaining to the history and life of Provence—antiquities, furniture, costumes, paintings, and so forth.

It was in Arles in 1909, the fiftieth birthday of *Mirèio*, that Mistral, then seventy-nine years old, may be said to have reached the summit of his romantic fame. A great festival was held in his honour, in which the most distinguished men of France took part. A dramatized version of his *Mirèio* was played in the old Roman amphitheatre, and a striking statue of him was unveiled in the antique public square, the Place du Forum, with the shade of Constantine looking on, one might feel, from his mouldering palace hard by.

In Arles Mistral is a well-known, beloved figure, for it is his custom, every Saturday, to come there from Maillane, to cast his eye over the progress of his museum, the pet scheme of his old age. One wonders how it must seem to pass that figure of himself, pedestaled high in the old square. To few men is it given to pass by their own statues in the street. Sang a very different poet—

> They grind us to the dust with poverty,
> And build us statues when we come to die.

But poor Villon had the misfortune to be a poet of the "langue d'oil," and the Montfaucon gibbet was the only monument of which he stood in daily expectation. Could the lines of two poets offer a greater contrast? Blessed indeed is he who serves the rural gods, Pan and Old Sylvanus and the sister nymphs—as Virgil sang; and Virgilian indeed has been the golden calm, and sunlit fortunes, as Virgilian, rather than Homeric, is the gracious art, of the poet whom his first Parisian admirer, Adolphe Dumas, called "the Homer of Provence"—as Virgilian, too, seemed the landscape through which at length, one April afternoon, we found ourselves on pilgrimage to the home of him whose name had been on the lips of every innkeeper, shopkeeper, and peasant, all the way from Marseilles to Tarascon.

Yes! the same golden peace that lies like a charm

across every page of his greatest poem lay across that sun-steeped, fertile plain, with its walls of cypress trees, its lines of poplars, its delicate, tapestry-like designs of almond trees in blossom, on a sombre background of formal olive orchards, its green meadows, lit up with singing water-courses, or gleaming irrigation canals, starred here and there with the awakening kingcup, or sweet with the returning violet—here and there a farmhouse ("mas," as they call them in Provence) snugly sheltered from the mistral by their screens of foliage— and far aloft in the distance, floating like a silver dream, the snow-white shoulder of Mont Ventoux —the Fuji Yama of Provence.

At last the old, time-worn village came in sight— it lies about ten miles north-east of Tartarin's Tarascon—and we entered it, as was proper, with the "Master's" words on our lips: "Maillane is beautiful, well-pleasing is Maillane; and it grows more and more beautiful every day. Maillane is the honour of the countryside, and takes its name from the month of May.

"Who would be in Paris or in Rome? Poor conscripts! There is nothing to charm one there; but Maillane has its equal nowhere—and one would rather eat an apple in Maillane than a partridge in Paris."

It was Sunday afternoon, and the streets were full of young people in their Sunday finery, the girls wearing the pretty Arlésien caps. At first sight of us, with our knapsacks, they were prepared to be amused, and saucy lads called out things in mock English; but when it was understood that we were seeking the house of the "Master" we inspired immediate respect, and a dozen eager volunteers put themselves at our service and accompanied us in a body to where, at the eastern edge of the village, there stands an unpretentious square stone house of no great antiquity, surrounded by a garden and half hidden with trees.

We stood silently looking at the house for a few minutes, trying to realize that there a great poet had gone on living and working, in single-minded devotion to his art and his people, for full fifty years—there in that green, out-of-the-way corner of the world. The idea of a life so rooted in contentment, so continuously happy in the lifelong prosecution of a task set to itself in boyhood, and so independent of change, is one not readily grasped by the hurrying American mind.

Then we pushed open the iron gate and passed into the garden. A paved walk led up to the front door, but that had an unused look, and, gaining no response there, we walked through a shrubbery around the side of the house, and as we turned the corner came on what was evidently the real entrance, facing a sunny slope of garden where hyacinths and violets told of the coming of spring. Here we were greeted by some half a dozen friendly dogs, whose demonstrations brought to the door a neat little, keen-eyed peasant woman, with an expression in her face that suggested that she was the real watch dog, on behalf of her master, standing between him and an intrusive world. As a matter of fact, as we afterward learned, that is one of her many self-imposed offices, for, having been in the Mistral household for many years, she has long since been as much a family friend as a servant, and generally looks after the Master and Mme. Mistral as if they were her children, nursing and "bossing" them by turns. "Elise"—I think her name is—is a "character" almost as well know in Provence as the Master himself.

So she looked sharply at us, while I produced a letter to M. Mistral which had been given me by a humble associate of the "félibres," a delightful *chansonnier* we had met at Les Baux. With this she went indoors, presently to return with a face of still cautious welcome, and invited us in to a little square hall hung with photographs of various distinguished friends of the poet and two bronze medallions of himself, one representing him with his favourite dog.

Then a door to the right opened, revealing a typical scholar's study, lined with books from ceiling to floor, books and papers on tables and chairs, and framed photographs again on the free wall space. The spring sunshine poured in through long windows, and in this characteristic setting stood a tall old man, astonishingly erect, his distinguished head, with its sparse white locks, its keen eyes, and strong yet delicate aquiline features, pointed white beard and mustache, suggesting pictures of some military grand seigneur of old time. His carriage had the same blending of soldier and nobleman, and the stately kindliness with which he bade us welcome belonged, alas! to another day.

At his side stood a tall, handsome lady, with remarkable, dark, kind eyes, evidently many years his junior. This was Mme. Mistral, in her day one of those "queens of beauty" whom the "félibres" elect every seven years at their floral fêtes. Mme. Mistral was no less gracious to us than her husband, and joined in the talk that followed with much animation and charm.

We had a little feared that M. Mistral, as he declines to write in anything but Provençal, might carry his artistic creed into his conversation too. To our relief, however, he spoke in the most polished French—for you may know French very well, but be quite unable to understand Provençal, either printed or spoken. This had sometimes made our journeying difficult, as we inquired our way of peasants along the road.

It was natural to talk first to Mistral of literature. We inquired whether he read much English. He shook his head, smiling. No! outside of one or two of the great classics, Shakespeare and Milton, for example, he had read little. Yes! he had read one American author—Fenimore Cooper. *Le Feu-Follet* had been a favourite book of his boyhood. This we identified as *The Fire-Fly*.

318 A Memory of Frédéric Mistral

He seemed to wish to talk about America rather than literature, and seemed immensely interested in the fact that we were Americans, and he raised his eyes, with an expression of French wonderment, at the fact of our walking our way through the country —as also at the length of the journey from America. Evidently it seemed to him a tremendous undertaking.

"You Americans," he said, "are a wonderful people. You think nothing of going around the world."

We were surprised to find that he took the keenest interest in American politics.

"It must be a terribly difficult country to govern," he said. And then he asked us eagerly for news of our "extraordinary President." We suggested Mr. Wilson.

"Oh, no! no!" he explained. "The extraordinary man who was President before him."

"Colonel Roosevelt?"

Yes, that was the man—a most remarkable man that! So Colonel Roosevelt may be interested to hear that the poet-king of Provence is an enthusiastic Bull Mooser.

Of course, we talked too of the "félibrige," and it was beautiful to see how M. Mistral's face softened at the mention of his friend Joseph Roumanille, and with what generosity he attributed the origin of the great movement to his dead friend.

"But you must by all means call on Mme. Roumanille," said he, "when you go to Avignon, and say that I sent you"—for Roumanille's widow still lives, one of the most honoured muses of the "félibrige."

When it was time for us to go on our way, nothing would satisfy M. and Mme. Mistral but that we drink a glass of a cordial which is made by "Elise" from Mistral's own recipe; and as we raised the tiny glasses of the innocent liqueur in our hands, Mistral drank "A l'Amérique!"

Then, taking a great slouch hat from a rack in the hall, and looking as though it was his statue from Arles accompanying us, the stately old man led us out into the road, and pointed us the way to Avignon.

On the 30th of this coming September that great old man—the memory of whose noble presence and beautiful courtesy will remain with us forever—will be eighty-three.

February, 1913.

XXVI

IMPERISHABLE FICTION

THE longevity of trees is said to be in proportion to the slowness of their growth. It has to do no little as well with the depth and area of their roots and the richness of the soil in which they find themselves. When the sower went forth to sow, it will be remembered, that which soon sprang up as soon withered away. It was the seed that was content to "bring forth fruit with patience" that finally won out and survived the others.

These humble, old-fashioned illustrations occur to me as I apply myself to the consideration of the question provoked by the lightning over-production of modern fiction and modern literature generally: the question of the flourishing longevity of the fiction of the past as compared with the swift oblivion which seems almost invariably to overtake the much-advertised "masterpieces" of the present.

I read somewhere a ballade asking—where are the "best sellers" of yesteryear? The ballad-maker might well ask, and one might re-echo with Villon:

"Mother of God, ah! where are they?" During the last twenty years they have been as the sands on the seashore for multitude, yet I think one would be hard set to name a dozen of them whose titles even are still on the lips of men—whereas several quieter books published during that same period, unheralded by trumpet or fire-balloon, are seen serenely to be ascending to a sure place in the literary firmament.

What can be the reason? Can the decay of these forgotten phenomena of modern fiction, so lavishly crowned with laurels manufactured in the offices of their own publishers, have anything to do with the hectic rapidity of their growth, and may there be some truth in the supposition that the novels, and books generally, that live longest are those that took the longest to write, or, at all events underwent the longest periods of gestation?

Some fifteen years or so ago one of the most successful manufacturers of best sellers was Guy Boothby, whose *Dr. Nikola* is perhaps still remembered. Unhappily he did not live long to enjoy the fruits of his industrious dexterity. I bring his case to mind as typical of the modern machine-made methods.

I had read in a newspaper that he did his "writing" by phonograph, and chancing to meet him somewhere, asked him about it. His response was to invite me to come down to his charming country house on the Thames and see how he did it. Boothby was a fine, manly fellow, utterly without "side" or any illusions as to the quality of his work. He loved good literature too well—Walter Pater, incongruously enough, was one of his idols —to dream that he could make it. Nor was the making of literature by any means his first pre-occupation, as he made clear, with winning frank-ness, within a few moments of my arriving at his home.

Taking me out into his grounds, he brought me to some extensive kennels, where he showed me with pride some fifty or so prize dogs; then he took me to his stables, his face shining with pleasure in his thoroughbreds; and again he led the way to a vast hennery, populated with innumerable prize fowls.

"These are the things I care about," he said, "and I write the stuff for which it appears I have a certain knack only because it enables me to buy them!"

Would that all writers of best sellers were as engagingly honest. No few of them, however, write no better and affect the airs of genius into the bargain.

Then Boothby took me into his "study," the entire literary apparatus of which consisted of three phonographs; and he explained that, when he had dictated a certain amount of a novel into one of them, he handed it over to his secretary in another room, who set it going and transcribed what he had spoken into the machine; he, meanwhile, proceed-ing to fill up another record. And he concluded airily by saying with a laugh that he had a novel of 60,000 words to deliver in ten days, **and was** just on the point of beginning it!

Boothby's method was, I believe, somewhat unusual in those days. Since then it has become something like the rule. Not so much as regards the phonograph, perhaps, but with respect to the breathless speed of production.

I am informed by an editor, associated with magazines that use no less than a million and a half words of fiction a month, that he has among his contributors more than one writer on whom he can rely to turn off a novel of 60,000 words in six days, and that he can put his finger on twenty novelists who think nothing of writing a novel of a hundred thousand words in anywhere from sixty to ninety days. He recalled to me, too, the case of a well-known novelist who has recently contracted to supply a publisher with four novels in one year, each novel to run to not less than a hundred thousand words. One thinks of the Scotsman with his "Where's your Willie Shakespeare now?"

Even Balzac's titanic industry must hide its diminished head before such appalling fecundity; and what would Horace have to say to such frog-like verbal spawning, with his famous "labour of the file" and his counsel to writers "to take a subject equal to your powers, and consider long what your shoulders refuse, what they are able to bear." It is to be feared that "the monument more endur-

ing than brass" is not erected with such rapidity.
The only brass associated with the modern best
seller is to be found in the advertisements; and,
indeed, all that both purveyor and consumer seem
to care about may well be summed up in the publisher's recommendation quoted by Professor
Phelps: "This book goes with a rush and ends with
a smash." Such, one might add, is the beginning
and ending of all literary rockets.

Now let us recall some fiction that has been
in the world anywhere from, say, three hundred
years to fifty years and is yet vigorously alive,
and, in many instances, to be classed still with the
best sellers.

Don Quixote, for example, was published in 1605,
but is still actively selling. Why? May it perhaps be that it was some six years in the writing,
and that a great man, who was soldier as well as
writer, charged it with the vitality of all his blood
and tears and laughter, all the hard-won humanity of years of manful living, those five years as a
slave in Algiers (actually beginning it in prison
once more at La Mancha), and all the stern struggle
of a storm-tossed life faced with heroic stead-
fastness and gaiety of heart?

Take another book which, if it is not read as
much as it used to be, and still deserves to be, is
certainly far from being forgotten—*Gil Blas*.
Published in 1715—that is, its first two parts—it
has now two centuries of popularity to its credit, and
is still as racy with humanity as ever; but, though

Le Sage was a rapid and voluminous writer, over this one book which alone the world remembers it is significant to note that he expended unusual time and pains. He was forty-seven years old when the first two parts were published. The third part was not published till 1724, and eleven years more were to elapse before the issue of the fourth and final part in 1735.

A still older book that is still one of the world's best sellers, *The Pilgrim's Progress*, can hardly be conceived as being dashed off in sixty or ninety days, and would hardly have endured so long had not Bunyan put into it those twelve years of soul torment in Bedford gaol. *Robinson Crusoe* still sells its annual thousands, whereas others of its author's books no less skilfully written are practically forgotten, doubtless because Defoe, fifty-eight years old at its publication, had concentrated in it the ripe experience of a lifetime. Though a boy's book to us, he clearly intended it for an allegory of his own arduous, solitary life.

"I, Robinson Crusoe," we read, "do affirm that the story, though allegorical, is also historical, and that it is the beautiful representation of a life of unexampled misfortune, and of a variety not to be met with in this world."

The Vicar of Wakefield, as we know, was no hurried piece of work. Indeed, Goldsmith went about it in so leisurely a fashion as to leave it neglected in a drawer of his desk, till Johnson rescued it, according to the proverbial anecdote;

and even then its publisher, Newbery, was in no hurry, for he kept it by him another two years before giving it to the printer and to immortality. It was certainly one of those fruits "brought forth with patience" all round.

Tom Jones is another such slow-growing masterpiece. Written in the sad years immediately following the death of his dearly loved wife, Fielding, dedicating it to Lord Lyttelton, says: "I here present you with the labours of some years of my life"; and it need scarcely be added that the book, as in the case of all real masterpieces, represented not merely the time expended on it, but all the accumulated experience of Fielding's very human history.

Yes! Whistler's famous answer to Ruskin's counsel holds good of all imperishable literature. Had he the assurance to ask two hundred guineas for a picture that only took a day to paint? No, replied Whistler, he asked it for "the training of a lifetime"; and it is this training of a lifetime, in addition to the actual time expended on composition, that constitutes the reserve force of all great works of fiction, and is entirely lacking in most modern novels, however superficially brilliant be their workmanship.

For this reason books like George Borrow's *Lavengro* and *Romany Rye*, failures on their publication, grow greater rather than less with the passage of time. Their writers, out of the sheer sincerity of their natures, furnished them, as by magic, with an inexhaustible provision of life-giving "ichor." To quote from Milton, "a good book is the precious life-blood of a master spirit, embalmed and treasured up on purpose to a life beyond life."

Of this immortality principle in literature Milton himself, it need hardly be said, is one of the great exemplars. He was but thirty-two when he first projected *Paradise Lost,* and through all the intervening years of hazardous political industry he had kept the seed warm in his heart, its fruit only to be brought forth with tragic patience in those seven years of blindness and imminent peril of the scaffold which followed his fiftieth birthday.

The case of poets is not irrelevant to our theme, for the conditions of all great literature, whatever its nature, are the same. Therefore, we may recall Dante, whose *Divine Comedy* was with him from his thirty-fifth year till the year of his death, the bitter-sweet companion of twenty years of exile. Goethe, again, finished at eighty the *Faust* he had conceived at twenty.

Spenser was at work on his *Faerie Queene,* alongside his preoccupation with state business, for nearly twenty years. Pope was twelve years translating Homer, and I think there is little doubt that Gray's *Elegy* owes much of its staying power to the Horatian deliberation with which Gray polished and repolished it through eight years.

If we are to believe Poe's *Philosophy of Composition,* and there is, I think, more truth in it than is generally allowed, the vitality of *The Raven*, as that, too, of his genuinely imperishable fictions, is less due to inspiration than to the mathematical painstaking of their composition.

But, perhaps, of all poets, the story of Virgil is most instructive for an age of "get-rich-quick" *littérateurs*. On his *Georgics* alone he worked seven years, and, after working eleven years on the *Æneid*, he was still so dissatisfied with it that on his death-bed he besought his friends to burn it, and on their refusal, commanded his servants to bring the manuscript that he might burn it himself. But, fortunately, Augustus had heard portions of it, and the imperial veto overpowered the poet's infanticidal desire.

But, to return to the novelists, it may at first sight seem that the great writer who, with the Waverley Novels, inaugurated the modern era of cyclonic booms and mammoth sales, was an exception to the classic formula of creation which we are endeavouring to make good. Stevenson, we have been told, used to despair as he thought of Scott's "immense fecundity of invention" and "careless, masterly ease."

"I cannot compete with that," he says——"what makes me sick is to think of Scott turning out *Guy Mannering* in three weeks."

Scott's speed is, indeed, one of the marvels of literary history, yet in his case, perhaps more than in that of any other novelist, it must be remembered that this speed had, in an unusual degree, that "training of a lifetime" to rely upon; as from his earliest boyhood all Scott's faculties had been consciously as well as unconsciously engaged in absorbing and, by the aid of his astonishing memory, preserving the vast materials on which he was able thus carelessly to draw.

Moreover, those who have read his manly autobiography know that this speed was by no means all "ease," as witness the almost tragic composition of *The Bride of Lammermoor*. If ever a writer scorned delights and lived laborious days, it was Walter Scott. At the same time the condition of his fame in the present day bears out the general truth of my contention, for there is little doubt that he would be more widely read than he is were it not for those too frequent *longueurs* and inert paddings which resulted from his too hurried workmanship.

Jane Austen is another example of comparatively rapid creation, writing three of her best-known novels, *Pride and Prejudice*, *Sense and Sensibility*, and *Northanger Abbey* between the ages of twenty-one and twenty-three. Yet *Pride and Prejudice*, which practically survives the others, took her ten months to complete, and all her writings, it has again to be said, had first been deeply and intimately "lived."

Charlotte Brontë was a year in writing *Jane Eyre*, spurred on to new effort by the recent rejection of *The Professor;* but to write such a book in a year cannot be called over-hasty production when one considers how much of *Jane Eyre* was drawn from Charlotte Brontë's own life, and also how she and her sisters had been experimenting with literature from their earliest childhood.

Thackeray considered an allowance of two years sufficient for the writing of a good novel, but that seems little enough when one takes into account the length of his best-known books, not to mention the perfection of their craftsmanship. Dickens, for all the prodigious bulk of his output, was rather a steady than a rapid writer. "He considered," says Forster, "three of his not very large manuscript pages a good, and four an excellent, day's work."

David Copperfield was about a year and nine months in the writing, having been begun in the opening of 1849 and completed in October, 1850. *Bleak House* took a little longer, having been begun in November, 1851, and completed in August, 1853. *Hard Times* was a hasty piece of work, written between the winter of 1853, and the summer of 1854, and it cannot be considered one of Dickens's notable successes.

. George Meredith wrote four of his greatest novels in seven years, *Richard Feverel*, *Evan Harrington*, *Sandra Belloni*, and *Rhoda Fleming* being produced between 1859 and 1866. His poem, *Modern Love*, was also written during that period.

George Eliot was a much-meditating, painstaking writer, though *Adam Bede* cost her little more than a year's work. Her novels, however, as a rule, did not come forth without prayer and fasting, and, in the course of their creation, she used often to suffer from "hopelessness and melancholy." *Romola*, to which she devoted long and studious preparation, she was often on the point of giving up, and in regard to it she gives expression to a literary ideal to which the gentleman with the contract for four novels a year, referred to in the outset of this paper, is probably a stranger.

It may turn out [she says], that I can't work freely and fully enough in the medium I have chosen, and in that case I must give it up; for I will never write anything to which my whole heart, mind, and conscience don't consent; so that I may feel it was something—however small—which wanted to be done in this world, and that I am just the organ for that small bit of work.

Charles Kingsley who, if not a great novelist, has to his credit in *Westward Ho!* one romance at least which, in the old phrase, "the world will not willingly let die," was as conscientious in his work as he was brilliant.

Says a friend who was with him while he was writing *Hypatia:*

"He took extraordinary pains to be accurate. We spent one whole day in searching the four folio volumes of Synesius for a fact he thought was there, and which was found there at last."

The writer of perhaps the greatest historical

novel in the English language, *The Cloister and the Hearth*, was what one might call a glutton for thoroughness. Of himself Charles Reade has said: "I studied the great art of fiction closely for fifteen years before I presumed to write a line. I was a ripe critic before I became an artist." His commonplace books, on the entries in which and the indexing he was accustomed to spend one whole day out of each week, cataloguing the notes of his multifarious reading and pasting in cuttings from newspapers likely to be useful in novel-building, completely filled one of the rooms in his house. In his will he left these open to the inspection of literary students who cared to study the methods which he had found so serviceable.

To name one or two more English novelists: Thomas Hardy's novels would seem to have the slow growth of deep-rooted things. His greatest work, *The Return of the Native*, was on the stocks for four years, though a year seems to have sufficed for *Far from the Madding Crowd*.

The meticulous practice of Stevenson is proverbial, but this glimpse of his method is worth catching again.

The first draft of a story [records Mr. Charles D. Lanier], Stevenson wrote out roughly, or dictated to Lloyd Osbourne. When all the colours were in hand for the complete picture, he invariably penned it himself, with exceeding care. . . . If the first copy did not please him, he patiently made a second or a third draft. In his stern, self-imposed apprenticeship of phrase-making he had prepared himself for these workmanlike methods by the practice of rewriting his trial stories into dramas and then reworking them into stories again.

Nathaniel Hawthorne brought the devoted, one might say, the devotional, spirit of the true artist to all his work, but *The Scarlet Letter* was written at a good pace when once started, though, as usual, the germ had been in Hawthorne's mind for many years. The story of its beginning is one of the many touching anecdotes in that history of authorship which Carlyle compared to the Newgate Calendar. Incidentally, too, it witnesses that an author occasionally meets with a good wife.

One wintry autumn day in Salem, Hawthorne returned home earlier than usual from the custom-house. With pale lips, he said to his wife: "I am turned out of office." To which she—God bless her!—cheerily replied: "Very well! now you can write your book!" and immediately set about lighting his study fire and generally making things comfortable for his work.

The book was *The Scarlet Letter*, and was completed by the following February, Hawthorne, as his wife said, writing "immensely" on it day after day, nine hours a day. When finished, Hawthorne seems to have been dispirited about the story, and put it away in a drawer; but the good James T. Fields chanced soon to call on him, and asked him if he had anything for him to publish.

"Who," asked Hawthorne gloomily, "would risk publishing a book from me, the most unpopular writer in America?"

"I would," was Field's rejoinder, and after some further sparring, Hawthorne owned up.

"As you have found me out," said he, "take what I have written and tell me if it is good for anything"; and Fields went away with the manuscript of what is, without any question, America's greatest novel.

Turning to the great novelists of France, with one or two exceptions, they all bear out the theory of longevity in literature which I have been endeavouring to support. It must reluctantly be confessed that one of the most fascinatingly vital of them all, Alexandre Dumas, is one of the exceptions, born improvisator as he was; yet immense research, it needs hardly be said, went to the making of his enormous library of romance—even though, it be allowed, that much of that work was done for him by his "disciples."

George Sand was another facile, all too facile, writer. Here is a description of her method:

To write novels was to her only a process of nature. She seated herself before her table at ten o'clock, with scarcely a plot and only the slightest acquaintance with her characters, and until five in the evening, while her hand guided a pen, the novel wrote itself. Next day, and the next, it was the same. By and by the novel had written itself in full and another was unfolding.

Whether George Sand is still alive as a novelist, apart from her place as an historic personality, I leave others to decide; but I am very sure that she would be read a great deal more than she is if she had not so confidently left her novels—to write themselves. Different, indeed, was the method of Balzac, toiling year after year at his colossal task of *The Human Comedy*, sometimes working eighteen hours a day, and never less than twelve, and that "in the midst of protested bills, business annoyances, the most cruel financial straits, in utter solitude and lack of all consolation." But then Balzac was sustained by one of those great dreams, without whose aid no lasting literature is produced, the dream, "by infinite patience and courage, to compose for the France of the nineteenth century, that history of morals which the old civilizations of Rome, Athens, Memphis, and India have left untold."

To fulfil this he was able to live, for a long period, on a daily expenditure of "three sous for bread, two for milk, and three for firing." But doubtless it had been different if his dream had been prize puppies, a garage full of motor-cars, or a translation into the Four Hundred.

Victor Hugo, again, was one of the herculean artists, working, in Emerson's phrase, "in a sad sincerity," with the patience of an ant and the energy of a volcano. Of his *Les Misérables*—perhaps the greatest novel ever written, as it is, I suppose, easily the longest—he said, "it takes me nearly as long to publish a book as to write one"; and he was at work on *Les Misérables*, off and on, for nearly fifteen years. Of his writing *Notre Dame* (that other colossus of fiction) this quaint picture has been preserved. He had made vast historical preparations for it, but ever there seemed still more to make, till at length his publisher grew impatient, and under his pressure Hugo at last made a start—after this fashion:

He purchased a great grey woollen wrapper that covered him from head to foot, he locked up all his clothes lest he should be tempted to go out, and, carrying off his ink-bottle to his study, applied himself to his labour just as if he had been in prison. He never left the table except for food and sleep, and the sole recreation that he allowed himself was an hour's chat after dinner with M. Pierre Leroux, or any other friend who might drop in, and to whom he would occasionally read over his day's work.

Daudet, whose *Tartarin* bids fair to remain one of the world's types, like *Don Quixote* or *Mr. Micawber*, for all his natural Provençal gift of improvisation and, indeed, from his self-recognized necessity of keeping it in check, was another strenuous artist. He wrote each manuscript three times over, he told his biographer, and would write it as many more if he could; and his son, in writing of him, has this truth to say of his, as of all living work:

The fact is that labour does not begin at the moment when the artist takes his pen. It begins in sustained reflection and in the thought which accumulates images and sifts them, garners and winnows them out, and compels life to keep control over imagination, and imagination to expand and enlarge life.

Zola is perhaps unduly depreciated nowadays, but certainly, if Carlyle's "infinite capacity for taking pains" as a recipe for genius ever was put to the test, it was by the author of the Rougon-Macquart series. Talking of rewriting, Prosper Mérimée, best known for *Carmen*, is said to have rewritten his *Colomba* no less than sixteen times; as our Anglo-Saxon Kipling, it used to be told, wrote his short stories seven times over.

But, of course, the classical example of the artist-fanatic in modern times was Gustave Flaubert. His agonies in quest of the *mot propre*, the one and only word, are proverbial, and are said literally to have broken down his nerves. Mr. Huneker has told of him that "he would annotate three hundred volumes for a page of facts. . . . In twenty pages he sometimes saved three or four from destruction," and, in the course of twenty-six years' polishing and pruning of *The Temptation of Saint Anthony*, he reduced his original manuscript of 540 pages down to 136, even reducing it still further after its first publication.

On *Madame Bovary* he worked six years, and in writing *Salâmmbo*, which took him no less time, he studied the scenery on the spot and exhausted the resources of the Imperial Library in his search for documentary evidences.

Flaubert may be said to have carried his passion for perfection to the point of mania, and it will be a question with some whether, with all his pains, he can be called a great novelist, after all.   But that he was a great stylist and a master in the art of making terrible and beautiful bas-reliefs admits of no doubt.

To be a great world-novelist you need an all-embracing humanity as well, such as we find in Tolstoy's *War and Peace*—but that great book, need one say, came of no slipshod speed of improvisation.   On the contrary, Tolstoy corrected and recorrected it so often that his wife, who acted as his amanuensis, is said to have copied the whole enormous manuscript no less than seven times!

Yes! though it be doubtless true, in Mr. Kipling's famous phrase, that

> There are nine and sixty ways
> Of inditing tribal lays,
> And every blessed one of them is right,

I think that the whole nine and sixty of them include somewhere in their method those sole preservative virtues of truth to life and passionate artistic integrity.   The longest-lived books, whatever their nature, have usually been the longest growing; and even those lasting things of literature that have seemed, as it were, to spring up in a night, have been long in secret preparation in a soil mysteriously enriched and refined by the hid processes of time.

XXVII

THE MAN BEHIND THE PEN

BULWER'S deservedly famous phrase, "The pen is mightier than the sword," beneath its surface application, if you think it over, has this further suggestion to make to the believer in literature—that, as the sword is of no value as a weapon apart from the man that wields it, so, and no less so, is it with the pen. A mere pen, a mere sword— of what use are they, save as mural decorations, without a man behind them?

And that recalls a memory of mine, which, as both great men are now drinking wine in Valhalla out of the skulls of their critics, there can be no harm in recalling.

Some years ago I was on an unforgettable visit to Björnson, at his country home of Aulestad, near Lillehammer. This is not the moment to relive that beautiful memory as a whole. All that is pertinent to my present purpose is a remark in regard to Ibsen that Björnson flashed out one day, shaking his great white mane with earnestness, his noble face alight with the spirit of battle. We had been talking of his possibly too successful

340

attempt to sever Norway from Sweden, and Ibsen came in somehow incidentally.

"Ibsen," said he, "is not a man. He is only a pen."

There is no necessity to discuss the justice of the dictum. Probably, if ever there was a man behind a pen, it was Ibsen; but Ibsen's manhood concentrated itself entirely behind his pen, whereas Björnson's employed other weapons also, such as his gift of oratory, and was generally more dramatically in evidence. Björnson and Ibsen, as we know, did not agree on a number of things. Thus Björnson, like a human being, was unjust. But his phrase was a useful one, and I am using it. It was misapplied to Ibsen; but, put in the form of a question, I know of no better single test to apply to writers, dead or alive, than—

"Is this a man? Or is it only a pen?"

Said Walt Whitman, in his familiar "So Long" to *Leaves of Grass:*

> Camerado, this is no book;
> Who touches this touches a man.

And, of course, Walt was right about his own book, whether you like the man behind *Leaves of Grass* or not; but also that assertion of his might be chalked as a sort of customs "O. K." on all literary baggage whatsoever that has passed free into immortality. There is positively no writer that has withstood the searching examination of time, on whose book that final stamp of literary reality may not be placed. On every classic, Time has scrawled ineffaceably:

> This is no book;
> Who touches this touches a man.

I raise the question of reality in literature in no merely academic spirit. For those who not only love books, but care for literature as a living thing, the question is a particularly live issue at the present time, when not only the quantity of writing is so enormous, but the average quality of it is so astonishingly good, when technique that would almost humble the masters, and would certainly dazzle them, is an accomplishment all but commonplace. At any rate, it is so usual as to create no special surprise. If people write at all, it is taken for granted, nowadays, that they write well. And the number of people at the present time writing not only well, but wonderfully well, is little short of appalling.

In this, for those who ponder the phenomena of literature, there is less matter for congratulation than would seem likely at first sight. There is, indeed, no little bewilderment, and some disquietude. Confronted with short stories—and novels also, for that matter—told with a skill which makes the old masters of fiction look like clumsy amateurs; confronted, too, with a thousand poets— the number is scarcely an exaggeration—with accomplishments of metre and style that make some famous singers seem like clodhoppers of the muse, one is obliged to ask oneself:

"Are these brilliant writers really greater than those that went before?"

If for some reason, felt at first rather than defined, we answer "no," we are forced to the conclusion that, after all, literature must be something more than a mere matter of writing. If so, we are constrained to ask ourselves, what is it?

The men who deal with manuscripts—editors, publishers' readers, and publishers, men not only expert witnesses in regard to the printed literature of the day, but also curiously learned in the story of the book unborn, the vast mass of writing that never arrives at print—are even more impressed by what one might call the uncanny literary brilliance of the time. They are also puzzled by the lack of a certain something missing in work which otherwise possesses every nameable quality of literary excellence. One of these, an editor with an eye as sympathetic as it is keen, told me of an instance to the point, typical of a hundred others.

He had been unusually struck by a story sent in to him by an unknown writer. It was, he told me, amazing from every purely literary point of view— plot, characterization, colour, and economy of language. It had so much that it seemed strange that anything at all should be lacking. He sent for the writer, and told him just what he thought.

"But," he ended, after praise such as an editor seldom risks, "there is something the matter with it, after all. I wonder if you can tell me what it is."

The writer was, for a writer so flattered, strangely modest. All he could say, he answered, was that he had done his best. The editor, agreeing that he certainly seemed to have done that, was all the more curious to find out how it was that a man who could do so well had not been able to add to his achievement the final "something" that was missing.

"What puzzles me," said the editor finally, "is that, with all the rest, you were not able to add—humanity. Your story seems to have been written by a wonderful literary machine, instead of by a man."

And, no doubt, the young story-writer went away sorrowful, in spite of the acceptance of his story—which, after all, was only lacking in that quality which you will find lacking in all the writing of the day, save in that by one or two exceptional writers, who, by their isolation, the more forcibly point the moral.

A wonderful literary machine! The editor's phrase very nearly hits off the situation. As we have the linotype to set up the written words with a minimum of human agency, we really seem to be within measurable distance of a similar automaton that will produce the literature to be set up without the intrusion of any flesh-and-blood author. In this connection I may perhaps be permitted to quote a sentence or two from myself, written *à propos* a certain chameleonesque writer whose deservedly popular works are among the contemporary books that I most value:

A peculiar skill seems to have been developed among writers during the last twenty years—that of writing in the manner of some master, not merely with mimetic cleverness, but with genuine creative power. We have poets who write so like Wordsworth and Milton that one can hardly differentiate them from their masters; and yet—for this is my point—they are no mere imitators, but original poets, choosing, it would seem, some old mask of immortality through which to express themselves. In a different way from that of Guy de Maupassant they have chosen to suppress themselves, or rather, I should say, that, whereas De Maupassant strove to suppress, to eliminate, himself, their method is that of disguise.

In some respects they remind one of the hermit-crab, who annexes some beautiful ready-made house, instead of making one for himself. But then they annex it so brilliantly, with such delightful consequences for the reader, that not only is there no ground for complaint, but the reader almost forgets that the house does not really belong to them, and that they are merely entertaining tenants on a short lease.

It is not that one is not grateful to writers of this type. Indeed one is. They not only provide us with genuine entertainment, but, by the skill born of their fine culture, they make us re-taste of the old masters in their brilliant variations. One has no complaint against them. Far from it. Only one wonders why they trouble to attach their own merely personal names to their volumes, for, so far as those volumes are concerned, there is no one to be found in them answering to the name of the ostensible author.

Suppose, for example, that the author's name on the title-page is "Brown." Well, so far as we can find out by reading, "Brown" might just as well be "Green." In fact, there is no "Brown" discoverable—no individual man behind the pen that wrote, not out of the fulness of the heart, or the originality of the brain, from any experience or knowledge or temperament peculiar to "Brown," but out of the fulness of what one might call a creatively assimilated education, and by the aid of a special talent for the combination of literary influences.

We have had a great deal of pleasure in the reading, we have admired this and that, we may even have been astonished, but I repeat—there is no "Brown." In private life "Brown" may be a forceful and fascinating personality, but, so far as literature is concerned, he is merely a "wonderful literary machine." He has been able, by his remarkable skill, to conjure every other writer into his book—except himself. The name "Brown" on his title-page means nothing. He has not "made his name."

The phrase "to make a name" has become

so dulled with long usage that it is worth while to pause and consider what a reality it stands for. What it really means, of course, is that certain men and women, by the personal force or quality of their lives, have succeeded in charging their names —names given them originally haphazard, as names are given to all of us—with a permanent significance as unmistakable as that belonging to the commonest noun. The name "Byron" has a meaning as clear and unmistakable as the word "mutton." The words "dog" and "cat" have a meaning hardly more clearly defined than the name "Burns" or "Voltaire." An oak-tree can no more be mistaken for a willow than Shakespeare can be confused with Spenser. If we say "Coleridge," there is no possibility of any one thinking that perhaps we meant "Browning."

The reason, of course, is that these names are as unmistakably "made" as a Krupp gun or a Sheffield razor. Sincere, intense life has passed into them, life lived as the men who bore those names either chose, or were forced, to live it; individual experience, stern or gentle, in combination with an individual gift of expression.

All names that are really "made" are made in the same way. You may make a name as Napoleon made his, through war, or you may make it as Keats made his, by listening to the nightingale and worshipping the moon. Or you may make it as Charles Lamb made his, merely by loving old

folios, whist, and roast pig.   All that is necessary—
granted, of course, the gift of literary expression—
is sincerity, an unshakable faithfulness to yourself.

In really great writers—or, at all events, in
those writings of theirs by which they immortally
exist—there is not one insincere word.   The perishable parts of great writers will, without exception,
be found to be those writings which they attempted
either in insincere moments, or at the instigation of
some surface talent that had no real connection
with their deep-down selves.

All real writing has got to be lived before it is
written—lived not only once or twice, but lived
over and over again.   Mere reporting won't do in
literature, nor the records of easy voyaging
through perilous seas.   Dante had to walk through
hell before he could write of it, and men today
who would write either of hell or of heaven will
never do it by a study of fashionable drawing-
rooms, or prolonged sojourns in the country houses
of the great.

On the other hand, if you wish to write convincingly about what we call "society," those
lords and ladies, for example, who are just as real
in their strange way as coal-heavers and mechanics,
it is of no use your trying, unless you were fortunate enough to be born among them, or have been
unfortunately associated with them all your life.
To write with reality about the most artificial
condition necessitates an intimate acquaintance
with it that, at its best, is tragic.   Those who

would write about the depths and the heights must have dared them, not merely as visitors, but as awestricken inhabitants. Similarly, those who would write about the plain, the long, low levels of commonplace human life, must have dwelt in them, have possessed the dreary, unlaurelled courage of the good bourgeois, have known what it is to live out the day just for the day's sake, with the blessed hope of a reasonably respectable and comfortable conclusion.

Probably it seldom occurs to us to think what a tremendously rooted life is needed to make even one lasting lyric, though the strangeness of the process is but the same strangeness that accompanies the antecedent preparation of a flower.

> How many suns it takes
> To make one speedwell blue—

was no mere fancy of a poet. It is a fact of the long sifting and kneading to which time subjects the material of its perfect things.

One could not get a better example of what I mean than Lovelace's song *To Lucasta, Going to the Wars*, without which no anthology of English verse could possibly be published. Why does generation after generation say over and over, and hand on to its children:

> Yet this inconstancy is such
>   As you too shall adore;
> I could not love thee, dear, so much
>   Loved I not honour more.

Is it merely because it is so well written, or because it embodies a highly moral sentiment suitable to the education of young men?   No, it is because the sword and the pen for once met together in the hand of a man, because a soldier and a lover and a poet met together in a song.   One might almost say that Lovelace wrote his lyric first with his sword, and merely copied it out with his pen.   At all events, he was first a man and incidentally a poet; and every real poet that ever sang, whether or not he wielded the weapons of physical warfare, has been just the same.   Otherwise he could not have been a poet.

When one speaks of the man behind the pen, one does not necessarily mean that the writer must be a man of dominant personality, suggestive in every sentence of "the strenuous life," and muscle, and "punch."   Literature might be described as the world in words, and as it takes all kinds of men to make a world, so with the world of literature.   All we ask is that we should be made aware of some kind of a man.   Numerous other qualities besides "the punch" go to the making of living literature, though blood and brawn, not to say brutality, have of late had it so much their own way in the fashionable literature of the day— written by muscular literary gentlemen who seem to write rather with their fists than their pens— that we are in danger of forgetting the reassuring truth.

J. M. Barrie long ago made a criticism on

Rudyard Kipling which has always stayed by me as one of the most useful of critical touchstones.

"Mr. Kipling," said he, "has yet to learn that a man may know more of life staying at home by his mother's knee than swaggering in bad company over three continents."

Nor is successful literature necessarily the record of the successful temperament. Some writers, not a few, owe their significance to the fact that they have found humanly intimate expression for their own failure, or set down their weakness in such a way as to make themselves the consoling companions of human frailty and disappointment through the generations. It is the paradox of such natures that they should express themselves in the very record of their frustration. Amiel may be taken as the type of such writers. In confiding to his *Journal* his hopeless inability for expressing his high thought, he expressed what is infinitely more valuable to us—himself.

Nor, again, does it follow that the man who thus gets himself individualized in literature is the kind of man we care about or approve of. Often it is quite the contrary, and we may think that it had been just as well if some human types had not been able so forcibly to project into literature their unworthy and undesirable selves. Yet this is God's world, and nothing human must be foreign to the philosophical student of it.

All the "specimens" in a natural history museum are not things of beauty or joy. So it is in the

world of books.   François Villon cannot be called
an edifying specimen of the human family, yet he
unmistakably belongs there, and it was to that
prince of scalawags that we owe not merely
that loveliest sigh in literature— "Where are the
snows of yester-year?"—but so striking a picture
of the underworld of medieval Paris that without
it we should hardly be able to know the times as
they were.

The same applies to Benvenuto Cellini—bully,
assassin, insufferable egoist, and so forth, as well
as artist.   If he had not been sufficiently in love
with his own swashbuckler rascality to write his
amazing autobiography, how dim to our imaginations, comparatively, would have been the world
of the Italian Renaissance!

Again, in our own day, take Baudelaire, a
personality even less agreeable still—morbid, dis-
eased, if you will, wasting, you may deem, immense
poetic powers on revealing the beauty of those
"flowers of evil" which had as well been left in
their native shade.   Yet, it is because he saw
them so vividly, cared to see little else, dwelt in
his own strange corner of the world with such an
intensity of experience, that he is—Baudelaire.
Like him or not, his name is "made."   A queer
kind of man, indeed, but not "only a pen."

Certain writers have made a cult of "imperson-
ality" in literature.   They would do their utmost
to keep themselves out of sight, to let their subject-
matter tell its own tale.   But such a feat is an

impossibility. They might as well try to get out of their own skins. The mere effort at suppression ends in a form of revelation. Their mere choice of themes and manner of presentation, let them keep behind the scenes as assiduously as they may, will in the end stamp them. However much a man may hide behind his pen, so that indeed his personality, compared with that of more subjective writers, remains always somewhat enigmatic, yet when the pen is wielded by a man, whatever his reticence or his mask, we know that a man is there—and that is all that concerns us.

On the other hand, of course, there are companionable, sympathetic writers whose whole stock-in-trade is themselves, their personal charm, their personal way of looking at things. Of these, Montaigne and Charles Lamb are among the great examples. It matters to us little or nothing what they are writing about; for their subjects, so far as they are concerned, are only important in relation to themselves, as revealing to us by reflection two uncommonly "human" human beings, whom it is impossible to mistake for any one else; just as we enjoy the society of some whimsical talker among our living friends, valuing him not so much for what he says, but for the way he says it, and because it is he, and no one else, that is talking.

Again, there are other men whose names, in addition to their personal suggestion, have an impersonal significance as marking new eras

23

of human development, such as Erasmus or Rousseau or Darwin; men who embodied the time-spirit at crucial moments of world change, men who announced rather than created, the heralds of epochs, men who first took the new roads along which the rest of mankind were presently to travel, men who felt or saw something new for the first time, prophets of dawn while yet their fellows slept.

Sometimes a man will come to stand for a whole nation, like Robert Burns or Cervantes; or a great, half-legendary age of the world, like Homer; or some permanent attitude of the human spirit, like Plato.

No fixed star, great or small, in the firmament of literature ever got there without some vital reason, or merely by writing, however remarkable. The idea that literature is a mere matter of writing is seen to be the hollowest of misconceptions the moment you run over any list of enduring names. Try any such that you can think of, and in every case you will find that the name stands for something more than a writer. Of course, the man had to have his own peculiar genius for writing, but the peculiarity was but the result of his individual being, his own special way of living his life or viewing the world.

Take Horace, for example. Does he live merely because of his unique style, his masterly use of the Latin tongue? By means of that, of course, but only secondarily. Primarily, he is as alive today as he was when he sauntered through the streets of Rome, because he was so absolutely the type of the well-bred man of the world in all countries and times. He lived seriously in the social world as he found it, and felt no idealistic craving to have it remoulded nearer to the heart's desire. He was satisfied with its pleasures, and at one with its philosophy. Thus he is as much at home in modern Paris or London or New York as in ancient Rome, and his book is, therefore, forever immortal as the man of the world's Bible.

Take a name so different as that of Shelley. We have but to speak it to define all it now stands for. Though no one should read a line of Shelley's any more, the dream he dreamed has passed into the very life-blood of mankind. Wherever men strive for freedom, or seek to attune their lives to the strange spiritual music that breathes through all things—music that none ever heard more clearly than he—there is Shelley like the morning star to guide them and inspire.

Think what Wordsworth means to the spiritual thought of the modern world. In his own day he was one of the most lonely and laughed at of poets, moping among his lakes and mountains and shepherds. Yet, as Matthew Arnold said, "we are all Wordsworthians nowadays," and the religion of nature that he found there for himself in his solitude bids fair to be the final religion of the modern world.

It is the same with every other great name one

can think of, be it Bunyan or Heine, Schopenhauer or Izaak Walton. One has but to cast one's eyes over one's shelves to realize, as we see the familiar names, how literally the books that bear them are living men, merely transmigrated from their fleshly forms into the printed word. Shakespeare and Milton, yes, even Pope; Johnson, Fielding, Sterne, Scott, Dickens, Thackeray, Carlyle, Dumas, Balzac, Emerson, Thoreau, Hawthorne, Poe—their very faces seem to look out at us from the bindings, such vividly human beings were they, with a vision of the world, or a definition of character, so much their own and no one else's. One might almost call them patented human beings—patentees of spiritual discoveries, or of aspects of humanity, whose patents can never be infringed for all our cleverness.

Said Tennyson, in bitter answer to criticism that began to depreciate him because of the glibness of his imitators:

> All can grow the flower now,
> For all have got the seed.

And certainly, as I have already said, the art of literary impersonation is carried to a pitch today that almost amounts to genius. Yet you have only to compare the real flower with the imitation, and you will soon understand the difference.

Take Walter Scott. It is a commonplace to say how much better we do the historical novel nowadays than he did. At first sight, we may seem to; in certain technical particulars, no doubt we do; but read him again, read *Rob Roy* or *Quentin Durward* again, and you will not be quite so sure. You will realize what an immortal difference there is, after all, between the pen with a man behind it, and the most brilliant literary machine.

Yes, "the mob of gentlemen that write with ease" is once more with us, but no real book was ever yet written with ease, and no book has ever survived, or ever can, in which we do not feel the presence of the fighting, dreaming, or merely enjoying soul of a man.

XXVIII

BULLS IN CHINA-SHOPS

THERE are some people of great value and importance in their own spheres, who, on the strength of the distinction gained there, are apt to intrude on other spheres of which they have no knowledge, where in fact they are irrelevant, and often indeed ridiculously out of place. This, however, does not prevent their trying to assert an authority gained in their own sphere in those other spheres where they simply do not belong; and such is the power of a name that is won for any one thing that the multitude, unaccustomed to make distinctions, accepts them as authorities on the hundred other things of which they know nothing.

Thus, to take a crude example, the New York Police, which is, without doubt, learned in its own world, and well-adapted and equipped for asserting its authority there, sometimes intrudes, with its well-known *bonhomie*, into the worlds of drama and sculpture, and, because it is an acknowledged judge of crooks and grafters, presumes to be a judge and censor also of new plays and nude statues.

358

Of course, the New York Police is absurd in such a character, absurd as a bull in a china-shop is absurd; yet, as in the case of the bull with the china, it is capable of doing quite a lot of damage.

I take the New York Police merely, as I said, as a crude example of, doubtless, well-meant, but entirely misplaced energy. Actually, however, it is scarcely more absurd than many similar, if more distinguished, bulls gaily crashing about on higher planes.

Such are statesmen who, because they are Prime Ministers or Presidents, deem themselves authorities on everything within the four winds, doctors of divinity, and general *arbitri elegantiarum.*

Such a bull in a china-shop in regard to literature was the late Mr. Gladstone. It is no disrespect towards his great and estimable character to say, that while, of course, he was technically a scholar— "great Homeric scholar" was the accepted phrase for him—there were probably few men in England so devoid of the literary sense. Yet for an author to receive a post-card of commendation from Mr. Gladstone meant at least the sale of an edition or two, and a certain permanency in public appreciation. Her late Gracious Majesty Queen Victoria was Mr. Gladstone's only rival as the literary destiny of the time. To Mr. Gladstone we owe Mrs. Humphry Ward, to Her Majesty we owe Miss Marie Corelli.

John Ruskin, much as we may admire him for his moral influence, and admire, or not admire, him for his prose, was a bull in a china-shop when he made his famous criticism on Whistler, and thus inadvertantly added to the gaiety of nations by provoking that delightful trial, which, farcical as it seemed at the moment, not merely evoked from Whistler himself some imperishable dicta on art and the relation of critics to art, but really did something towards the long-drawn awakening of that mysterious somnolence called the public consciousness on the strange mission of beauty in this world, and, incidentally of the status of those "eccentric" ministers of it called artists.

I do not mean to say that bulls in china-shops are without their uses. John Ruskin is a shining example to the contrary.

One of his contemporaries, Thomas Carlyle, for all his genius, was on one important subject— that of poetry—as much of a bull in a china-shop as Ruskin was in art. Great friends as were he and Tennyson, the famous anecdote *à propos* of Tennyson's publication of *The Idylls of the King*— "all very fine, Alfred, but when are you going to do some work"—and many other such written deliverances suffice to show how absolutely out of court a great tragic humorist and rhetorician may be on an art practised by writers at least as valuable to English literature as himself, say Wordsworth, Shelley, Coleridge, and Keats. Carlyle was a great writer, but the names of these four gentlemen who, according to his standard, never did any "work" have a strangely permanent look about them compared with that of the prophet-journalist of Chelsea and Ecclefechan.

A similar "sage," another of the great conversational brow-beaters of English literature, Samuel Johnson, though it was his chief business to be a critic of poetry, was hardly more in court on the matter than Carlyle. In fact, Dr. Johnson might with truth be described as the King Bull of all the Bulls of all the China-shops. There was no subject, however remote from his knowledge or experience on which he would hesitate to pronounce, and if necessary bludgeon forth, his opinion. But in his case, there is one important distinction to be made, a distinction that has made him immortal.

He disported his huge bulk about the china-shop with such quaintness, with such engaging sturdiness of character, strangely displaying all the time so unique a wisdom of that world that lies outside and encloses all china-shops, so unparalleled a genius of common sense, oddly linked with that good old-time quality called "the fear of God," that in his case we felt that the china, after all, didn't matter, but that Dr. Samuel Johnson, "the great lexicographer," supremely did. His opinions of Scotsmen or his opinions of poetry in themselves amount to little—though they are far from being without their shrewd insight—and much of the china—such as Milton's poetry— among which he gambolled, after the manner of

Behemoth, chanced to be indestructible. Any
china he broke was all to the ultimate good of the
china-shop. Yet, if we accept him so, is it not
because he was such a wonderful bull in the china-
shop of the world?

There have been other such bulls but hardly
another so great, and with his name I will, for the
moment at least, put personalities aside, and refer
to droves rather than to individual bulls. A familiar type of the bull in the china-shop is the modern
clergyman, who, apparently, insecure in his
status of saint-hood, dissatisfied with that spiritual
sphere which so many confiding human beings
have given into his keeping, will be forever pushing
his way like an unwelcome, yet quite unauthori-
tative, policeman, into that turmoil of human
affairs—of which politics is a sort of summary—
where his opinion is not of the smallest value,
though, perforce, it is received with a certain
momentary respect—as though some beautiful
old lady should stroll up to a battery of artillery,
engaged in some difficult and dangerous attack,
and offer her advice as to the sighting and management of the guns. The modern clergyman's
interference in the working out of the secular
problems of modern life has no such picturesque
beauty—and it is even less effective.

One would have thought that to have the care of
men's souls would be enough. What a world of
suggestiveness there was in the old phrase "a cure
of souls"! Men's souls need saving as much to-

day as ever. Perhaps they were never in greater danger. Therefore, as the proverbial place for the cobbler is his last, so more than ever the place for the clergyman is his church, his pulpit, and those various spiritual offices for which he is presumably "chosen." His vows do not call upon him either to be a politician or a matinée idol, nor is it his business to sow doubt where he is paid for preaching faith. If the Church is losing its influence, it is largely because of its inefficient interference in secular affairs, and because of the small percentage of real spirituality amongst its clergy.

But there is a worse intrusion than that of clergymen into secular affairs. There is the intrusion of the cheap atheist, the small materialistic thinker, into a sphere of which certainly no clergyman or priest has any monopoly, that sphere of what we call the spiritual life, which, however undemonstrable by physical tests, has been real to so many men and women whose intellects can hardly be called negligible, from Plato to Newman. I have too much respect for their courageous sincerity, their nobility of character, as well as for the necessary, if superficial, destructive work they did, when to do such work meant no little personal peril and obloquy to themselves, to class Robert Ingersoll and Charles Bradlaugh with the small fry that resemble them merely in their imitative negations; yet this is certainly true of both of them that they were bulls in the china-shop to this extent—that they confounded real religion

with the defective historical evidences of one religion, and the mythologic assertions and incongrui-
ties of its sacred book.   They did splendid work
in their iconoclastic criticim of "the letter" that
"killeth," but of "the spirit" that "giveth life"
they seem to have had but little inkling. To make
fun of Jonah and the whale, or "the Mistakes of
Moses," had no doubt a certain usefulness, but it
was no valid argument against the existence of
God, nor did it explain away the mysterious
religious sense in man—however, or wherever
expressed. Neither Ingersoll nor Bradlaugh saw
that the crudest Mumbo-Jumbo idolatry of the
savage does really stand for some point of rap-
port between the seen and the unseen, and that,
so long as the mysterious sacredness of life is
acknowledged and reverenced, it matters little
by what symbols we acknowledge it and do it
reverence.

One may consider that the present age is an
age of spiritual eclipse, though that is not the
writer's opinion, and question with Matthew
Arnold:

> What girl
> Now reads in her bosom as clear
> As Rebekah read, when she sate
> At eve by the palm-shaded well?
> Who guards in her breast
> As deep, as pellucid a spring
> Of feeling, as tranquil, as sure?

What bard,
At the height of his vision, can deem
Of God, of the world, of the soul,
With a plainness as near,
As flashing as Moses felt
When he lay in the night by his flock
On the starlit Arabian waste?
Can rise and obey
The beck of the Spirit like him.

Yet the sight of one who sees is worth more than the blindness of a hundred that cannot see. Some people are born with spiritual antennæ and some without. There is much delicate wonder in the universe that needs special organizations for its apprehension. "One eye," you remember, that of Browning's *Sordello*—

one eye
In all Verona cared for the soft sky.

In these imponderable and invisible matters, many are in a like case with Hamlet's mother, when she was unable to see the ghost of his father which he so plainly saw. "Yet all there is I see!" exclaimed the queen—though she was quite wrong, as wrong as Mr. Ruskin when he could see nothing in that painting of Whistler's but a cockscomb throwing a paint-pot at a canvas and calling it a picture!

Many people who have sharp enough eyes and ears for their own worlds are absolutely blind and

deaf when introduced into other worlds for which
nature has not equipped them. But this by no
means prevents their pronouncing authoritative
opinions in those worlds, opinions which would be
amazing if they were not so impertinent. Many
literary people proclaim their indifference to and
even contempt for music—as if their announcement
meant anything more than their music deafness,
their unfortunate exclusion from a great art.
Mark Twain used to advertise his preference for
the pianola over the piano—as if that proved
anything against the playing of Paderewski.
Similarly, he acted the bull in the china-shop in
regard to Christian Science, which cannot be the
accepted creed of millions of men and women
of intelligence and social value without deserv-
ing even in a critic the approach of some
respect.

But humorists are privileged persons. That,
no doubt, accounts for the astonishing toleration
of Bernard Shaw. Were it not that he is a *far-
ceur*, born to write knock-about comedies—his
plays, by the way, might be termed knock-about
comedies of the middle-class mind—he would
never have got a hearing for his common-place
blasphemies, and cheap intellectual antics. He
is undeniably "funny," so we cannot help laughing, though we are often ashamed of ourselves for
our laughter; for to him there is nothing sacred—
except his press-notices, and—his royalties.

His so-called "philosophy" has an air of danger-.

ous novelty only to those innocent middle-classes born but yesterday, to whom any form of thought is a novelty. Methusaleh himself was not older than Mr. Shaw's "original ideas." In England, twenty years ago, we were long since weary óf his egotistic buffooneries. Of anything "fine" in literature or art he is contemptuously ignorant, and from understanding of any of the finer shades of human life, or of the meaning of such words as "honour," "gentleman," "beauty," "religion," he is by nature utterly shut out. He laughs and sneers to make up for his deficiencies, like that Pietro Aretino who threw his perishable mud at Michael Angelo. So is it always with the vulgarian out of his sphere. Once he dared to talk vulgarly of God to a great man who believed in God—Count Tolstoi.

He had written to Tolstoi *à propos* his insignificant little play *The Showing up of Blanco Posnet*, and in the course of his letter had said: "Suppose the world were only one of God's jokes, would you work any less to make it a good joke instead of a bad one?" Tolstoi had hitherto been favourably inclined towards Shaw, owing to his friend and biographer Mr. Aylmer Maude; but this cheapjack sacrilege was too much for the great old man, who seemed to know God with almost Matthew Arnold's

> plainness as near
> As flashing as Moses felt,

and he closed the correspondence with a rebuke which would have abashed any one but the man to whom it was sent.

Tolstoi was like Walt Whitman—he "argued not concerning God." It is a point of view which people like Mr. Shaw can never understand; any more than he or his like can comprehend that there are areas of human feeling over which for him and other such bulls in china-shops should be posted the delicate Americanism—KEEP OUT.

XXIX

THE BIBLE AND THE BUTTERFLY

ONCE, in my old book-hunting days, I picked up, on the Quai Voltaire, a copy of the *Proverbs of King Solomon.* Then it was more possible than today to make finds in that quaint open-air library which, still more than any library housed within governmental or diplomaed walls, is haunted by the spirit of those passionate, dream-led scholars that made the Renaissance, and crowded to those lectures filled with that dangerous new charm which always belongs to the poetic presentation of new knowledge—those lectures, "musical as is Apollo's lute," being given up on the hill nearby, by a romantic young priest named Abelard.

My copy of the Great King's Wisdom was of no particular bibliographical value, but it was one of those thick-set, old-calf duodecimos "black with tarnished gold" which Austin Dobson has sung, books that, one imagines, must have once made even the Latin Grammar attractive. The text was the Vulgate, a rivulet of Latin text surrounded by meadows of marginal comments of the Fathers

24   369

translated into French,—the whole presided over, for the edification of the young novice, to whom my copy evidently belonged, by a distinguished Monseigneur who, in French of the time of Bossuet, told exactly how these young minds should understand the wisdom of Solomon, told it with a magisterial style which suggested that Solomon lived long ago—and, yet, was one of the pillars of the church.   But what particularly interested me about the book, however, as I turned over its yellow pages, was a tiny thing pressed between them, a thing the Fathers and the Monseigneur would surely have regarded as curiously alien to their wisdom, a thing once of a bright, but now of a paler yellow, and of a frailer texture than it had once been in its sunlit life—a flower, I thought at first, but, on looking closer, I saw it was, or had once been, a yellow butterfly.

What young priest was it, I wondered, that had thus, with a breaking heart, crushed the joy of life between these pages! On what spring morning had this silent little messenger hovered a while over the high garden-walls of St. Sulpice, flitting and fluttering, and at last darted and alighted on the page of this old book, at that moment held in the hands of a young priest walking to and fro amid the tall whispering trees— delivering at last to him on the two small painted pages of its wings a message he must not read. . . .

The temptation was severe, for spring was calling all over Paris, and the words of another book of the Great King whose wisdom he held in his hand said to him in the Latin that came easily to all manner of men in those days: *Lo! the winter is past, the rain is over and gone; the flowers appear on the earth; the time of the singing of birds is come, and the voice of the turtle is heard in our land. . . . Arise, my love, my fair one, and come away.*

The little fluttering thing seemed to be saying that to him as it poised on the page, and, as his eyes went into a dream, began to crawl softly, like a rope-walker, up one of his fingers, with a frail, half-frightened hold, while, high up, over the walls of the garden the poplars were discreetly swaying to the southern wind, and the lilac-bushes were carelessly tossing this way and that their fragrance, as altar-boys swing their censers in the hushed chancel,—but ah! so different an incense.

The flowers appear on the earth, he repeated to himself, beguiled for a moment, *the flowers appear on the earth; and the time of the singing of birds is come. . . .*

But, suddenly, for his help against that tiny yellow butterfly there came to him other stern everlasting words:

The grass withereth, the flower fadeth, but the word of our Lord endureth forever.

Then it was, if I imagine aright from my old book, that my young novice of St. Sulpice crushed the joy of life, in the frail form of its little messenger, between the pages of the book he held in his hand just then, the book I held in my hand for a while a hundred and fifty years or so after—the book I bought that morning on the Quai Voltaire—guarding that little dead butterfly even more than the wisdom of Solomon. I wonder if, as he crushed that butterfly, he said to himself—in words that have grown commonplace since his time—the words of that strange emperor Hadrian—*Animula, vagula, blandula!*

Perhaps I should not have remembered that book-hunting morning in Old Paris on the Quai Voltaire, when I bought that beautiful old copy of the *Proverbs of Solomon*—with the butterfly so strangely crushed between its pages—had it not been for a circumstance that happened to me, the other day, in the subway, which seemed to me of the nature of a marvel. Many weary men and women were travelling—in an enforced, yet in some way humorously understanding, society — from Brooklyn Bridge to the Bronx. I got in at Wall Street. The "crush-hour" was near, for it was 4:25—still, as yet, there were time and space granted us to observe our neighbours. In the particular car in which I was sitting, there was room still left to look about and admire the courage of your fellow-passengers. Weary men going home—many of them having used them all day long—have little wish to use their eyes, so all the men in my car sat silently and sadly, contemplating the future. As I looked at them, it seemed to me that they were thinking over the day's work they had done, and the innumerable days' work they

had still to do. No one smiled. No one observed
the other. An automatic courtesy gave a seat
here and there, but no one gave any attention to
any business but his own thoughts and his own
sad station.

It was a car, if I remember aright, occupied
almost entirely by men-passengers, and, so far as
I could see, there were no evidences that men knew
women from men, or *vice versa*, yet, at last, there
seemed to dawn on four men sitting in a row that
there was a wonderful creature reading a book on
the other side of the aisle—a lovely young woman,
with all the fabled beauty of the sea-shell, and the
rainbow, that enchantment in her calm pearl-like
face, and in the woven stillness of her hair, that has
in all times and countries made men throw up
sails and dare the unknown sea, and the unknown
Fates. The beauty, too, that nature had given
her was clothed in the subdued enchantments of
the rarest art. All unconscious of the admiration
surrounding her, she sat in that subway car, like a
lonely butterfly, strangely there in her incongruous
surroundings, for a mysterious moment, — to
vanish as swiftly as she had come—and, as she
stepped from the car, leaving it dark and dazzled—

bright with her past presence yet —

I, who had fortunately, and fearfully, sat by her
side was aware that the book she had been reading
was lying forgotten on the seat. It was mine by

right of accident,—treasure-trove. So I picked it up, braving the glares of the four sad men facing me.

Naturally, I had wondered what book it was; but its being bound in tooled and jewelled morocco, evidently by one of the great bookbinders of Paris, made it unprofitable to hazard a guess.

I leave to the imagination of lovers of books what book one would naturally expect to find in hands so fair. Perhaps *Ronsard*—or some other poet from the Rose-Garden of old France. No! it was a charmingly printed copy of The New Testament.

The paradox of the discovery hushed me for a few moments, and then I began to turn over the pages, several of which I noticed were dog eared after the manner of beautiful women in all ages. A pencil here and there had marked certain passages. *Come unto me,* ran one of the underlined passages, *all ye that are heavy laden, and I will give you rest,*—and I thought how strange it was that she whose face was so calm and still should have needed to mark that. And another marked passage I noted—*He was in the world, and the world was made by Him, and the world knew Him not.* Then I put down the book with a feeling of awe—such as the Bible had never brought to me before, though I had been accustomed to it from my boyhood, and I said to myself: "How very strange!" And I meant how strange it was to find this wonderful old book in the hands of this wonderful young beauty.

It had seemed strange to find that butterfly in that old copy of the *Proverbs of King Solomon,* but how much stranger to find the New Testament in the hands, or, so to speak, between the wings, of an American butterfly.

I found something written in the book at least as wonderful to me as the sacred text. It was the name of the butterfly—a name almost as beautiful as herself. So I was enabled, to return her book to her. There is, of course, no need to mention a name as well-known for good works as good looks. It will suffice to say that it was the name of the most beautiful actress in the world.

There is a moral to this story. Morals—to stories—are once more coming into fashion. The Bible, in my boyhood, came to us with no such associations as I have recalled. There were no butterflies between its pages, nor was it presented to us by fair or gracious hands. It was a very grim and minatory book, wielded, as it seemed to one's childish ignorance, for the purpose which that young priest of St. Sulpice had used the pages of his copy of the *Proverbs of King Solomon,* that of crushing out the joy of life.

My first acquaintance with it as I remember, was in a Methodist chapel in Staffordshire, England, where three small boys, including myself, prisoned in an old-fashioned high-back pew, were endeavouring to relieve the apparently endless *ennui* of the service by eating surreptitious apples. Suddenly upon our three young heads descended what seemed like a heavy block of wood, wielded by an ancient deacon who did not approve of boys. We were, each of us, no more than eight years old, and the book which had thus descended upon our heads was nothing more to us than a very weighty book—to be dodged if possible, for we were still in that happy time of life when we hated all books. We knew nothing of its contents—to us it was only a schoolmaster's cane, beating us into silence and good behaviour.

So the Bible has been for many generations of boys a book even more terrible than Cæsar's *Commentaries* or the *Æneid* of Virgil—the dull thud of a mysterious cudgel upon the shoulders of youth which you bore as courageously as you could.

So many of us grew up with what one might call a natural prejudice against the Bible.

Then some of us who cared for literature took it up casually and found its poetic beauty. We read the *Book of Job*—which, by the way, Mr. Swinburne is said to have known by heart; and as we read it even the stars themselves seemed less wonderful than this description of their marvel and mystery;

Canst thou bind the sweet influences of Pleiades or loose the hands of Orion?

Canst thou bring forth Mazzaroth in his season? or canst thou guide Arcturus with his sons?

Or we read in the 37th chapter of the *Book of Ezekiel* of that weird valley that was full of bones—

"and as I prophesied, there was a noise, and behold a shaking, and the bones came together bone to bone," surely one of the most wonderful visions of the imagination in all literature.

Or we read the marvellous denunciatory rhetoric of Jeremiah and Isaiah, or the music of the melodious heart-strings of King David; we read the solemn adjuration of the "King Ecclesiast" to remember our Creator in the days of our youth, with its haunting picture of old age: and the loveliness of *The Song of Songs* passed into our lives forever.

To this purely literary love of the Bible there has been added within the last few years a certain renewed regard for it as the profoundest book of the soul, and for some minds not conventionally religious it has regained even some of its old authority as a spiritual guide and stay. And I will confess for myself that sometimes, as I fall asleep at night, I wonder if even Bernard Shaw has written anything to equal the Twenty-third Psalm.

THE END

Memories and Anecdotes

By Kate Sanborn

8°. Illustrated. $1.75

A gossipy, informing, waggish, and altogether delightful volume,---the retrospect of
a woman who is interesting in herself and
who attracted other interesting people.
Among those who appear in the lively pages
of the volume are—to mention only a few—
President Barnard, Henry Ward Beecher,
Mrs. Anne C. L. Botta, William Cullen Bry-
ant, Hezekiah Butterworth, Mark Twain,
Ralph Waldo Emerson, Edward Everett
Hale, James T. Fields, Horace Greeley, John
Hay, Thomas Wentworth Higginson, Wen-
dell Phillips, and Vereshchagin.

G. P. Putnam's Sons

New York   :-:   :-:   :-:   London

Lightning Source UK Ltd.
Milton Keynes UK
UKHW020557131218
333915UK00011B/644/P